THE *Nursing Mother's Companion*

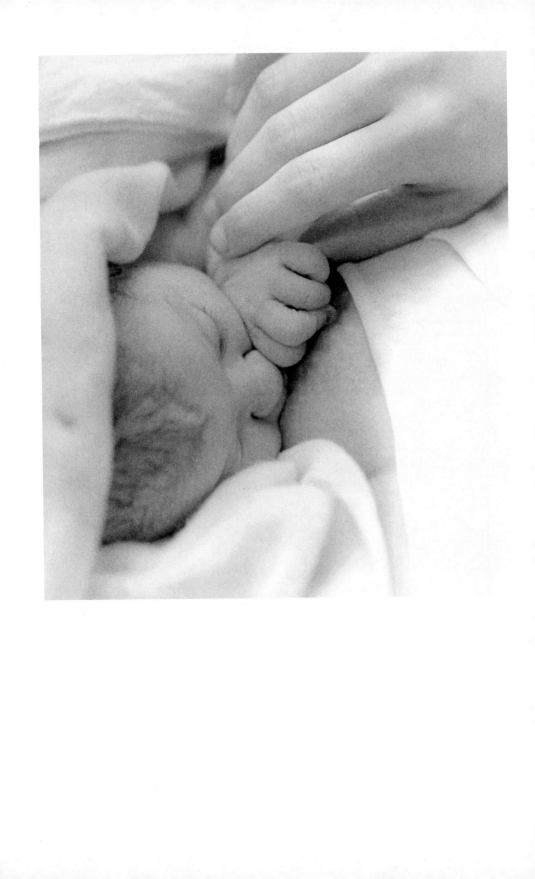

THE *Nursing Mother's Companion*

FOURTH REVISED EDITION

Kathleen Huggins

Foreword by Ruth A. Lawrence
Photographs by Harriette Hartigan

THE HARVARD COMMON PRESS
Boston, Massachusetts

The Harvard Common Press
535 Albany Street
Boston, Massachusetts 02118

Printed in the United States of America

Library of Congress Cataloging-in-Publication Data

Huggins, Kathleen.
  The nursing mother's companion / Kathleen Huggins ;
foreword by Ruth A. Lawrence ; photographs by Harriette
Hartigan.—4th ed.
    p. cm.
    Includes bibliographical references and index.
    ISBN 1-55832-151-9 (hc.).—ISBN 1-55832-152-7 (pbk.)
    1. Breast feeding. I. Title.
RJ216.H845 1999
649'.33—dc21   98-51793
                                                    CIP

Special bulk-order discounts are available on this
and other Harvard Common Press books.
Companies, organizations, and health-care
providers may purchase books for premiums or for
resale, or may arrange a custom edition, by
contacting the Marketing Director at the address
above.

Drawings by Susan Aldridge
Cover design by Jackie Schuman
Text design by Linda Ziedrich

10 9 8 7

To the nursing mothers of San Luis Obispo,
who have been my teachers

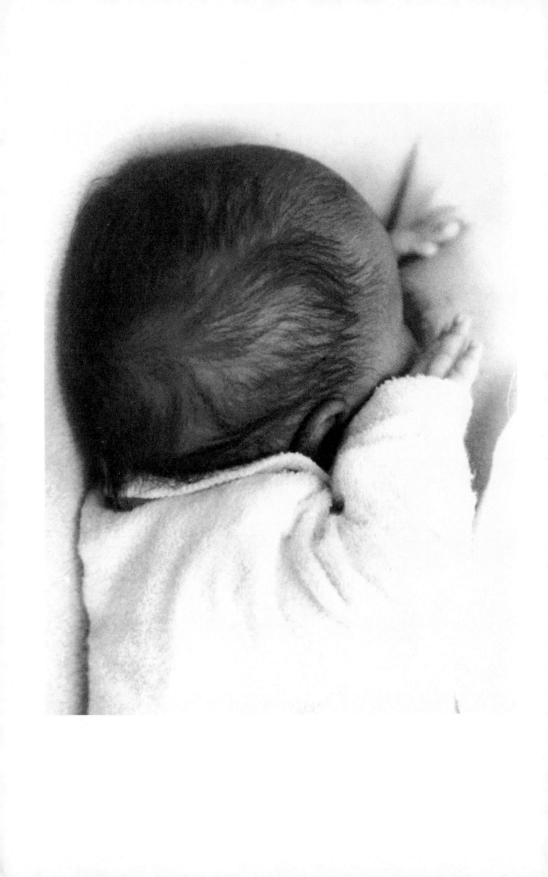

Contents

Foreword

Centuries ago few women faced decisions about how to feed their babies: the newborn's only means of survival was mother's milk. Today, however, there are safe alternatives to nursing, and so a woman needs to think about how she wishes to feed her baby and what method is really best for them both. If she decides to nurse her baby as her ancestors did theirs, she must make an effort to learn how. Breastfeeding is the physiologic continuation of the normal reproductive cycle, and babies are born knowing how to find the nipple and to suck; their mothers, however, do not instinctively know how to nurse. Many women today have never seen a baby breastfed and have little access to experienced nursing mothers. Today's mothers have to learn what to do.

An expectant mother must first learn about alternative feeding methods so she can make an informed choice. With this book Kathleen Huggins helps the mother through the decision-making process by providing sound information about the practical advantages of breastfeeding, its importance to a baby's health, and the very special emotional rewards it offers both mother and baby.

As a woman progresses through her pregnancy and makes preparations for her baby, she may wonder how she should also prepare for breastfeeding. Inexperienced though well-meaning friends may offer abundant but conflicting advice. This book, on the contrary, provides sensible guidelines for preparing to breastfeed, as well as an explanation of the process by which nature prepares the breast for nursing. Understanding how the breast functions prepares a woman for the physiologic changes that occur as the baby is born, the placenta is delivered, and lactation begins. It is also important that the expectant mother discuss her plans to breastfeed with her physician or midwife. The health-care provider can work together with the mother to plan the details of delivery and postpartum care to facilitate lactation.

Having made the decision to breastfeed and having prepared herself for it, a woman must learn *how* to nurse her new baby. Included here are chapters that cover methods of increasing milk production and release, or let-down, and what to do when small problems arise. The author also describes more complicated problems, though these are rare, and explains the course of treatment a doctor or midwife is likely to recommend. It is important to recognize when a situation warrants medical attention, since early appropriate management can usually minimize a problem and facilitate its resolution.

The author, who has breastfed her own children, is also a perinatal nurse who has counseled thousands of new mothers through a breastfeeding clinic and telephone hot line. With her practical experience enhanced by her formal study of lactation, she is especially qualified to prepare this manual for mothers.

A new mother needs to be confident that she is doing the best for her baby. This book will give her the knowledge that is vital to developing that confidence. With the rich store of information herein, every mother should be able to experience the joy of breastfeeding.

RUTH A. LAWRENCE, M.D.

University of Rochester

Preface

Not long ago, a first-time nursing mother came to me about a difficulty she was having breastfeeding her baby. After we successfully resolved it, she suggested I write a book on breastfeeding that included problem-solving techniques. Although I was flattered, such a project seemed monumental. But later, as I recalled her enthusiasm, I began to consider the insights I had gained over years of assisting so many mothers, first as a maternity and newborn nurse and later after founding a breastfeeding clinic and telephone counseling service. Certainly, I was more than familiar with the common concerns of mothers who are learning to breastfeed, as well as with the occasional problems that can interfere with the development of a successful nursing relationship. The next day I wrote my rough outline.

Many excellent books had already been written on the benefits of nursing over artificial feeding methods. I set out, however, to provide mothers with a practical guide for easy reference throughout the nursing period. The first part of the book provides basic information about the breast, preparation for nursing, and nursing during the first week; the remainder of the book is intended for reading as the baby and the nursing relationship grow and develop. There are chapters on each of the three later phases of nursing—from the first week through the second month, from the second month through the sixth, and after the sixth month. Following each of these chapters is a Survival Guide—a quick yet thorough reference for almost any problem you or your baby may encounter during the phase covered. Although you may rarely need to consult the Survival Guides, I have included them to ensure that, when you do, you will be able to identify and resolve your problem as quickly as possible. Because many nursing women occasionally find themselves in need of medication, Dr. Philip Anderson has provided an appendix on drugs and their safety for the breastfed baby.

During the year I spent writing this book, I received a great deal of encouragement and guidance. I am tremendously indebted to Lynn Moen for her support along the way. I also wish to thank

Penny Simkin, R.P.T., and my editor, Linda Ziedrich, for their many efforts on my behalf.

For their thoughtful review of the text I thank Marian Tompson; Andrea Herron, R.N., M.S., C.L.C.; Kathleen Rodriquez Michaelson, B.A., C.L.C.; Vicki McDonald, R.D.; Judith La Vigna; Julie Merrill, R.N.; Tom Robinson; and Kathleen Auerbach, Ph.D.

Jim Litzenburger; Vicki Gadberry, R.N., C.N.M.; Marilynn Schuster, R.N.; Kathleen Long, M.D.; and Dawn Edwards, R.N.C., are most appreciated for their encouragement as well as their friendship.

I am grateful to Donna Janetski for her commitment to this project in preparing the manuscript. My thanks also to Mike Sims for his generosity, and to Susan and Kirk Graves for their efforts on my behalf.

This book would never have been possible without my husband, Brad, whose love, patience, and faith sustained me. Kate, my beautiful daughter and former nursing companion, was my inspiration throughout.

NOTE TO THE SECOND EDITION: For help in preparing this edition I would like to thank Trina Vosti, I.B.C.L.C., and Andrea Van-Outryve, I.B.C.L.C. And thanks to John, my current nursing companion.

NOTE TO THE THIRD EDITION: For their extensive review of the text I wish to thank Olga Mireles, R.N., C.L.C., and Ellen ("Binky") Petok, I.B.C.L.C.

NOTE TO THE FOURTH EDITION: For their generous assistance with revisions, I thank the following women: Dayna Ravalin, R.D.; Sue Petracek, B.S. Ed.; Paula Meier, D.N.Sc., R.N., F.A.A.N.; Lois D. W. Arnold, M.P.H., I.B.C.L.C.; Jan Barger, R.N., I.B.C.L.C.; Darillyn Starr; and Rachel Vireday.

THE Nursing Mother's Companion

Introduction

SINCE THE BEGINNING OF HUMANKIND, WOMEN HAVE PUT THEIR infants to breast. Extending the physical bond that begins at conception, they have nourished and protected their young with their bodies. These tender moments, in return, have brought pleasure and fulfillment to the task of mothering. If you are now pregnant, you are probably looking forward to the time in which you will nourish, comfort, and protect your child in the same way as others before you—at the breast.

Perhaps you already feel committed to the idea of nursing. For you, there is no question that you'll breastfeed your baby. Or perhaps, like many women, you have some uncertainties, but still feel it's worth a try. Your outlook depends on many things—the value you place on breastfeeding, how your partner feels about it, how your friends have fed their babies, your lifestyle, your feelings about yourself and your body.

You probably also have some notions about what nursing will be like. Perhaps you think it will be easy and convenient. Maybe you worry that it might not fit in with your activities and plans. You may have concerns about your ability to nurse. Probably you know of other women who tried to nurse but soon gave up. Whatever your attitudes, expectations, and concerns about breastfeeding, these may become powerful determinants in your ultimate success or failure to nurse your baby happily.

Is Breastfeeding Really Better?

You may be under the impression that the decision to breastfeed or bottle-feed is simply a matter of personal preference. Don't let anyone fool you into believing that breast milk and formula are equally good—they are not. Without a doubt, mother's milk alone promotes optimum health and development for babies. It is uniquely designed to meet the complete nutritional needs of the growing human infant. It also protects the infant against illness throughout the entire first year and beyond, as long as nursing continues.

Although babies do grow on processed infant formulas, formula manufacturers are continually challenged to include all of the nutrients in breast milk that scientists are gradually identifying as important to infant growth and development. But artificial infant milks, whether based on cow's milk or soybeans, will never be able to duplicate nature's formula. Human milk contains proteins that promote brain development and specific immunities against human illness. In contrast, cow's milk contains proteins that favor muscular growth and specific immunities to bovine disease. Babies, like all young mammals, do best with milk from their own species. Babies on a formula diet are at greater risk for illness and hospitalization. Diarrheal infections and respiratory illnesses are more frequent and serious among these babies. Formula-fed babies develop many more ear infections, which may lead to later speech and reading problems. Urinary tract infections and bacterial meningitis are more common among artificially fed infants. Formula feeding appears to be one of several factors implicated in Sudden Infant Death Syndrome (SIDS). Formula-fed infants also have higher incidences of colic, constipation, and allergic disorders. In fact, a significant number of babies are allergic to formulas, both those based on cow's milk and those based on soy. There is also mounting evidence that artificially fed infants more often experience learning disorders and lower levels of intellectual functioning.

Bottle feeding with formula more commonly leads to overfeeding and obesity, which may well persist into childhood, adolescence, and adulthood. Tooth decay, malocclusion (improper meeting of the upper and lower teeth), and distortion of the facial muscles may also directly result from sucking on bottles.

Some studies suggest the benefits of breastfeeding also extend into adulthood. Breastfed babies have lower cholesterol levels and less coronary artery disease, on average, when they become adults. Breastfeeding is also protective against chronic digestive disorders, such as Crohn's Disease and ulcerative colitis. Although asthma rates are not significantly different between breastfed and non-breastfed babies, there is a lower rate of asthma in adults who were breastfed. Breastfed babies also have a smaller chance of developing Type 1 (juvenile-onset) diabetes and cancer of the lymph glands. For all of these reasons, the American Academy of Pediatrics recommends that infants be offered only breast milk for the first six months after birth, and that breastfeeding continue throughout the first year and then as long as mutually desired.

Establishing a close bond and meeting the emotional needs of a child are certainly an essential part of mothering. The nursing woman is thought to produce hormones that promote a physiologic bonding between mother and child. And in what better way can a baby be nurtured, comforted, and made to feel secure than snuggled within his mother's loving arms, against the warmth of her breast? Although some rationalize that bottle-feeding mothers can capture a similar warm feeding relationship, in reality they do not. This is partly because bottle feeding doesn't require much human contact. The bottle-fed baby generally receives less stroking, caressing, and rocking than the breastfed baby. He is talked to less often and he spends more time in his crib away from his parents. Although it is unknown how prevalent the practice of propping bottles for the young infant is, probably the overwhelming majority of babies who are able to hold their own bottles become almost entirely responsible for feeding themselves.

Practical Considerations

Although you may already be convinced nursing is best for your baby, you may have heard it will be a bother for you.

Which is more convenient, breastfeeding or bottle feeding? Whereas formula-feeding mothers feel they are less "tied down," most experienced nursing mothers are grateful they don't have to shop for formula and prepare bottles. It's difficult to believe that getting up at night to fix a bottle is more convenient than pulling the baby to the breast and dozing off again. Outings with a nursing baby mean not having to cart around formula, bottles, and nipples wherever you go. Just because the breastfed baby is easy to take along doesn't mean she can't be left behind; you can leave milk for your infant at times the two of you must be apart.

Mothers who plan to return to work often worry whether they will be able to continue nursing. Today, a growing number of women are combining motherhood, nursing, and working, and doing it quite successfully. Having a healthy baby is especially important to a working mother, and breastfed babies are sick less often. And after several hours spent apart, moreover, nursing becomes a loving reunion between a working mother and her child (see Chapter 5).

Expectant mothers often hear stories about women who tried to nurse their babies but failed. Perhaps you know women who claim that they didn't produce enough milk, that it wasn't rich enough, that their milk supply dried up one day, that their milk didn't agree with their baby, or that the baby suddenly decided he wanted a bottle instead. You may even have heard that women with small breasts or those who are "nervous types" aren't able to nurse.

Maybe you put no stock in these common myths, and believe instead that because nursing a baby is natural it must be easy. Sometimes it isn't. Today close to half of all mothers who start out nursing their babies give it up within the first six weeks. The reason for this failure is rarely that the mother is unable to produce enough milk. Typically it is because she is alone in her efforts to nurse. All too many new mothers know little about the nursing process and the breastfed infant, have little or no guidance, and lack support while they are learning. Although breastfeeding is natural, it is not instinctive—it must be learned.

When anticipating nursing, some women worry about modesty. Although we all know making milk is the natural function of our breasts, most of us feel embarrassed about exposing them. At first you may be more comfortable nursing in private, but most women find that, with a little time and experience, nursing in the presence of others can be discreet and comfortable. Techniques for discreet nursing are discussed in Chapter 5.

You may have heard that nursing can be painful. Normally, women find it comfortable and pleasurable. Some women worry about developing sore nipples during the early days of nursing, but most soreness can be avoided by correctly positioning the baby at the breast (see Chapter 2). You may have also heard that babies sometimes bite their mothers while nursing. When a baby is sucking, his tongue covers his lower gums and teeth so he cannot bite. Still, some babies do occasionally bite at the end of feeding, usually during a period of teething. Most babies learn very quickly not to do this.

Pregnancy typically causes the breasts to enlarge, and sometimes to develop stretch marks. During the first few months of nursing, women whose breasts are normally small or medium-sized generally find them to be bigger. Women whose breasts are normally large can usually expect them to stay about the same size as they were late in pregnancy. As the baby gets older and begins nursing less often, most women notice their breasts reduce in size. At weaning, the breasts typically appear smaller still and somewhat droopy, but within six months they generally resume their usual size and shape. Whether you nurse or not, however, you may notice a change in the firmness of your breasts after you have a baby. Childbearing, not nursing, is along with age and heredity a major determinant of the breasts' ultimate appearance.

What's in It for Mom?

Although the health of an infant and the emotional benefits of breastfeeding are certainly reason enough to nurse, mothers frequently have other motives.

Experienced nursing mothers boast about the ease and convenience of breastfeeding. They are often quick to add that information, guidance, support, and reassurance were essential at the start. After the first few weeks, however, nursing a baby simplifies life considerably.

Many women worry about how they will look after they have had a baby. The fat you accumulate during pregnancy is intended for caloric reserves while nursing. Although vigorous dieting is not a good idea during the nursing period, most mothers find that they gradually lose weight while they are breastfeeding, so long as they are not overeating.

Many studies report lower rates of ovarian cancer and premenopausal breast cancer among women who have breastfed, and it appears that the risk of cancer decreases the longer a woman nurses. There is some evidence, too, that nursing offers protection against osteoporosis (brittle bones), which can occur later in life. And breastfeeding generally lengthens the time before menstrual periods resume. Most nursing women find they don't have a menstrual cycle for several months to two years after delivery, so long as they are nursing frequently.

All nursing mothers appreciate the money they save by not buying formula. Mothers committed to providing their children with wholesome, natural foods see breast milk as a sound beginning. Some mothers are repelled by the smell and taste of many formula preparations, not to mention the unpleasant odor of the bowel movements and spit-up milk of the formula-fed baby, and the stains formula may leave on clothing.

Mothers who nurse do so not only because they want the very best nourishment and protection for their babies and because they personally derive many practical benefits from breastfeeding, but simply because they enjoy the experience. The loving relationship established between mother and infant at the breast is emotionally fulfilling and pleasurable. You'll know no greater reward as a mother than witnessing your child grow from your body—first in the womb, and then at the breast.

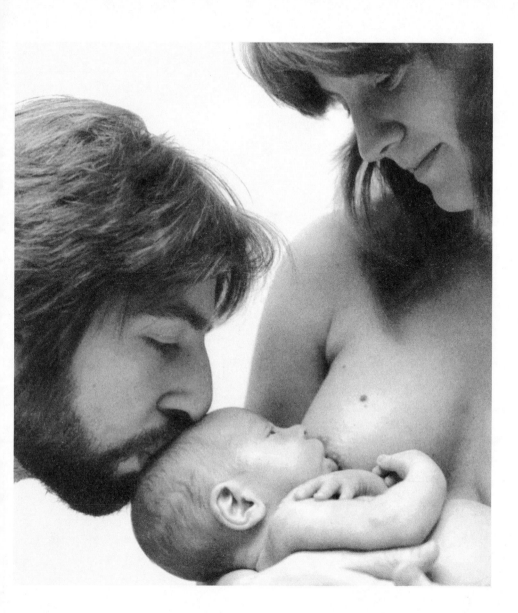

Sweet voice, sweet lips, soft hands, and softer breast.

John Keats

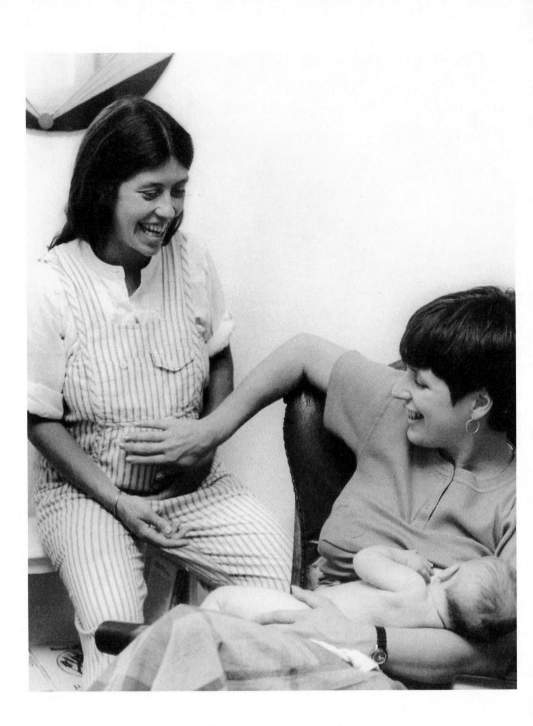

CHAPTER ONE

Looking Forward: Preparations during Pregnancy

YOU MAY HAVE DECIDED TO NURSE YOUR BABY LONG BEFORE YOU became pregnant. Or perhaps you have just begun to consider breastfeeding. Although nourishing a baby at the breast is natural, many new mothers are surprised to find it is a learned skill—one that usually takes several weeks to master.

Success at nursing often depends upon a woman's confidence and commitment. You can develop your confidence by learning as much as possible about breastfeeding ahead of time. You can strengthen your commitment to nurse by developing a strong support system for yourself.

Learning about Breastfeeding

Generations ago, most new mothers turned to their own mothers for support and guidance on breastfeeding. Unfortunately, few women today can do this. For many, the art of breastfeeding is learned alone—by trial and error. All too often this leads to frustration and discouragement.

There are several ways you can learn about nursing ahead of time. Reading about it is certainly beneficial. In some communities breastfeeding classes are offered. Expectant mothers are also most welcome to attend La Leche League meetings, which are held monthly in most areas. La Leche League is the organization of nursing mothers whose purpose is to support breastfeeding worldwide. In some areas, other groups, such as the Nursing Mothers Counsel, provide classes and telephone counseling for pregnant and nursing women. These groups are listed in Appendix A. In addition, hospitals, county health departments, and WIC (Women, Infants, and Children Supplemental Nutrition) programs may sponsor prenatal breastfeeding classes. See Appendix A for more information about WIC.

Another excellent way to learn about breastfeeding is to spend time with women who are nursing their babies. It may be that you have never seen, close up, a mother and baby breastfeeding. Most nursing mothers will delight in your interest, and one or two may become good sources of information and support for you in the days to come. Be sure to ask them about their first weeks of nursing. Most likely you will hear of a variety of experiences, and perhaps you will develop a sense of what the early period of breastfeeding can be like.

Your Breasts

During pregnancy many changes occur in your breasts in preparation for nourishing your baby. Initially, you probably noticed they were more full and tender than usual. Their increasing size during the first few months of pregnancy is caused by the development of the milk-making structures within them. With this growth the blood flow to the breasts increases, and veins in the breasts may become clearly visible. Some women develop stretch marks on their breasts like the ones that can occur on the abdomen during pregnancy.

The nipple and the area around the nipple, the areola, may double in size and deepen in color; this darkening may serve as a visual cue to the newborn. Also during this time, small glands located in the areola, known as Montgomery's tubercles, become pronounced. Their function is to secrete an antibacterial lubricant that keeps the nipple moist and protected during pregnancy and breast-feeding. This is why soaps and special creams are unnecessary in caring for your breasts, and may even be harmful: soaps remove the breast's natural lubricant, and creams may interfere with its antibacterial action.

The nipples often become more sensitive during pregnancy in preparation for nursing. Some women may find that their nipples

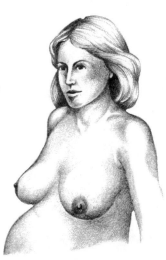

In pregnancy the breasts become enlarged, and veins and stretch marks may become visible.

are overly sensitive and even hurt when touched. Other women enjoy this sensitivity and feel great pleasure when their breasts are fondled during lovemaking.

By the fifth or sixth month of pregnancy, the breasts are fully capable of producing milk. Some women begin to notice drops of fluid on the nipple at this time. This fluid, known as colostrum, comes from the many tiny openings in the nipple and is the food your baby will receive during the first few days after birth. Some women do not leak colostrum, but it is there in the breasts just the same.

As women, we all receive messages about our bodies and what they "ought" to look like. These messages affect our self-image, including our feelings about our breasts and how they look. You can probably remember how you felt about your breasts as they developed in early adolescence. You may have felt proud as they grew larger and you began wearing a bra. Perhaps you were embarrassed if they developed earlier or grew larger than the other girls'. You may have felt anxious if they took a long time to grow, or self-conscious if they were small.

Even now you may wish that your breasts were smaller or larger, fuller or less droopy. You may not resemble the women with "perfect" breasts portrayed in photographs of nursing mothers. Women with large breasts, especially, often feel insecure about nursing, fearing that their breasts will grow much larger still or

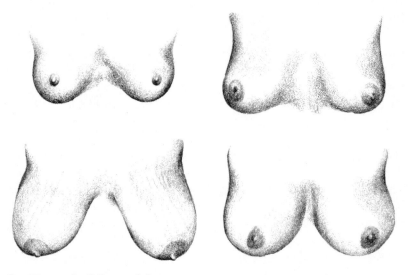

Breasts come in all sizes and shapes.

leak milk excessively. Actually, large breasts seldom grow larger after delivery, and they tend to leak less than small breasts.

Each woman's breasts are very different from all others, but the breast, regardless of size, is perfectly designed for its ultimate purpose—to nourish and nurture our children. The breasts not only provide an infant with superb nutrients for growth and development, but offer the warmth, the comfort, and the security that every growing baby needs. In this respect, they are most beautiful.

Caring for your breasts. During the last months of pregnancy, just rinse your breasts during your bath or shower. Avoid soaping them, since soaps tend to dry the nipples and the areola. If your breasts are dry or itchy, a mild cream or lotion may feel soothing, but avoid getting it on the nipple or areola.

Many women prefer to wear a supportive bra during pregnancy, although some are just as comfortable without one.

The making and giving of milk. After the birth of your baby, colostrum is readily available for her first nursings. Colostrum is the ideal food for her first days; it is both perfect nutritionally and important for protection against infection. Milk generally appears by the second or third day, but occasionally not until the fourth or fifth.

Your body is signaled to initiate milk production with the delivery of the placenta. This causes the hormone prolactin to activate the milk-producing cells of the breast. The initial manufacture of milk occurs whether the baby nurses or not. Continued milk production is another matter. This depends on frequent and regular stimulation of the breast and the drainage of milk. The baby's sucking stimulates the nerve endings in the breast, which in turn trigger the release of the two hormones essential to milk production and release—prolactin and oxytocin.

Prolactin, as mentioned previously, activates the milk-producing cells in the breast to manufacture milk. Oxytocin is responsible for the release of the milk from the tiny sacs where the milk is made. This release is referred to as the ejection or let-down reflex. As the baby nurses, the milk is propelled forward to the sinuses beneath the areola. It is the baby's job to get the milk out of the sinuses by compressing the areola with her tongue and gums as she nurses.

During the early months of her life, your baby will receive plenty of milk as long as she nurses frequently, at least eight times in 24

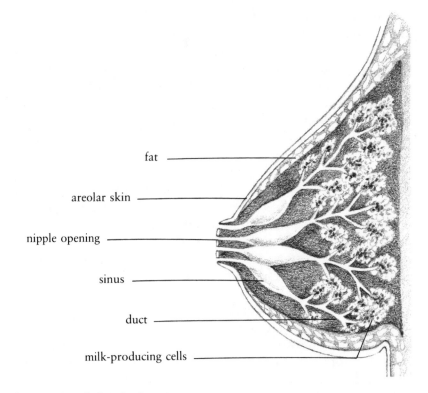

fat

areolar skin

nipple opening

sinus

duct

milk-producing cells

Cross-section of a lactating breast.

hours, is latched on and sucking properly, and is allowed a sufficient amount of time to complete each feeding. This is because breastfeeding works by supply and demand. The more your breasts are stimulated and emptied by the baby's sucking, the more milk you will produce.

Planning for the First Days

Nipple preparation. Often mothers who plan to breastfeed are advised to prepare their nipples during pregnancy. In fact, studies have shown that nipple "toughening" maneuvers such as brisk rubbing or twisting do little to prevent soreness during early breastfeeding. Whether or not they have especially sensitive skin, blondes and redheads do not generally experience any more nipple soreness than other women. Sore nipples are usually prevented by correct attachment of the baby at the breast during nursing (see Chapter 2).

One preparation is very important during pregnancy: you should make sure your nipples can extend outward. Your baby may have difficulty grasping the breast if the nipples do not protrude enough on their own or cannot be made to protrude. Do not assume because your nipples appear to extend outward that all is well. Even if you had a breast exam earlier in your pregnancy, your nipples may not have been fully checked. Take the time to perform your own assessment.

First, look at both your nipples. They may protrude, or one or both may be flat, dimpled, folded in the center, or inverted. Next, do the "pinch test": gently squeeze just behind the nipple with your thumb and forefinger. This imitates the motion your baby will make while nursing. See how both nipples respond. If your nipples are flat, pull them outward to determine if they can lift away from the inner mass of the breast. The following chart will help you determine whether you need to take further steps to minimize initial nursing difficulties.

Usual nipple appearance	Appearance when pinched	
	Satisfactory	*Needs correction*
Protruding	Nipple stays protruded	———
Flat	Nipple can be pinched outward	Nipple moves inward or cannot be pinched outward
Dimpled or folded	Entire nipple extends outward	Nipple moves inward or flattens
Inverted	Entire nipple extends outward	Nipple extends out only slightly, remains inverted, or inverts further

When nipples need correction. The flat nipple that cannot be pinched outward, or the nipple that moves inward or flattens when compressed, is said to be "tied" to the inner breast tissue by tiny adhesions. The physical changes of pregnancy help the nipples to stand out, but one or both may still need correction. In this case, special plastic breast shells may solve the problem before breast-feeding begins.

Worn inside the bra, breast shells exert a steady but gentle pressure on the areola and cause the nipple to extend outward through the opening in the shell. This helps to loosen the adhesions beneath the nipple. Breast shells should be worn as soon as you have determined that improvement is needed, ideally from about mid-pregnancy on. They can be purchased in most maternity shops (see Appendix A for information on ordering them). Gradually work up to wearing the shells most of the day, letting comfort be your guide.

The postpartum setting. Too few mothers realize ahead of time the tremendous effect the immediate postpartum experience—in a hospital, in a birth center, or at home—can have on their breast-feeding success. It is most worthwhile to evaluate the situation you

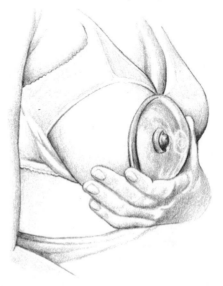

Breast shells can improve nipple shape.

will be in after delivery to make any necessary arrangements for early nursing.

Some women have the opportunity to select among several hospitals or birth centers for their delivery. If you are making such a choice, be sure to get a recommendation from your childbirth educator or a breastfeeding counselor. She will probably know which places are most supportive of nursing mothers and infants. Even if only one hospital is available to you—and many birth attendants practice at only one—it is well worth your time to ask about the policies of the maternity unit. This will help assure that your nursing gets off to the best possible start.

Take advantage of the maternity tours, teas, and classes that most hospitals and birth centers offer, or call the postpartum unit (make sure the nurse has time to talk) to learn about policies and routines. Be sure to inquire:

- How soon after delivery will I be able to nurse? What if I have a cesarean birth?
- How often is nursing encouraged during the day and at night?
- Can the baby stay in the room with me? If not, how often and for how long will we be together?
- What assistance with breastfeeding is offered by the nursing staff?
- Does the staff avoid supplemental bottle feeding?
- Is there a lactation professional on staff?

In 1990, the United Nations Children's Fund (Unicef) and the World Health Organization created an award of recognition for those hospitals worldwide that have enacted ten policies to support breastfeeding mothers and babies. Hospitals that have implemented the "Ten Steps" are awarded the designation "Baby Friendly." At this writing, over seventy hospitals in the United States have applied for baby-friendly status, but only seventeen have passed inspection so far. When inquiring about a hospital's breastfeeding policies, ask if it has applied for the Baby-Friendly certificate. If it has, you can be assured that the nurses are committed to your breastfeeding success. If it hasn't, perhaps your inquiry will inspire the hospital to enact baby-friendly policies.

If the nurse is friendly and receptive to your questions, you might also ask which pediatricians she feels are particularly knowledgeable about breastfeeding and supportive of it.

Ideally, the maternity unit's policies encourage mothers and babies to remain together for the first few hours after birth, or at least assure that nursing takes place within the first two hours, when the baby is likely to be alert and eager to suck. Breastfeeding goes best when nursing is frequent, every one to three hours, during both day and night. "Rooming in" with the baby, at least during the day and evening, is conducive to frequent nursing and allows the mother and baby to become better acquainted before going home. Preferably, the nursing staff does not routinely give the babies water or formula supplements, as this lessens their interest in nursing and sometimes interferes with their ability to breastfeed. It can be an added bonus if the nurses enjoy assisting breastfeeding mothers or if one nurse is specifically responsible for breastfeeding counseling.

If you are planning an early discharge from a hospital or birth center, or will be delivering at home, you may also want to inquire about home visits by a nurse, lactation professional, or midwife during the first few days.

The baby's doctor. Your breastfeeding experience can be greatly influenced by your choice of physician for your child. You may want a pediatrician for your baby, or you may prefer to use a family practitioner (you may certainly choose to continue with a family practitioner who attended your baby's birth). In selecting a doctor, start by getting the names of those who are known to have a positive attitude about breastfeeding. Ask your obstetrician, midwife, childbirth educator, or a lactation professional for recommendations. You might also inquire about physicians in your area who work with nurse practitioners. These nurses have advanced education and training in well-baby care, and they usually provide mothers with extra attention and counseling on a variety of parental concerns, including breastfeeding.

Most doctors and nurse practitioners will set aside time for a preliminary visit with expectant parents. Usually this is free of charge; they realize you are "looking and choosing." Be sure to visit at least two before making a final decision, even if the first one seems nice. By all means meet the office nurse. She will often be the one who will answer your questions or concerns when you call during office hours. She can be a good resource for you, especially if she has breastfed successfully herself or has a special interest in nursing.

Let the doctor or nurse practitioner know that you are going to nurse your baby. To gauge his or her overall support of nursing mothers, ask what the recommendations would be should you experience difficulty in breastfeeding. The best pediatric practitioners offer practical assistance with breastfeeding or referrals to lactation professionals. Other practitioners provide reassuring words about feeding infant formula. Take time to discuss your preferences for feeding the baby in the hospital. If the maternity unit's policies are not ideal, ask about written orders to allow early nursing and rooming-in, and to prevent the feeding of supplements to your baby.

There may be other questions you will want to ask about the hospital or birth center, or about well-baby care. Bring a list with you so you don't forget any of them. Be sure to inquire about any necessary procedures for notifying the doctor or nurse practitioner when the baby is born. It is often said that the pediatrician takes care of the parents perhaps even more than the child. Trust your intuition when making your final choice about which pediatrician, family doctor, or nurse practitioner is right for you.

Nursing bras and pads. During the early weeks of breastfeeding, the average breast weighs three to four times as much as it did before pregnancy. Although a bra isn't an absolute necessity in this period, you'll probably be more comfortable in one, at least if it fits well. If you leak milk and want to use breast pads, you'll definitely need a bra to hold them in place. A stretch bra that can be pulled out of the way may work fine if you're small-breasted, but otherwise you may prefer a nursing bra, with its removable cup flaps.

Pregnancy changes not only the size of the breasts but also the size of the rib cage. After you give birth, both measurements change again. If you buy a nursing bra in early pregnancy, it may not fit when milk production begins. A better time to shop for nursing bras is during the last month of pregnancy. To be on the safe side, limit your purchase to two or three bras; you'll be more sure of the size and style that suits you after a week or so of nursing.

The salesperson in the maternity shop or department may be able to help you choose a bra that will fit well while you are nursing. If she doesn't know a lot about bras, though, you can figure out your size yourself by following these guidelines: while standing, wearing an unpadded bra and breathing normally, measure

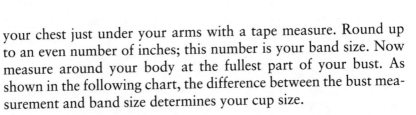

A nursing bra makes the breast available with only the motion of one hand.

your chest just under your arms with a tape measure. Round up to an even number of inches; this number is your band size. Now measure around your body at the fullest part of your bust. As shown in the following chart, the difference between the bust measurement and band size determines your cup size.

Up to 1-inch difference	A cup
1- to 2-inch difference	B cup
2- to 3-inch difference	C cup
3- to 4-inch difference	D cup
4- to 5-inch difference	DD or E cup
5- to 6-inch difference	F cup
6- to 7-inch difference	G cup
7- to 8-inch difference	H cup

Since finding larger bra sizes can be difficult, you may have to use a mail-order supplier. To locate one, see Appendix A.

To check a bra for fit, fasten it on the outside row of hooks. Before raising the straps over your shoulders, bend forward, allowing your breasts to fill the cups. Now stand straight, and adjust the straps.

Check the cup fit. When the flaps of a nursing bra are hooked at their highest points, the cups should have just a little extra room at the top for when milk production begins. If the cups are roomier than this, try a smaller cup size. If your breasts are overflowing at the top, outsides, or center, you need a larger cup size.

Next check the bottom band. While fastened on the outside row of hooks, the band should be snug; an inner row of hooks will allow you to tighten the band as your rib cage contracts after birth. Check to see that the band is level all around or slightly lower in the back. If the bra rides up in the back, the shoulder straps may be too tight. Otherwise, try a larger cup size.

Aside from a good fit, other valuable features of a bra for breast-feeding include all-cotton cups to absorb moisture, non-elastic straps for better support, and front-flap fasteners that are manageable with one hand.

A word about underwire bras: poorly fitted ones are associated with plugged milk ducts and breast infections. If you want to wear an underwire bra while nursing, it is very important to get one that fits properly. The bend of the wire must be wide enough to fall where there are no milk ducts—that is, well behind the breast tissue. If you have a lot of breast tissue below the armpits, as many women do, a soft-cup bra is definitely preferable. If you do use an underwire bra while nursing, rotate it with a soft-cup bra, and never wear the underwire bra during sleep.

You may also wish to purchase breast pads before delivery, to keep your bra and clothing dry during the early weeks of nursing (not all women leak, so you may want to start with just one pack). These pads come in two varieties, disposable and reusable. Whichever you select, be sure the pads do not contain plastic or waterproof liners, as these can contribute to nipple soreness. Some women prefer to use handkerchiefs or cut-up cloth diapers instead of commercial pads.

Sometimes mothers consider using plastic breast shells instead of pads to keep dry. The primary purpose of these shells is to improve nipple shape. When they are routinely worn in place of pads, milk may leak excessively.

Other purchases you may be considering. The arms of an adult are never a safe place for an infant or small child riding in an automobile. If you use a car, buy an infant restraining seat; every U.S. state now requires the use of one. Although all infant car seats sold today must meet federal safety standards, the seats vary considerably in both features and price. Look for latches you can operate easily; you may also prefer a washable cover. If you're considering a secondhand car seat, check its label to be sure it meets safety standards. Some communities and hospitals offer car seat rental and loan programs.

Don't pay extra for a car seat that also functions as a general-purpose infant carrier. In the past decade, plastic carriers, many of which double as car seats, have become one of the most harmful types of baby equipment. Parents use them both to carry their babies outside the home and to contain them within the home, whether the babies are awake or asleep. Some babies spend many hours each day in these carriers. The problem is that the carriers limit babies' movements and thereby delay their muscular and sensory-motor development. Babies need to spend most of their time in a horizontal position, in someone's arms or on a level surface. The constant upright position fails to stimulate the lower brain and delays physical coordination. A bouncer seat, bassinet, or blanket on the floor is a better place to leave your baby for extended periods. Or carry your baby in a pouch or sling, keeping your arms free for other things. Holding, rocking, and carrying your baby against your body will stimulate his physical and mental development while strengthening the loving bond between you.

You'll want to either buy diapers or arrange for diaper service for the first few weeks. Besides being ecologically safer than disposable diapers, cloth diapers are more economical as well, if you own or have access to a washer and dryer. Full diaper service is usually no more expensive than disposable diapers and is a luxury all new parents deserve.

A comfortable armchair can make positioning your newborn at the breast much easier and provide more support for you while nursing. Many couches are too deep to sit up straight on. Propping yourself against your headboard or sitting on the edge of the bed could make it hard to position your baby well and contribute to poor posture and muscle fatigue. An upholstered living-room, dining-room, or office chair with arms, or a wooden rocking chair, may make a great place for nursing your baby. If your breasts are large, a recliner may be most comfortable. Consider borrowing an appropriate chair or buying one secondhand if you can't afford to buy a new one.

Many mothers have found that a foot stool specially designed for nursing is very helpful in reducing the strain of holding the baby at the breast. The angled stool raises the mother's feet and legs, lifting her lap. This relaxes her abdomen and supports her lower back, preventing arm and shoulder strain. Nursing stools can be bought through some catalogs and from a major breast pump manufacturer (see Appendix A for information on ordering them).

Some mothers buy breast pumps before delivery. Although a pump is not a necessity, you may at some time want to use one. Or you may prefer to learn the technique of manual expression, which is described in Chapter 5. If you do decide to purchase a pump ahead of time, see Chapter 5 for a review of various popular models, and information on obtaining them. Many mothers are disappointed with the pumps that are widely available in drugstores and baby shops.

Some mothers need a fully automatic electric breast pump in the first few days after delivery. Whether you buy another sort of pump or not, know where you can rent an electric pump should the need arise. If your baby isn't nursing well upon leaving the hospital or is at risk of underfeeding for another reason (see pages 39–41), you should go home with an electric pump. You can locate a rental station by calling the toll-free numbers in Appendix A.

Planning for the First Weeks

During your first few weeks of motherhood, caring for the baby and yourself will take just about all of your time and energy. Most new mothers find they are often tired and have emotional highs and lows. Planning ahead can make these important first weeks go much more smoothly for both you and your family.

If your partner can possibly manage to take time off from work, by all means encourage him to do so. Not only can he help in fixing meals, managing the household, and caring for any other children at home, but he also needs and deserves time to get to know the baby. And he can be a great source of support and encouragement while you are learning to breastfeed.

Other family members can also make these weeks easier, but invite them to stay with you only if you feel they will make a positive contribution and be supportive of your nursing.

Perhaps some of your friends in the area have already offered to help when the baby arrives. There are many things they can do, like fixing a meal, washing a load or two of laundry, running errands, minding any older children, or spending an hour or so straightening up your house.

When you're pregnant, a nursing friend can be a great source of information and inspiration.

It's also a good idea to stock up on groceries before the birth. Include foods that are easy to prepare and plenty of things to drink. You may also want to plan some simple menus or freeze some dinners ahead of time.

Your support system. About half of American women who start out breastfeeding give up and begin bottle feeding within the first two months after birth. As said so well by Dana Raphael (1976), "The odds in our culture today are stacked heavily against success-ful breastfeeding, and the emotional price for failure is high." Mothers frequently give up breastfeeding in the learning stage be-cause they have little information, guidance, and support.

When a nursing mother is encouraged and cared for by others, her motivation can carry her through almost any difficult situa-tion. When she feels alone and unsupported, however, the nursing relationship seems to fall apart at the slightest provocation.

As enthusiastic as you may feel now, you probably have diffi-culty imagining that during the early weeks you may sometimes doubt your ability to nurse. In fact, many new mothers experience periods of anxiety while they are learning to breastfeed. If you are lucky you can turn to your own mother for advice and reassurance about nursing. Many of our mothers, however, nursed us only a few weeks, if at all. You may hear from today's grandmothers that "no one nursed back then," "the doctor said the bottle was eas-ier," "I just didn't make enough milk," or "the doctor said my milk wasn't rich enough." Comments such as these reflect an era when women received little encouragement and support in their efforts to nurse, especially from their male doctors. Consider for a moment the idea of giving birth all alone. Awful, right? It is proba-bly important to you that someone you love and trust will be with you, encouraging you each step of the way. During your early weeks of breastfeeding you need the same kind of support—the presence of someone who provides reassurance, guidance, and en-couragement.

You may be fortunate enough to have friends who have nursed—or are nursing—their babies, and a partner who believes with you that breastfeeding is healthy and natural. Even so, you may discover in time that not everyone in your life shares your feelings about breastfeeding. In fact, many people feel indifferent, and some downright opposed, to this way of feeding and nurturing a baby. Your partner, mother, or best friend may not be entirely enthusiastic about your decision. Some people may even try to discourage you along the way. Perhaps they feel a bit threatened, fearful, or even jealous of the intimate relationship you will be establishing with the baby. The sad fact of the matter is that despite the renewed enthusiasm of young women today toward breastfeeding, many new mothers still get too little support—from family, friends, health professionals, and society in general.

Develop a support system for yourself ahead of time. Let your partner and other family members know how much breastfeeding means to you and how important they will be to your success. If they have concerns or fears about nursing, find out what they are and provide them with the information they need to correct any misconceptions. If you have older children, talk with them about nursing so they know what to expect.

Be sure to identify sources of guidance. Perhaps you are close to women who have successfully nursed their babies. Many WIC (Women, Infants, and Children Supplemental Nutrition) programs provide breastfeeding support and guidance (see Appendix A for more information about WIC). Take time to find the names of lactation professionals in your community. Your childbirth educator, your maternity unit, or your obstetrician's or pediatrician's nurse may know of some, and WIC programs sometimes have lactation professionals on staff. Two breast pump companies, Medela and Hollister, have geographically arranged lists of lactation professionals. The companies' toll-free numbers are listed in Appendix A. When you have gathered these supports, you will have stacked the odds in your favor.

CHAPTER TWO

Off to a Good Start: The First Week

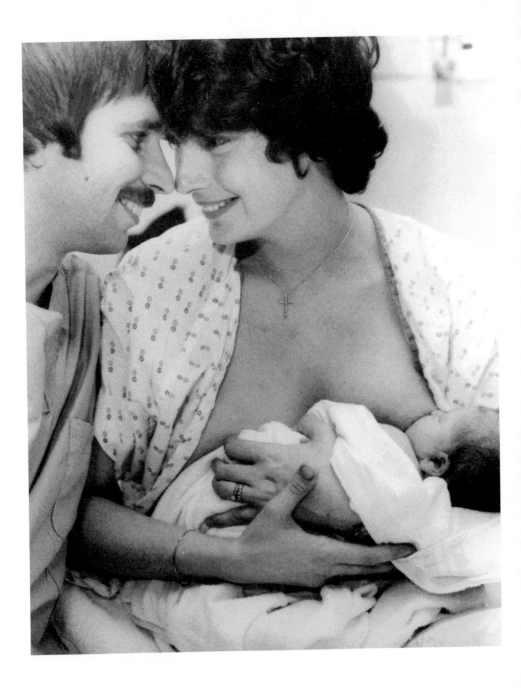

YOU MIGHT EXPECT THAT AFTER THE WORK OF LABOR AND BIRTH a mother and her newborn infant would be too exhausted to greet each other. But no matter how fatigued birth may have left her, the mother usually brightens with renewed energy to explore her baby. Some mothers seem to meet their infants for the first time with puzzlement, as if searching for some sign of familiarity. Others react as if they have always known this tiny being and are overjoyed to meet him at long last.

After several minutes of adjustment to breathing, the temperature change, and lights and sounds, the infant likewise becomes alert, opening his eyes and moving his mouth. Soon he is actively rooting about. With his fists to his mouth, or perhaps his lips against the blanket or his father's arm, he seeks out the comfort of the breast.

In the Beginning

Throughout the first two hours after birth, the infant is usually alert and eager to suck. At this time he is most ready for his first nursing.

Colostrum. It is not unusual to hear a first-time mother tell a nurse, "I don't think I have anything yet to feed the baby." Although small in amount, colostrum is available in the breast in quantities close to the stomach capacity of the newborn. This "liquid gold," which is often yellow but may be clear, resembles blood more than milk in that it contains protective white blood cells capable of attacking harmful bacteria. Colostrum also acts to "seal" the inside of the baby's intestines, preventing the invasion of bacteria, and provides the baby with high levels of antibodies from the mother. Not only does colostrum thus offer protection from sickness, but it is the ideal food for the newborn's first few days of life. It is high in protein and low in sugar and fat, making it easy to digest. Colostrum is also beneficial in stimulating the baby's first bowel movement. The black, tarry stool, called meconium, contains bilirubin, the substance that causes newborn jaundice. Colostrum in frequent doses helps eliminate bilirubin from the body and may lessen the incidence and severity of jaundice.

In the hospital this first nursing may take place in the delivery room, the birthing room, or the recovery area. With minimal assistance from your nurse or partner, the baby will probably latch on eagerly to the breast and suck. He will be more willing if he is unbundled; snuggled within your arm and next to your body, he is unlikely to get too cold (unless perhaps the room is air-conditioned). The purple color of his hands and feet is normal; it is caused by changes in blood circulation that take place at delivery. If you or the nurse is concerned about the cold, place a blanket over the baby after he has begun to nurse.

Many specialists believe that when the first nursing is delayed much beyond the first two hours, the infant may be somewhat reluctant to take the breast thereafter. Most babies fall asleep about two hours after birth, and become more difficult to rouse over the next few hours. Nursing without delay also boosts the confidence of the mother, and stimulates the action of hormones that cause the uterus to contract and remain firm after delivery. These contractions may help speed delivery of the placenta and minimize blood loss afterward (breastfeeding alone is insufficient, however, in the case of postpartum hemorrhage, when prompt intervention by the medical staff is essential). During the first few days after birth, some mothers feel these contractions, or "afterpains," while nursing. Mothers who have had other children may be especially uncomfortable with afterpains.

Should you not have the opportunity to nurse right after delivery, or if you can't persuade your baby to take the breast, don't get discouraged. Many mothers have established successful nursing hours or days after giving birth.

Just the breast. When you have finished your first nursing in the hospital, let the nurses know (if you have not done so previously) that you prefer your baby be given no supplementary bottles of water or formula and no pacifiers. Water or formula is unnecessary, and artificial nipples may confuse your baby while he is learning to breastfeed.

Newborns do not normally require any fluids other than colostrum (the exception is the baby who has low blood sugar—because her mother is diabetic, her birth weight was low, or she underwent unusual stress during labor or delivery). Supplemental feedings, moreover, can be harmful: they may cause the baby to lose interest in the breast and to nurse less frequently than needed. This is because bottle nipples may (1) lessen the baby's instinctive efforts to open her mouth wide, (2) condition her to wait to suck until she feels the firm bottle nipple in her mouth, and (3) encourage her to push her tongue forward—the opposite of what she needs to do while nursing. The baby who has sucked on bottle nipples may also become frustrated while nursing, since milk does not flow as rapidly from the breast as it does from the bottle.

Giving newborns large amounts of water is dangerous. Because young babies can't excrete water quickly, large amounts can lower sodium levels in their bodies, causing complications that include low body temperature and seizures.

A newborn trained to take a pacifier may fail to recognize her mother's soft, short nipple, and therefore have trouble latching on to the breast. Introducing a pacifier now could lead to later problems, too. Recent studies associate the use of pacifiers with early weaning, and older babies who use pacifiers are more likely than others to have repeated ear infections.

Some hospitals now have policies against giving bottles and pacifiers to nursing newborns, but not all do. To be sure all the nurses know of your preference, ask them to place a sign on the baby's crib like this one:

To all my nurses:

While I'm here and learning to breastfeed, PLEASE, NO BOTTLES OR PACIFIERS. My mom will be happy to nurse me whenever I fuss.

Thanks!!
Baby Reynolds

Time at the breast. Many doctors and nurses tell mothers that to prevent sore nipples they should limit their nursing time during the first several days. Probably nothing else about breastfeeding is as poorly understood as the causes of sore nipples. It may be explained that keeping feedings short will prevent soreness and will help "toughen" the nipples. Actually, sore nipples usually result from improper positioning of the baby on the breast, not from long nursings. Another myth often heard by new mothers is that the breast "empties" in a prescribed number of minutes. Most newborns require 10 to 45 minutes to complete a feeding. As long as your positioning is correct and nursing is comfortable, there is no need to restrict your nursing time. Besides being unnecessary, limiting nursing time may frustrate the baby and lead to increased engorgement when milk production begins.

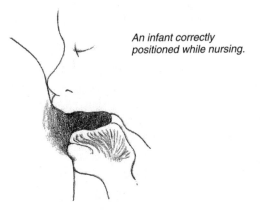

An infant correctly positioned while nursing.

Positioning at the breast. A baby is correctly positioned at the breast when he has come on to it with a wide-open mouth, so that his lower gum is well below the base of the nipple on the areola, the dark area around the nipples. In this position he will compress the sinuses located beneath the areola to draw out milk. If he instead latches on only to the nipple and starts "chewing," the nipple will probably become sore and cracked, and perhaps even bleed. The baby will also be unable to compress the sinuses beneath the areola and may therefore get too little milk.

Probably the most important skill for you to master, initially, is that of getting the baby on the breast correctly. Some mothers can do this easily, but many need practice.

The "cradle hold," or "cuddle hold," in which the baby's head is held in the crook of the mother's arm, is considered the classic breastfeeding position. I have come to believe that for most new mothers and babies this position is neither the easiest nor the most

It's hard to control a newborn's head using the cradle hold.

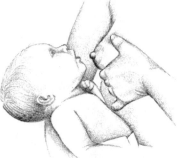

effective for getting a baby well latched on to the breast. In the first few weeks after birth, a baby hasn't developed enough muscular coordination to easily latch on without help; she needs a good deal of direction from her mother. But it is difficult to direct a newborn's head accurately with the inside of one's forearm. Although most mothers sooner or later begin using the cradle hold for most of their daytime nursings, in the early days of breastfeeding the cross-over and football holds are generally more useful.

The cross-over hold. Take time to position yourself comfortably. If you are nursing in a hospital bed, sit up as straight as possible with a pillow behind you. As soon as you are able, sit in a chair with arms (most couches are too deep). Unwrap your baby; this will encourage his interest in latching on and make it easier for you to check his position. Place one or two pillows on your lap so that the baby is at the level of your breast. Lay him on his side with his chest and abdomen against your body.

Instead of placing the baby's head in the bend of your elbow as in the cradle hold, hold him with the opposite arm, so that your hand rests between the shoulder blades and supports the back of his neck and head. Place your thumb behind and below one ear and your other fingers behind and below the other. Now shift the baby, if necessary, so that his nose—not his mouth—is right in front of your nipple. In this position he is most likely to latch on with his lower jaw far back of the nipple.

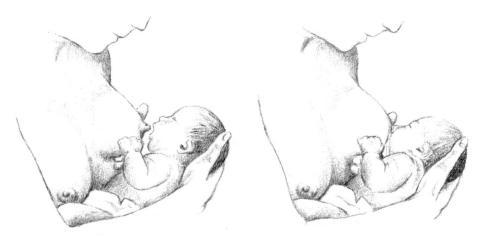

Cross-over hold.

If you're starting on the left breast, hold it with your left hand so that your thumb is positioned at the margin of the areola, about 1½ inches from the nipple, at the spot where the baby's nose will touch the breast (or at about two o'clock, if you imagine a clock face printed on your breast). Place your index finger the same distance from the nipple at the spot where the baby's chin will touch the breast (or at about eight o'clock). Gently compress the breast to match the shape of your baby's open mouth.

Before you bring the baby onto the breast, you must stimulate him to "root." Touch the baby's upper lip to your nipple, and wait until he opens his mouth wide. When his lower jaw is dropped all the way down, quickly bring his shoulders and head together to the breast. His head should be tipped slightly back, so his chin reaches the breast first. Don't lean into the baby. Keep the areola compressed until he begins sucking. You'll know that he is well latched on if his lips are far apart and flared, if he has more of the bottom of the areola in his mouth than the top, and if you feel comfortable.

You may need to repeat this process several times before the baby latches on correctly. Common mistakes include lining up the baby's mouth rather than the nose with the nipple, pulling the baby on before his mouth is wide open, not pulling him on quick enough far enough, and letting go of the breast before he is well latched on.

Once the baby is actively nursing, you'll probably need to support the breast for him, by gently pressing your fingers against the underside. If your breasts are small, though, you may be able to let go of the breast or even switch arms and continue nursing using the cradle hold.

Hand position for the cross-over hold.

Football hold. The football hold is a great position to use when—

- You have had a cesarean birth and want to avoid placing the baby against your abdomen.
- You need more visibility in getting the baby to latch on.
- Your breasts are large.
- You are nursing a small baby, especially if he is premature.
- You are nursing twins.

Sit in a comfortable armchair with a pillow at your side to help support your arm and lift the baby. Support the baby in a semisitting position facing you, with her bottom at the back of the chair. Your arm closest to your baby should support her back, with your hand holding her neck and head. Place your thumb behind and below one ear and your other fingers behind the other. Position the baby with her head just below the breast and her nose in front of the nipple. This way she'll latch on to the areola with her lower jaw far back of the nipple.

Support your breast with your free hand so that your thumb is about 1½ inches above the nipple, at twelve o'clock, and your index finger is the same distance below the nipple, at six o'clock. Compress the areola with your thumb and index finger so that your hand forms a C-shape. This will more closely match your breast to the shape of your baby's mouth, so she can take in more of the breast. As with the cross-over hold, stimulate the baby to open her mouth wide, and bring her up onto the breast.

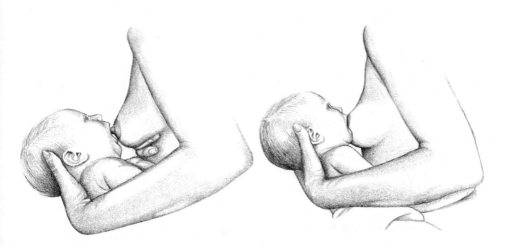

Football hold.

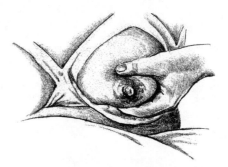

Hand position for the football hold.

Side-lying position. The side-lying position is an especially good choice for nursing when—

- You must be flat after a cesarean birth.
- You are uncomfortable sitting up.
- You need help from someone else to get the baby latched on.
- The baby is sleepy and reluctant to begin nursing or stay awake very long.
- You are nursing during the night.

You and your baby lie on your sides, tummy to tummy, as with the cuddle hold. Place your fingers beneath the breast and lift upward, then pull the baby in close after he roots with a wide open mouth.

The side-lying position becomes much easier after four to six weeks, when the baby has better head control and can come onto the breast without much assistance.

Ending the feeding. Waiting until your baby lets go of the nipple is the ideal way to end a feeding. If the baby does not come off the breast by himself after 20 to 25 minutes on a side, and you want to switch breasts or rest awhile, you can take him off by first breaking the suction. Even if he is not actively sucking, his hold on the nipple is tremendously strong. To release the suction, insert your finger into the corner of his mouth, pushing your finger between his gums until you hear or feel the release. You can also try placing your finger on the corner of the baby's mouth and pulling the skin gently towards his ear.

After taking the baby off the breast, leave your bra flaps down

Side-lying position.

so that the air can dry your nipples. Air drying helps to maintain healthy nipples.

After a cesarean birth. Whether or not your cesarean is planned, your milk will come in just as if you had delivered vaginally, and you can breastfeed your baby. Because you will be recovering from surgery, you will face some discomfort and possibly some difficulty maneuvering the baby to your breast. If you are expecting a cesarean, you may want to ask to share a hospital room with another woman who has had one. Some hospitals make such arrangements routinely.

If you are awake for your delivery, let the staff and the baby's physician know you wish to nurse as soon as possible. As long as the baby is not having any difficulties, there is no reason to delay nursing. If you can't sit up, you can nurse in the side-lying position with some help from your partner or the nurse.

If you are not fully conscious during the delivery, or if the baby is kept in the nursery by the doctor's orders, you can still begin nursing after your initial separation. Medication for pain is important for your comfort during the first few days; it will not hurt the baby. If you take the medication right after you nurse, moreover, a minimal amount will be in your milk at the next feeding. After a couple of days you may want to keep the baby in the room with you. Remember to ask for help whenever you need it. Sometimes the staff may forget you gave birth by cesarean section.

You may prefer to nurse at first in the side-lying position. Leave the side rails of the bed up so that turning will be easier. A pillow behind your back and one between your legs may be helpful. When you begin sitting up to nurse, a pillow on your lap will make you more comfortable. The football hold works well while sitting if you want to keep the baby off your abdomen.

Insuring Your Milk Supply

Frequent nursing. Your baby should be nursing often, at least eight times in 24 hours. Until your milk comes in your baby needs frequent feedings of colostrum. After your milk comes in, about 72 hours after the birth, a good feeding every few hours will help ensure a plentiful milk supply.

During the first few days after birth, many babies are sleepy. If your newborn has not nursed after three hours (counted from the start of the last feeding), unwrap her from her blankets, rub her back, and talk to her. She will probably then become interested in nursing.

In the hospital, keeping the baby with you in your room helps insure frequent nursing. If you are not rooming-in with your baby, ask the nurses to bring her to you at least every three hours (more often if she fusses), including whenever she wakens in the night.

Encourage the baby to have a good feeding each time you nurse her. Until your milk is in, you can probably persuade her to take both breasts at each feeding. Listen for the sound of your baby swallowing; when you hear it you will know that she is taking colostrum or milk. When your baby has released the nipple, or when you have nursed her for at least 20 minutes and she is no longer swallowing, burp her. Hold her up over your shoulder and pat her back, or sit her upright, bent slightly forward with your hand supporting her lower jaw, and firmly pat her lower back. After burping, she will probably regain interest in nursing and take the second breast. If she doesn't burp within a few minutes, just switch sides. If she refuses to nurse on the second breast or nurses only a short time, be sure to start her on that side at the next feeding.

You can burp the baby by sitting her up, one hand under her jaw. Firmly pat her back with the other hand.

The first days of milk production are the critical period for determining whether a mother ends up with a generous milk supply or an inadequate one. If little milk is removed from the breast, the resulting pressure causes the breast to slow down production. If no milk is removed, milk production stops entirely. (This is how women who don't nurse stop producing milk.) So ensuring a good milk supply depends on having a vigorous nursing baby (or an effective breast pump) that drains at least one breast every few hours around the clock.

Avoiding supplements. Another way to help insure your milk supply is to avoid supplemental feedings. Some babies become very confused when a bottle nipple is introduced during the first few days (see "Just the Breast"). Glucose (sugar) water offers few calories and may discourage the baby's interest in nursing. Also, babies fed glucose water more frequently develop jaundice in the first few days after birth. After taking formula, a baby frequently will not want to nurse for four hours or longer, since formula takes longer to digest than breast milk. The decrease in breast stimulation may decrease milk production.

Babies who may not get enough. Some babies at risk for underfeeding can be identified even before the milk comes in. These babies may be unable to drain the breasts adequately during feedings:

- babies who are born three weeks or more before the due date;
- babies who weigh less than six pounds at birth;

- babies who may have poor muscle tone, such as those with Down syndrome;
- babies who have unusual conformations in their mouths, such as a short frenulum (the string of tissue on the underside of the tongue) near the tongue's tip, a recessed lower jaw, a high palate, or a cleft lip or palate;
- babies whose mothers have large nipples (as large or larger in diameter than a quarter); and
- babies who aren't yet latching on or sustaining sucking 24 hours after birth.

If you or your baby falls into one of these risk groups, a few days of sluggish nursing and limited milk removal could have a devastating effect on your milk production. Consider renting a fully automatic electric breast pump, which may be more reliable than your baby in stimulating continued milk production. Starting on the third day after birth, pump for five minutes on each breast right after each daytime and evening nursing. This "insurance pumping" should assure that you'll have an abundant milk supply even if your baby's sucking is on the sluggish side. You can freeze the pumped milk for later use.

Watch your baby closely for the reassuring signs of adequate milk intake listed near the end of this chapter. The baby should be weighed at 10 to 12 days of age, or sooner if you suspect that he may not be taking enough milk. If he has regained his birth weight, you can gradually stop pumping over a few days (before returning the pump, though, make sure the baby has gained an ounce a day since the last weighing). But if he is still below his birth weight at 10 to 12 days of age, supplement nursings with the pumped milk (see "Treatment Measures for Underfeeding" in "Survival Guide for the First Week").

Other babies who may not get enough milk are those whose mothers—

- have had previous breast surgery involving an incision around the nipple or areola, such as in some breast augmentation or reduction procedures (see "Nursing after Breast Surgery" in Chapter 3); or
- have breasts that appear underdeveloped, with a space of 1½ inches or more between them, especially if they grew little during pregnancy. Often, such *hypoplastic* breasts differ markedly from each other in size, and sometimes they have stretch marks.

Hypoplastic breasts may remain soft on the third day after birth, when a mother's breasts normally fill with milk. These breasts may contain insufficient glandular tissue to produce a full milk supply. Perhaps half of women identified with this condition, however, can develop full milk production by six weeks post partum.

If you have had breast surgery that may affect your ability to produce milk, or if you suspect you may have insufficient glandular tissue, observe your baby closely for signs of low milk intake, and use a fully automatic pump after each nursing to stimulate maximum milk production. Weigh your baby at three to four days of age and every couple of days thereafter until she is clearly gaining an ounce a day. If she loses 10 percent or more of her birth weight or does not gain an ounce a day after five days of age, she needs your pumped breast milk or formula as a supplement. See "Underfeeding and Weight Loss" in "Survival Guide for the First Week."

The First Week of Nursing

Although most babies are alert and eager to nurse during the first two hours after birth, during the next few days they may sleep much of the time. The average baby, after the first couple of days, begins to wake up to nurse about every one to three hours. At night, he will sleep from one to five hours at a stretch. If your baby is not waking on his own to nurse at least eight times in each 24-hour period, including at least once in the night, awaken him for feedings.

The typical length of a feeding varies greatly from baby to baby. A baby who is "all business"—who sucks and swallows with few pauses—may complete a feeding in as little as ten minutes. At the other extreme is the "dawdler," who sucks and swallows five or six times and then pauses. This pattern of frequent pausing may extend a feeding up to 45 minutes. Most babies' feedings fall between these extremes; the average is about 20 to 30 minutes. Although your baby may not fall asleep after feeding, he should seem content.

While the baby nurses, you should hear a lot of swallowing. Some babies gulp noisily, whereas others are more quiet. When babies are getting milk they take long, drawing sucks and can be heard swallowing or gulping. (They take short, choppy sucks when they are not swallowing milk.) These long, drawing sucks usually occur in bursts, that is, five to ten continuous sucks followed by a pause. Babies who are taking enough milk usually have several bursts of continuous sucking and swallowing during a feeding.

You should not hear clicking noises while your baby nurses. Clicking usually means that the baby is not sucking adequately and therefore may not be receiving enough milk. The baby should have such a strong hold on the breast that the nipple does not easily slip from his mouth when you pull him slightly away. His cheeks should remain smooth with each suck; dimples on the cheek while nursing are a sign of inadequate suction and faulty sucking (see "Survival Guide for the First Week" if your baby's cheeks are dimpling).

During the first day after birth, babies sometimes spit up mucus they have swallowed during delivery. Occasionally a baby will gag on this mucus. After the first 24 hours, this is usually no longer a problem.

Some babies also spit up colostrum or milk. The amounts are usually smaller than they seem, though you may wonder if your baby is keeping anything down. Spitting up a teaspoon or two after feedings is normal for some babies in the first week.

Babies also get hiccoughs, often after a feeding. If the baby starts hiccoughing after nursing at the first breast, it may be difficult to interest him in the other. You don't need to give him water or anything else. The hiccoughs are painless for him; just wait till they go away.

The baby's first stools, called meconium, are black and sticky. Stooling every day and having yellow stools by the fifth day usually indicates an adequate intake of colostrum, first, and then breast milk. This is one of the surest signs that a newborn is getting enough to eat. Most newborns have at least three bowel movements each day during the first month. Only after the first month is it normal for breastfed babies to go several days without having a bowel movement.

The yellow stools are soft, loose, or watery, and sometimes they look seedy. Babies normally strain and grunt when passing their stools—this does not mean they are constipated.

Wet diapers are usually infrequent in the first few days, but they should be more frequent and wetter by the fifth day. Eight or more diapers wet with pale urine each day, along with daily yellow stools, are usually a sign of sufficient milk intake. (This rule may not hold true if the baby is receiving water supplements.)

All newborns lose weight after birth. Expect your baby to lose about 5 to 9 percent of his birth weight. He should begin gaining weight by the fifth day, about an ounce a day.

Caring for your breasts. Your daily bath or shower is sufficient for cleaning your breasts. Avoid getting soap or shampoo on the nipple and areola; it tends to counteract the naturally occurring oils that cleanse this area. Antiseptic applications to the nipples are also unnecessary, but do take care to wash your hands before nursing.

You will probably want to wear a nursing bra for convenience and comfort, especially after your milk comes in. Again, bras with cotton rather than synthetic cups allow for better air circulation to the nipples.

If the baby does not come off the breast by herself when the nursing session is over, take care to release the suction with your finger. Leave your breasts exposed to the air for five or ten minutes before covering up. Air drying is soothing to the nipples.

During the past decade nursing mothers have been discouraged from using nipple creams, since some women develop sore nipples in reaction to preparations containing lanolin, vitamin E, or cocoa butter. Also, lanolin preparations were discovered to be contaminated with pesticide residues. Recently, however, a purified form of lanolin has been developed: it is nonallergenic and pesticide-free. Modified lanolin will not prevent nipple soreness, but it is very soothing to tender nipples and may promote healing. See Appendix A for ordering information.

For those women who leak milk, nursing pads are usually necessary during this time to prevent wet or spotted clothing. You can buy the pads in two varieties: reusable, washable types, and disposable types. (Remember: if you prefer disposable pads, stay away from those with plastic liners because they keep the nipple wet and may aggravate soreness.)

If you are using plastic breast shells to improve the shape of your nipples, you may find during the first few weeks that they cause your milk to leak excessively and keep your nipples damp. You might try placing the shells in your bra just 20 to 30 minutes before the feeding (milk collected this way must be discarded). Don't routinely use breast shells in place of nursing pads; this would probably cause more leakage. Breast shells should be washed after each nursing in hot soapy water and rinsed thoroughly.

When your milk comes in. Milk production generally begins on the second or third day post partum, but occasionally not until the fourth day. At first the milk will be mixed with colostrum, and so will be pale orange in color. After a few days the milk will become whiter. This mature milk will look more watery than cow's milk; it may resemble skim milk. If your milk hasn't come in by the fourth day after birth, see "Late Onset of Milk Production" in "Survival Guide for the First Week."

Most women notice that their breasts become larger, fuller, and more tender as the milk comes in. Large-breasted women may notice only a change in heaviness. This change, known as engorgement, is caused by increased blood flow to the breasts as well as beginning milk production. Fullness may be more apparent if your breasts are normally small or medium-sized. They may feel lumpy, and the lumpiness may extend all the way to your armpits, since milk glands are also located there. After nursing, your breasts should feel softer or lighter.

Engorgement normally lasts 24 to 48 hours. During this time a nursing bra will provide support and comfort. Frequent nursing, at least every two to three hours, is the best treatment. Heat treatments such as warm showers, hot packs, and heating pads may worsen the swelling. You may get relief, though, from gently massaging the breast while the baby is nursing. This will encourage more milk to let down. It is important to pay careful attention to the way the baby latches on while the breast is engorged. When latch-on is incorrect, because the baby isn't positioned well or the areola is overly full, soreness often follows. If the areola is hard, you can express some milk, by hand or with a pump. (For further advice on managing engorgement, see "Survival Guide for the First Week.")

When you put your baby to breast you may feel any of these normal sensations: warmth, relaxation, sleepiness, thirst, and even hunger.

It is normal for milk to leak from the breasts. When the baby nurses at one breast, milk may drip from the other. This leaking may continue for several weeks, or it may never happen at all.

From hospital to home. At the time of discharge it is customary in many hospitals to give new mothers an array of sample products that manufacturers would like them to try. It may appear that the staff endorses these products; this is not necessarily so. One of

Older children may be more of a help than a hindrance if you encourage them to feel that the baby is theirs, too.

these gifts is usually a package of formula, sometimes called a "breastfeeding kit." The "kit" contains formula, bottle nipples, and a pamphlet on breastfeeding. These pamphlets sometimes contain misleading information about nursing. Since you have chosen to breastfeed, it is best to leave the kit behind. You won't be needing it.

What are well worth taking home, however, are the names and telephone numbers of people who have a good reputation for helping nursing mothers and infants. Ask any nurse who has been encouraging or helpful with your early breastfeeding for this information. She may know of volunteers in La Leche League or the Nursing Mothers Counsel, or lactation professionals in your community.

At home. As any experienced nursing mother can tell you, the first few days at home with a baby are exhausting and, at times, emotional. These days are best spent caring only for yourself and the baby. Besides recovering from the birth, you are doing the important work of getting to know your baby and learning to breastfeed. Rest and a quiet, pleasant environment are important in preventing anxiety and "baby blues." Try to eat well, but don't worry if your appetite has lessened; this can be normal during the first couple of weeks after delivery. Ideally, you should spend the first several days nursing and resting with the baby, while a supportive partner or helper (or both) manages your home, meals, any other children, and callers.

It is not uncommon for things to suddenly "fall apart" shortly after a new mother comes home from the hospital. Suddenly responsible for a new baby, you may feel shaky at times and your confidence may vanish. The dramatic hormonal shift that begins immediately after birth may also affect your emotional state for a short time. You may find yourself exhausted and upset—especially if you've been taking responsibility for more than the baby and yourself.

The postpartum period is a time of physical and emotional adjustment. As with most changes in life, it is usually accompanied by some turmoil. It will take several weeks, and most of your time and energy, to get to know your baby and learn how to care for her. So don't do more than you must, and accept offers for help. Adjusting to motherhood is always easier when you are supported and cared for by others.

SURVIVAL GUIDE
for the First Week

Concerns about Yourself

Engorged Breasts

Late Onset of Milk Production

Sore Nipples

Breast Pain

Leaking Milk

Let-down Difficulty

Milk Appearance

Difficult Latch-on: Flat, Dimpled, or Inverted Nipples

Fatigue and Depression

Concerns about the Baby

Sleepy Baby

Bowel Movements

Jaundice

Difficult Latch-on: Refusal to Nurse

Sucking Problems

Fussiness and Excessive Night Waking

Underfeeding and Weight Loss

Concerns about Yourself

Engorged Breasts

At two or three days post partum the breasts usually become engorged, or temporarily swollen and uncomfortable. This is caused by the increased flow of blood to the breasts and the start of milk production. For some women the breasts become only slightly full, but for others they feel very swollen, tender, throbbing, and lumpy. Sometimes the swelling extends all the way to the armpit. Engorgement may cause the nipple to flatten, making it difficult for the baby to latch on. The problem usually lessens within 24 to 48 hours, but the swelling and discomfort may worsen if nursing is too brief or infrequent. If engorgement is unrelieved by nursing or pumping, milk production declines and ultimately stops altogether.

Although many health-care providers recommend applying direct heat (warm washcloths, heating pads, hot water bottles, or hot showers) to engorged breasts, this may actually aggravate engorgement.

Treatment Measures for Engorged Breasts

1. Wear a supportive nursing bra, even during the night. Be sure your bra is not too tight.

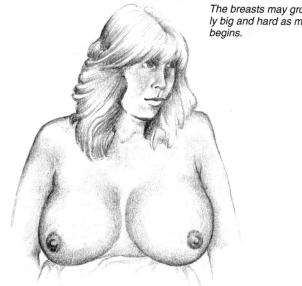

The breasts may grow astonishingly big and hard as milk production begins.

2. Nurse frequently, every one to three hours. This may mean waking the baby (see "Sleepy Baby").

3. Avoid having the baby latch on when the areola is very firm. To reduce the possibility of damage to your nipples, manually express or pump milk until the areola softens. Wearing plastic breast shells for half an hour before nursing also helps to soften the areola.

4. Encourage the baby to nurse at least 10 minutes or longer at each breast. It is preferable to nurse on just one side until the breast is soft, even if the baby then goes to sleep, than to limit the baby's nursing time on the first side so you can nurse from both sides in one feeding.

5. Gently massage the breast at which the baby is nursing. This will encourage the milk to flow and will help relieve some of the tightness and discomfort you feel.

6. To soothe the pain and help relieve swelling, apply a cold pack to the breast for a short period *after* nursing. You can use ice in a plastic bag, or soak a disposable diaper in water, shape it, and then freeze it. Lay a thin cloth over your breast before applying the cold diaper.

7. If you need to, take acetaminophen tablets (such as Tylenol), ibuprofen (such as Advil or Motrin), or another mild pain reliever.

8. If 48 hours after your milk has come in you still find yourself overly full right after nursing, use a pump to drain both breasts as completely as possible. In this first week, habitual pumping along with nursing is generally discouraged, as it can lead to more engorgement and chronic overproduction. But pumping after nursing once every 24 hours or so should relieve your engorgement, not prolong it.

9. If the baby is not nursing well enough to soften at least one breast every few hours, use an electric breast pump as necessary. Unrelieved engorgement causes milk production to stop.

Late Onset of Milk Production

Within 72 hours after birth, the production of mature milk normally begins. The breasts typically feel heavier and fuller, although large-breasted women may notice little change.

Occasionally milk production is delayed beyond 72 hours; sometimes it begins only days later. In the meantime, the breasts remain soft, and the baby sucks but gets little milk. In these circumstances, some babies seem sleepy and content, but most act hungry and dissatisfied. They have infrequent bowel movements and lose more weight than normally expected.

I suspect that events during labor and birth may influence the onset of milk production. Overhydration with intravenous fluids during a long or induced labor, or after a postpartum hemorrhage, may perhaps cause a delay in mature milk production.

If your milk is late in coming in, you may need to supplement with formula until it does. But you should continue to nurse frequently in the meantime.

Treatment Measures for Late Onset of Milk Production

1. If after 72 hours post partum you suspect that your milk is not in, have your baby weighed. If he has lost less than 10 percent of his birth weight (see the chart in Appendix B), continue to nurse frequently, every one to three hours, and monitor his weight daily.

2. If the baby has lost 10 percent or more of his birth weight, use an electric breast pump after each nursing. Feed your baby the colostrum you collect and any necessary formula (see Appendix A to determine how much your baby needs).

3. When your milk comes in, refer to "Underfeeding and Weight Loss," later in this Survival Guide, to estimate your production and wean your baby off formula and pumped milk.

Sore Nipples

There is no doubt about it: sore nipples can make a trial of what ought to be a joyous experience. For a few days after giving birth, you may feel slight tenderness during the first minute of nursing, when the baby latches on and the nipple stretches into her mouth. Such tenderness is normal at this time. (See "General Comfort Measures for Sore Nipples.")

If your nipples become really sore, however, they are probably damaged or irritated and require treatment beyond simple comfort measures. It is important for you to identify the cause of the problem so that you can help your nipples heal. At any time that you are unable to tolerate the pain, and the position changes recommended in the following pages do not help, consult a lactation professional. If none is available, you may want to stop nursing; pump your milk with a fully automatic electric pump for 24 to 72 hours, or until the nipples heal (see Chapter 5 on expressing milk).

There are two basic types of sore nipples: the traumatized nipple and the irritated nipple. The traumatized nipple may be blistered, scabbed, or cracked. The irritated nipple is very pink and often burns. Occasionally a mother may have both types of soreness at once.

In addition to the specific treatments listed for each category of sore nipples, the "General Comfort Measures for Sore Nipples" will speed healing and provide comfort.

General Comfort Measures for Sore Nipples

1. Take acetaminophen tablets (such as Tylenol), ibuprofen (such as Advil or Motrin), or a pain reliever prescribed by your doctor, a half hour before nursing.

2. Begin nursing on the least sore side (if there is one).

3. Avoid nipple shields for nursing. These often make the soreness worse, and they may decrease your milk supply. If nursing is too painful, rent a fully automatic electric pump.

4. Massage your breasts while nursing to encourage the milk to flow and to speed emptying.

5. Restrict nursing time to about ten to fifteen minutes per side if you are sore during the entire feeding. This will probably mean nursing more often (every hour or two).

6. Release the baby's suction hold carefully before removing the baby from the breast.

7. Air-dry the nipples after each feeding. Leave the nipples exposed to the air as much as possible between nursings. A cotton T-shirt worn without a bra, or with your bra flaps down, will provide good air circulation to the nipples.

8. Change nursing pads after each nursing and when they become wet. Make sure there are no plastic liners hidden in the pads; cut them open and check if you are not absolutely sure.

9. Wear cotton bras. Other fabrics do not allow adequate air circulation.

10. Wash plastic breast shells daily, if you use them at all. Shells may prevent the nipples from rubbing against your bra, but they may also encourage dripping, keep the nipples moist, and delay healing.

11. Avoid excessive washing of your nipples. Rinse them in your daily bath or shower, but avoid getting soap on them. Do take care to wash your hands before handling your breasts.

12. Leave scabs and blisters alone.

13. Do not delay nursings. Shorter, more frequent nursings (every hour to three hours) are easier on the nipples.

14. If you are using a breast pump during a period of soreness, pump your milk often—at least eight times a day—to keep up your supply. Again, anything other than a fully automatic pump (a rental pump) may not be effective enough to maintain your milk supply. Be sure to use the correct size shield for your nipple, and carefully center it before starting to pump (see Chapter 5).

Traumatized nipples. Cracks, blisters, and abrasions usually result because a baby is improperly positioned for nursing; her gums close on the nipple instead of the areola. Trauma can also occur when a baby fails to open her mouth wide enough or when her gums slide off the areola onto the nipple, commonly when the breast is engorged or not supported.

Babies who have a faulty suck or who are "tongue-tied" can also make nipples sore as they nurse (see the section on "tongue-tied" babies under "Difficult Latch-on," later in this Survival Guide). Cracking may also occur with irritated nipples and thrush nipples (see the sections on both).

Treatment Measures for Traumatized Nipples

1. Carefully review "Positioning at the Breast," in Chapter 2, so that you clearly understand the details of correct latch-on technique. The football or the cross-over hold is highly recommended.

2. If your breast is so full that the areola cannot be easily compressed, manually express or pump enough milk to soften the areola. This will allow the baby to get more of the areola into her mouth and will help to stimulate let-down.

3. Use the football or the cross-over hold to control the position of the baby's head through the entire feeding. This will allow you to prevent her gums from sliding down onto the nipple after she has latched on.

4. If your baby is reluctant to open her mouth wide, don't let her chew her way onto the breast. Patiently wait until she opens her mouth wide. Letting the baby suck on your finger for a few seconds may stimulate her sucking response and encourage her to open more enthusiastically.

5. Do not hesitate to take the baby off the breast as soon as you realize that she is not in the right position. You may need to help her latch on several times before you succeed at getting her far enough

onto the breast. Ask your partner, helper, or lactation professional to observe your latch-on technique. A helper can also guide your arm when the baby opens wide so that she is pulled in as close as possible.

6. After nursing, apply a thin coating of modified lanolin to your nipples to soothe them and promote healing. Review "General Comfort Measures for Sore Nipples."

Irritated nipples. Irritated nipples are reddened and sometimes slightly swollen, and *generally they burn.* Some mothers may feel burning between as well as during feedings. In severe cases, the nipples may be cracked, peeling, or oozing. Irritated nipples may be caused by dermatitis, thrush or yeast, or an underlying skin condition such as eczema or impetigo.

Thrush nipples. This problem occurs when a yeast *(monilia)* infection in the baby's mouth spreads to the mother's nipples. The nipples become reddened, swollen, tender, and sometimes cracked. Occasionally peeling or a red, dotty rash can be seen on the nipples. Some mothers complain of itching and flaking; others complain of burning.

When a mother's nipples become sore after weeks or months of comfortable nursing, thrush is the usual cause. But a thrush infection may also occur in the first weeks after delivery, and when it does it may be overlooked as the cause of the nipple soreness. A newborn with thrush may have picked up a yeast infection in the birth canal during delivery; this often happens if the mother is diabetic. A thrush infection may also result if a mother or her baby is given antibiotics (after a cesarean, antibiotics are often given in intravenous fluids).

If you suspect a case of thrush, carefully inspect the baby's mouth. You may see white patches on the inside of the cheeks, inside the lips, and possibly on the tongue. Sometimes a baby will have no symptoms in the mouth but will have a diaper rash caused by yeast. This rash, usually in the genital area, often resembles a mild burn; it may peel and does not respond to ordinary measures. Sometimes the rash looks like just a patch of red dots.

Treatment Measures for Thrush Nipples

1. Both the mother and the baby must be treated in order to prevent reinfection. The treatment usually recommended is 1 milliliter of

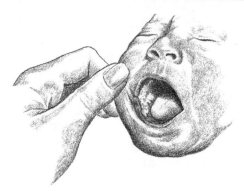

Thrush often appears as white, cheesy patches on the insides of the cheeks and lips.

nystatin suspension (Mycostatin) by dropper into the baby's mouth after every other nursing, or four times daily, for 14 days. Half the dose should be dropped into each side of the mouth. For the nipples, nystatin cream or ointment is recommended; the baby's medicine can also be used, but it may be less effective. The medication should be applied after each nursing. In either form, nystatin must be prescribed by a physician. Even though the symptoms may be gone after a few days, continue the treatment for the full 14 days.

If you cannot get your baby's doctor to prescribe nystatin cream for your nipples (and your baby's diaper rash, if present), call your obstetrician. Or use an over-the-counter antifungal cream such as Lotrimin AF, Micatin, or Monostat 7. Another treatment that is sometimes recommended is swabbing the baby's mouth with a 1-percent solution of gentian violet, which can be purchased at most drugstores without a prescription. Thoroughly swab the affected areas in the baby's mouth with a cotton-tipped applicator once or twice a day for three days. The solution will stain the baby's mouth and your breasts purple; take care in applying so that nothing else turns purple.

2. If you are using nystatin, it is best to wait for a few minutes after nursing before giving it to the baby so that it isn't washed out of his system with the milk. Some lactation professionals also recommend rinsing your nipples after each nursing the first few days with water or a mild solution of vinegar (one tablespoon vinegar to one cup water) before applying the cream or drops.

3. In addition to medication, brief exposure to the sun two or three times daily may hasten the healing of the nipples.

4. Changing the nursing pads at each feeding is a must to prevent reinfection.

5. Pacifiers, bottle nipples, and plastic breast shells must be boiled

for 5 minutes every day during treatment. If you are using nystatin, these nipples should be replaced at the end of the first week.

6. If you are using a pump, it is important to wash all pump parts thoroughly after each use. In addition, the parts that come in contact with the breast or the milk should be boiled for 5 minutes daily.

7. If nystatin suspension has not cleared thrush from your baby's mouth after five to six days of treatment, consider that this medication inhibits yeast growth for only about two hours after you swab the baby's mouth. Ask your doctor about more frequent dosing, or try using gentian violet (as described in item 1) in addition to the nystatin.

8. If your nipples are not significantly better after several days of the treatment just described, see a dermatologist for additional treatment.

Nipple dermatitis. A slight reddening and a burning feeling in the nipples, in the absence of thrush (yeast) or another underlying skin condition, usually indicates dermatitis. Nipple dermatitis can result from bacterial growth on the nipples or an allergic response to a nipple cream or oil.

Common offenders are vitamin E preparations—oils, creams, or capsules. Mothers allergic to chocolate may develop an allergic reaction to preparations with cocoa butter, such as Balm Barr. Unmodified lanolin may also cause an allergic response, usually in a mother who is allergic to wool (from which lanolin comes) or very sensitive to it. Lanolin is found in pure hydrous and anhydrous forms and in many commercial creams, such as Masse Cream, Mammol Ointment, Eucerin, and A & D Ointment. Modified lanolin, which has had the allergenic component removed, seldom causes allergic reactions.

Simply discontinuing use of the cream or oil may bring some relief, but usually additional measures are necessary.

Treatment Measures for Nipple Dermatitis

1. The ideal doctor to diagnose and treat this type of nipple soreness is a dermatologist. Usually, a moderate-strength or high-potency anti-inflammatory cream and an antibiotic cream are prescribed. Your obstetrician may give you a prescription, but if he is reluctant or his remedy ineffective, see a dermatologist.

2. Place cool, wet compresses on the nipples after nursing.

3. Apply the medication to the irritated areas after every other nursing, making sure your nipples are completely dry first. The cream

should be applied sparingly so that all of it is absorbed. If you see traces on your nipples when you are ready to nurse again, you are using too much. Dab the area with a tissue to absorb the excess.

4. Use the medication for as long as advised by your doctor. Although the pain may be gone in a day or two, the dermatitis may take from one to two weeks to completely heal.

5. Should you find that the medication aggravates your soreness, stop using it immediately. This may indicate that yeast is present and should be treated. (See "Thrush Nipples.")

6. Review "General Comfort Measures for Sore Nipples."

Eczema and impetigo. Eczema can appear on the nipple and areola, making the area burn, itch, flake, ooze, or crust. Women with a history or current outbreak of eczema elsewhere on the body are most often affected. Treatment from a dermatologist should be sought.

Impetigo is a severe infection that causes continual sloughing off of the skin. Impetigo on the nipples can be quickly cured with a prescription antibiotic cream.

Breast Pain

You may feel pain in your breasts if you become engorged, which usually happens two to four days after delivery (see "Engorged Breasts").

Occasionally mothers complain of breast pain while nursing. If you feel a burning pain and your nipples are pinker than normal, see "Irritated Nipples." If you feel a mild aching at the start of nursing, it is probably related to the beginning of let-down.

A deep pain, sometimes described as "shooting," that occurs soon after nursing is believed to be related to the sudden refilling of the breast. This discomfort is usually temporary and disappears after the first weeks of nursing.

Leaking Milk

During the early weeks of nursing, milk may drip, leak, or spray from the breasts. This is a normal sign of let-down. While the baby nurses at one breast, milk often drips or sprays from the other. Let-down, and leaking, may occur frequently and unexpectedly between nursings as well. Milk may leak during sleep. It may be stimulated by the baby's sounds, by thoughts about nursing, or by any routines associated with feeding time. A shower may stimulate let-down. Dripping, leaking, and spraying usually lessen considerably after a few weeks of nursing.

Some mothers' breasts do not leak. Mothers who have nursed previously may notice that their breasts leak less with subsequent children. Both of these situations are usually normal.

Coping Measures for Leaking Milk

1. Open both bra flaps while nursing and let the milk drip into a small towel or diaper.

2. Change nursing pads as soon as they become wet. Avoid those with plastic liners.

3. Avoid routine use of plastic breast shells if you do not need them to improve the shape of your nipples. They may keep your clothes dry, but they can cause excessive leaking and keep your nipples moist. Milk collected in the shells between nursings is unsafe for feeding. Only if the shells are boiled just prior to nursing and put in place during nursing can the milk be stored for later feedings.

4. Habitually pumping your breasts will not control leaking. In fact, it will stimulate greater milk production and possibly make your breasts fuller and more prone to leaking.

5. Place extra pads in your bra if your breasts leak during the night. You may want to spread a bath towel over the bed sheet to eliminate middle-of-the-night linen changes and to protect your mattress.

6. Do not try to stop leaking with the pressure of your fingers or forearm during the first few weeks, since this may inhibit milk let-down and may possibly lead to plugged milk ducts.

Let-down Difficulty

During the early weeks of breastfeeding, the let-down response is developing. Sometimes mothers are told that they must be happy, relaxed, and carefree for the let-down of milk to occur. If this were the case, few women would ever succeed at nursing. Although many mothers worry that their milk won't be available as needed, let-down failure is extremely rare among women who nurse regularly and often.

For the establishment and maximal functioning of the let-down reflex, nurse the baby every two to three hours around the clock during the first week. Make sure that she is positioned correctly and is compressing the sinuses beneath the areola, and that her feeding time is not limited. Ideally, the baby should be allowed—encouraged, if necessary—to drain one or both breasts well at each feeding.

It is also important that you are as comfortable as possible. The milk may not release completely if you are experiencing much pain—whether from sore nipples or from the trauma of delivery.

The signs of milk release during the first week will vary for each woman. They *may* include—

- mild uterine cramping during nursing;
- increased vaginal flow during nursing;
- dripping, leaking, or spraying of milk, especially during nursing;
- occasional sensations in the breast during nursing (usually not felt during the first week); and
- softening of the breasts after nursing.

The most reliable indicator of milk let-down is the sound of the baby swallowing. As the milk releases the baby will swallow after every one or two sucks. Most women, particularly first-time mothers, do not feel the let-down reflex during the first few weeks after birth.

Usually when a mother believes she is experiencing a let-down difficulty, the problem is actually with the baby's latch-on or sucking, or a low milk supply. See "Difficult Latch-on: Refusal to Nurse," "Sucking Problems," and "Underfeeding and Weight Loss" later in this chapter.

Milk Appearance

Whereas colostrum is usually clear, yellow, or orange, mature breast milk is white, sometimes with a bluish tint. If it resembles skim milk from the dairy, this does not mean your milk is "weak"; breast milk normally looks thin. Occasionally a mother discovers that her milk is green, blue, or pink. Such coloring is due to her intake of vegetables, fruits, food dyes, or dietary supplements, and is not harmful to the baby.

Blood in the milk can usually be traced to a bleeding nipple. Occasionally bleeding from the breast occurs during pregnancy or when breastfeeding begins. Frequently, a benign papilloma is the cause, and the bleeding generally stops within several days. Blood in the milk will not hurt the baby, though substantial amounts may make him vomit. If you are advised against nursing, pump for a few days. The problem will clear up on its own in a day or so.

Difficult Latch-on: Flat, Dimpled, or Inverted Nipples

Both mother and baby get frustrated when latching on to the breasts is difficult because of flat, dimpled, or inverted nipples. Typically, the problem is intensified if the breasts become engorged or overly full. When they do, even nipples that seemed normal may suddenly flatten or dimple. Frequently, one nipple proves to be more troublesome than the other. Persistence and patience help most mothers through this problem.

Mothers with problem nipples are often more prone to soreness. This is because latch-on becomes their number-one priority; they give little attention to correct positioning.

Treatment Measures for Flat, Dimpled, or Inverted Nipples

1. Put the baby to the breast within the first two hours after birth. The timing of the first nursing may be critical when the nipples are flat, dimpled, or inverted. Many babies are able to latch on easily to problem nipples during this initial period, and they continue to do well.

2. Avoid giving the baby an artificial nipple of any kind. Whether or not your baby has succeeded at latching on at first try, this is very important. An artificial nipple often makes his subsequent attempts more difficult.

3. Stimulate the nipples to help them stand out, by gently stroking or rolling them between your thumb and forefinger or by applying ice to the nipple just before the baby attempts to latch on.

4. To help the baby latch on, make a flat nipple stand out by pinching it between your thumb and forefinger. This won't work with a dimpled or inverted nipple, though; it may invert further when pinched. Instead, place your thumb about 1½ to 2 inches behind the nipple, with your fingers beneath, and pull back toward your chest. The cross-over or football hold will allow you the most visibility and control.

5. Wear breast shells in your bra at least a half-hour before nursing if your breasts are engorged; this is often essential for dimpled or inverted nipples. Many hospital maternity units have breast shells. If

To help the baby latch on to an inverted nipple, place your thumb above the areola and your fingers below, and push your breast against your chest wall.

Don't squeeze your thumb and forefinger together, or the nipple may invert further.

yours doesn't, send your partner or friend to any maternity shop for a pair. (See "Planning for the First Days" in Chapter 1.)

6. Pump your breasts just before nursing to pull the nipples out enough for the baby to latch on. Any pump can be used for this.

7. Express a few drops of colostrum or milk onto your nipple or onto the baby's lips if he is reluctant to latch on. Glucose water (available only in hospital nurseries) dripped over the nipple may also entice the baby, although it sometimes makes the nipple too slippery. At home, in a pinch, you can mix a teaspoon of refined sugar in a cup of warm boiled water, then drip the solution over your nipple. But *never* use honey or corn syrup on your nipple, as they have been associated with infant botulism.

8. Stop nursing if the baby is frantic, and calm him for a while. Dripping glucose water on his lips also helps to calm him and gain his interest in latching on.

9. If a nurse or another helper is working with you, use the side-lying position—or, if you're large-breasted, the football hold—to allow your helper maximum visibility and control. If your nipples are dimpled or inverted, ask the helper to pull back on the breast behind the nipple; pinching will usually result in further inversion. Sometimes these sessions become intense and upsetting, so let your helper know when you or your baby needs a break. If you are in the hospital, let a variety of nurses work with you; you can usually find one or two who are exceptionally skilled and sensitive.

10. Refuse any offers from nurses of rubber nipple shields or bottle nipples to place over your own nipple for nursing. Your baby will latch on and suck, but the shield may not allow for adequate stimula-

tion of your nipple, or for the necessary compression of the sinuses beneath the areola. The shield can thus inhibit the let-down of milk and adequate emptying of the breast, possibly leading to a poor milk supply and insufficient milk intake for the baby. In addition, some babies who begin nursing with a nipple shield will refuse to ever nurse without it.

If you want to try using a nipple shield to make your nipples stand out, wait at least 24 hours after the birth, to give the baby a chance to nurse on his own. Take the shield off after the baby has sucked for one to two minutes, and try to get him to latch on without it. Pumping just before nursing works just as well as nipple shields in making the nipples stand out.

Use a nipple shield throughout feedings only if (1) a lactation professional makes sure that the baby is taking enough milk while you're wearing the shield, or (2) you use a fully automatic electric pump after each nursing to guarantee that your breasts are being well emptied, and you have the baby weighed every few days to make sure he is gaining at least an ounce a day.

11. Begin bottle feedings 24 hours after birth if your baby still has not latched on. An electric pump is usually the best choice for collecting milk and improving the nipple shape. Continue putting the baby to breast.

12. Occasionally a mother and her baby are discharged from the hospital before nursing has occurred. If this happens to you, locate a fully automatic electric pump (see Appendix A) and use it at least eight times a day. (See Chapter 3 for guidelines on pumping, and refer to Appendix B for the approximate amount of milk your baby needs at each feeding.) Keep trying to nurse; once at home, short practice sessions at least three to four times per day, on a soft breast when the baby is not frantic, eventually pay off. In this situation you may need a great deal of support and encouragement. Finding this support will make all the difference. Seeing a lactation professional may be very helpful. It is very common for a baby to suddenly latch on one day, rewarding his mother's persistence.

Fatigue and Depression

During this first week, make your life as simple as possible. Your partner or helper is essential, of course, to your recovery and adjustment. He or she can be most helpful in assuring your rest by

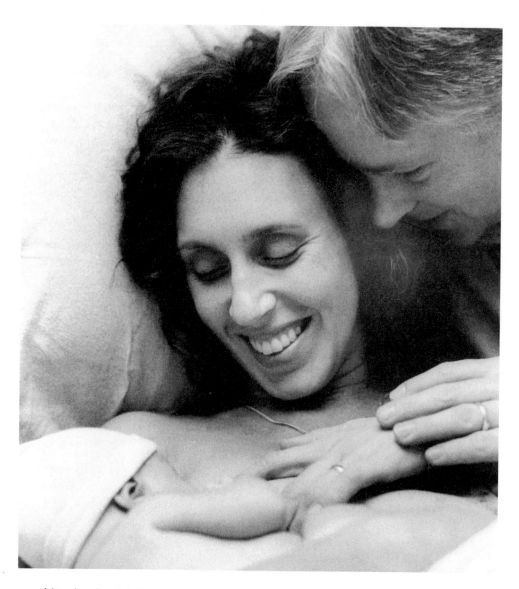

A loved one's admiration and encouragement help keep the baby blues at bay.

taking over family and household duties and limiting phone calls and visitors.

Rest is necessary to your ability to cope during the postpartum period. Make a commitment to take at least one nap a day, to make up for sleep lost in labor and afterward, due to frequent feeding demands. You may find that you are able to sleep better during naps and at night if you tuck the baby in with you. Babies often sleep better this way, too. An answering machine can be very helpful in preventing disruptions while you nap. It's also handy when you are busy with nursing and baby care.

Eat a good breakfast—perhaps your partner can prepare it for you. If you lack an appetite at mealtimes, frequent snacking throughout the day on high-protein foods will assist your own physical recovery and help maintain your energy level.

If you have had tearing or an episiotomy, or you have hemorrhoids, take several baths each day. Warm water is soothing and relaxing, and it will speed healing of your perineum.

Don't expect yourself to adjust to new parenthood on your own. Reach out for help or reassurance whenever you need it. Friends or relatives might welcome the opportunity to come and help out for a while, and you should feel free to call the hospital staff, a public health nurse, your childbirth instructor, or a breastfeeding counselor whenever you need assistance, reassurance, or support.

If you feel tired and overwhelmed, try not to keep it to yourself. Let your partner know—a good cry on someone's shoulder may leave you feeling much better. Avoid making your partner the target of your fears and anger; instead of criticizing, let him know exactly what you need. One mother put it very well: "I just need him to give me hugs and let me know I'm doing OK." Your partner, after all, may be feeling as much stress as you are.

Feeling depressed over a birth experience is not uncommon. You may be able to resolve some of your feelings by talking to your childbirth instructor or birth attendant. In a week or two, you might try to locate a postpartum or cesarean support group.

If you are alone with your baby during this first week, make a special effort to continue limiting your activities. Perhaps you can have a friend come by to fix you lunch. Let the dishes soak all day, and pick up the house for only ten minutes at a time, if you must. Unplug the phone and place a sign on your door when it's time for your nap. Perhaps you can afford to pay for light housekeeping once or twice a week for a short period.

Concerns about the Baby

Sleepy Baby

Most babies are sleepy during the first several days after birth. They may be so sleepy that they refuse to nurse or they fall asleep after just a few minutes of nursing. Sleepiness during the first few days may be related in part to recovery following labor and delivery. Pain medications and general anesthetics given to the mother during the birth process also lessen the baby's wakefulness and interest in nursing. When newborns are wrapped snugly, too, they usually sleep for long periods of time (that's why nurses bundle them tightly). Babies may act too sleepy to nurse when they feel full from water or formula supplements—or an air bubble. The newborn with jaundice may also be somewhat sleepy.

Although it may seem unkind, the sleepy baby should be wakened and fed at least every three hours. The sleepy baby needs a "mother-led" rather than a "demand" schedule until she begins waking on her own. This is necessary not only for her nutritional well-being but to insure milk production and supply. Frequent feedings will also help minimize jaundice.

Treatment Measures for the Sleepy Baby

1. Attempt nursing only after waking the baby. This is best accomplished by unwrapping and undressing her down to the diaper. Dim any bright lights, and sit the baby up on your lap by holding her under her chin. While talking to the baby, gently rub or pat her back (you may even get a burp).

2. Stroke the baby's forehead with a cool (not cold) washcloth to help waken the very persistent sleeper.

3. If the baby falls back asleep soon after latching on, use the side-lying position to encourage her to nurse for longer periods. You may need assistance from someone else to get the baby to latch on. The football hold may also be helpful in keeping the baby awake, though not as effective as side-lying nursing.

4. Burp the baby after nursing at one breast to encourage her to take the other. Sitting the baby up in your lap and bending her slightly forward usually works best. Change her diaper if needed.

5. Be persistent. If all else fails, which may happen, try again in a half hour.

6. Avoid supplements, pacifiers, and rubber nipple shields. All of these may increase the baby's reluctance to nurse.

7. While in the hospital, take advantage of the baby's normal sleeping and waking cycles by keeping her with you as much as possible.

8. Alert your physician if your baby is very lethargic and cannot be roused by the preceding techniques after five to six hours.

Bowel Movements

Your baby's first few stools are called meconium. Meconium is black, greenish-black, or dark brown, and is tarry or sticky. By the second or third day, after several good colostrum feedings, the baby will have passed most of the meconium; he may have a few greenish-brown or brownish-yellow transitional stools.

Once milk production is established and the baby is nursing well, stools take on their characteristic yellow or mustard color. This usually occurs by the fifth day, unless the baby is jaundiced and is receiving phototherapy, which makes the stools dark, or is not getting enough milk. Yellow stools by the fifth day are a sign that the baby is getting sufficient milk.

During the early days most babies have at least a few bowel movements daily. The stools of a breastfed baby are generally the consistency of yogurt. They are soft and may even be runny; they may appear curdled or seedy. This is not diarrhea. These stools have a sweet or cheesy odor.

Your baby may pass his stools easily, or he may fuss, grunt, and turn red in the face while having a bowel movement. This is not constipation. Constipation is not possible as long as your baby is totally breastfed.

If your baby doesn't have bowel movements every day, or if by the fifth day his stools are still dark, he may not be getting enough milk. See "Underfeeding and Weight Loss."

Jaundice

A yellowing of the skin and eyes, jaundice is caused by bilirubin, a yellow pigment that is present to some degree in all blood. The skin becomes yellowish when the amount of bilirubin is higher than normal.

Bilirubin comes from the red blood cells. These cells live only a short time; as they are destroyed, bilirubin is made. Bilirubin is then processed through the liver and finally eliminated in the stool. During pregnancy, the mother's liver processes bilirubin for the baby. After birth, the baby's liver has to learn to do the job. This usually takes a few days. Until the baby's liver is able to process bilirubin, it may increase in the baby's blood. This normal rise is referred to as physiologic jaundice. This is the most common form of jaundice, and about 40 percent of all babies develop it. It is usually noticed on the second or third day of life, and it generally disappears by one week of age.

Mild to moderate jaundice of this type will not hurt a baby, although many parents worry about it. However, the baby who nurses poorly or not at all during the first few days may become jaundiced from the lack of colostrum, which is important for the elimination of meconium. When meconium is retained in the bowel longer than usual, bilirubin cannot be eliminated as needed. The best way to treat this jaundice is to make sure the baby gets plenty of colostrum and breast milk (see "Underfeeding and Weight Loss").

Some babies develop jaundice for other reasons. One type of jaundice, ABO incompatibility, occurs when the mother's blood type is O and the baby's blood type is A, B, or AB. During pregnancy, maternal antibodies cross the placenta, break down red blood cells, and cause more bilirubin to be produced in the baby after birth. On the first or second day after delivery, the bilirubin level may rise rapidly. Other, less common blood incompatibilities also produce elevated bilirubin levels.

Babies with any bruises resulting from the birth process commonly develop jaundice. Also more prone to jaundice are babies who are sick right after birth or born prematurely, at low birth weights, or to diabetic mothers. Twins, too, are especially susceptible. Some drugs that are used during labor, including pitocin, can also cause jaundice.

Another type of jaundice, known as breast-milk jaundice, occurs in approximately one-third of all nursing babies. Breast-milk jaundice does not generally appear until the fifth day after birth. It usually lasts four to six weeks but can continue for as long as eight to ten weeks. The exact cause of this jaundice is still unknown, but it has never been known to cause any problem for a baby. When a baby's skin stays yellow beyond the first week, breast-milk jaundice is diagnosed by laboratory tests that rule out other forms of jaundice. Breastfeeding need not be interrupted to make this diagnosis.

If your baby looks jaundiced, the doctor may order tests to measure the level of bilirubin in the blood and determine whether treatment is necessary. If the baby was born at term and is otherwise healthy, many doctors will not order treatment unless the bilirubin level is over 20 milligrams per deciliter. Frequent breastfeeding may be all that is necessary.

Some babies may be treated with phototherapy. The "bili-lights," along with frequent nursing, help to destroy excess bilirubin. The baby usually lies under these lights from two to four days, her eyes covered with a protective mask. Often, the bilirubin level will stay constant for 24 hours and drop by 48 hours. The treatment is discontinued as soon as the bilirubin level has dropped to a normal level. Usually a baby is hospitalized for phototherapy, but in some communities home phototherapy services are available.

Rarely, usually in cases of blood incompatibility, the bilirubin climbs rapidly to high levels. On these occasions an exchange transfusion may be done to reduce the bilirubin. Over an hour or two, small amounts of the baby's blood are taken out and replaced with donated blood.

Some doctors ask the mother to stop breastfeeding temporarily whenever a baby becomes jaundiced. This is generally unwise, since breastfeeding is usually one of the most effective ways of eliminating jaundice. Calling a halt to nursing is also unfortunate for the mother, who may wonder if her milk is really best for her baby.

Mothers are also commonly told that their nursing babies need water supplements to help get rid of jaundice. Water supplements do not lower the level of bilirubin in the blood. Some studies sug-

Nurse often during phototherapy; taking the baby from under the bili-light for feedings will not slow her recovery from jaundice.

gest that water supplements are associated with higher bilirubin levels. Moreover, babies who are routinely given water tend to be nursed less frequently, and they have a higher rate of early weaning.

Since 1994, the American Academy of Pediatrics has recommended a different approach: healthy, full-term babies over 72 hours old with bilirubin levels below 20 milligrams per deciliter (or 340 micromoles per liter) should be nursed frequently, at least eight times every 24 hours, and should receive no water supplements.

Treatment Measures for Jaundice

1. Let the baby's physician know you prefer to continue nursing throughout the period of jaundice.

2. Nurse frequently, ideally every two to two and a half hours, and encourage the baby to suck at least 15 to 20 minutes at each breast. If your baby needs phototherapy, taking her from under the bili-light for these feedings will not delay the effectiveness of treatment. Intermittent phototherapy is thought to be as effective as continuous exposure.

3. If your baby is sleepy, as jaundiced babies sometimes are, see "Sleepy Baby."

4. Avoid water supplements, as these do not reduce bilirubin levels and may discourage the baby from nursing frequently.

5. To be sure your baby is getting enough milk, keep track of her bowel movements. She should have at least a few each day. She should have lost less than 10 percent of her birth weight, and she should gain an ounce a day after the fifth day. If she doesn't gain this much, refer to "Underfeeding," later in this Survival Guide.

6. If you are still hospitalized or you are welcome to stay in a hospital room while your baby is being treated, ask the nurses if you can have the baby's crib and light set up next to your bed so you can care for the baby and nurse frequently.

7. If you cannot stay 24 hours a day with your baby, express your milk every three hours (see Chapter 5). Take your milk to the hospital for the feedings you will miss.

8. If your doctor is firm in her desire for you to temporarily stop nursing, again, express milk every three hours to keep your supply up. Freeze your milk and save it for later. In this case a fully automatic electric pump is strongly recommended (see Appendix A).

Difficult Latch-on: Refusal to Nurse

Latch-on problems can originate with the baby or the mother. Most occur when the baby is sleepy (see "Sleepy Baby"); when the breast becomes overly full or engorged (see "Engorged Breasts"); when the mother and baby are not positioned well for latch-on; or when the mother has flat, dimpled, or inverted nipples (see "Difficult Latch-on: Flat, Dimpled, or Inverted Nipples"). Problems other than these are as follows.

The baby who has nursed earlier. During the first week, it is not uncommon for a baby who has already nursed to suddenly refuse one or both sides. He may simply act uninterested although he is awake, or he may protest furiously when put to one or both breasts. A baby who has been given a bottle or pacifier during the first week may become "nipple-confused" and refuse to nurse thereafter. Such a baby will likely start nursing again after a few hours uncoaxed or after one or more of the following measures are taken.

Treatment Measures for the Baby Who Stops Nursing

1. Soften the areola if your breasts are overly full or engorged by using manual expression or a pump just before putting the baby to breast.

2. Calm the frantic baby. A few drops of colostrum or glucose water (available only in hospital nurseries) on his lips or dripped over the nipple will often alert and encourage him. At home, in a pinch, you can mix a teaspoon of refined sugar in a cup of warm boiled water to entice the baby. Occasionally a very upset baby may need to be tightly swaddled in a thin blanket.

3. Pay attention to proper positioning (see Chapter 2). When the baby turns his face from side to side with mouth wide open, pull him in closer so his tongue can feel the nipple.

4. Try letting the baby suck on your finger for a few seconds just before putting him to breast.

5. If the baby seems to spit out the nipple with his tongue, try holding some ice against the nipple for a few minutes to firm it. This can be particularly effective for the baby who acts "nipple-confused."

6. Persist. The baby who is hiccoughing, having a bowel movement, or staring at his mother or something else interesting will usually be reluctant to latch on. Try again in a half hour or so.

7. Coax the baby who is suddenly refusing one breast by using the football hold on that side.

8. If you can't get the baby latched on, express your milk until you can. Refer to Appendix B for the approximate amounts of milk a baby needs at each feeding.

The baby who has not yet nursed. If a day or more has passed since the baby's birth and she still has not managed to latch on and suck, she probably has one of the specific problems described as follows.

Recessed jaw. Some babies are born with a very recessed lower jaw. This can best be seen by looking at the baby's face in profile. A recessed jaw is problematic because a baby can latch on only if her chin reaches the breast before her upper lip; otherwise she can't take enough breast tissue into her mouth.

When you try to get a baby like this to latch on, make sure your breast isn't overly full. Extend the baby's head slightly backward as you bring her onto the breast, so that her chin touches the breast first. Most babies overcome this problem by four to six weeks of age, when they are finally able to latch on and suck efficiently. In the meantime, you may need to pump your milk and feed it to your baby.

Tongue-tied. Some of the infants in this situation—mostly males— are tongue-tied. The frenulum, or string-like tissue that attaches to the underside of the tongue, is so short or connected so close to the tip of the tongue that the baby may not be able to extend his tongue past his bottom lip. Although he can suck on a finger or rubber nipple that extends well into his mouth, he may be unable to grasp the underside of his mother's nipple. Occasionally, a tongue-tied baby can manage to latch on to one breast but not the other.

The solution is simple: the frenulum should be clipped to release the tongue. Some physicians are reluctant or unwilling to perform this procedure, however, since studies made several years ago showed that tongue-tied infants rarely develop speech difficulties later in life; the studies concluded that tongue clipping was therefore unnecessary. Unfortunately, though, some tongue-tied babies are unable to breastfeed. If you cannot persuade your doctor to clip the frenulum, find another who will. An experienced surgeon or dentist may do this in his or her office. The procedure takes just a minute.

The tongue-tied baby may not be able to extend his tongue far enough to latch on to his mother's nipple.

Tongue thrusting (nipple confusion). Some babies push their tongues forward while trying to latch on or suck, and by doing so they spit the nipple out. Babies may do this from birth or as a result of sucking on a rubber nipple. When a rubber nipple is to blame, the problem is referred to as nipple confusion. Tongue-thrusting babies can usually relearn to nurse, with some assistance.

Protruding tongue. A few babies have tongues that protrude. The tongue may look longer than normal; it may be visible between the lips much of the time. Some mothers have described the protruding tongue as forming a hump in the mouth that the nipple is not able to get past.

You may be able to teach the baby to nurse by encouraging her to open wide with her tongue down and pulling back behind the areola just before latch-on. The football hold is recommended for the best visibility and control. If you manage to get the baby on the breast, be sure she is sucking adequately. This means she does not come off the breast easily; is making long, drawing sucks; and is audibly swallowing. A few babies suck with the nipple in the front of the mouth; they rarely swallow and get very little milk.

Tongue sucking. Other infants who have difficulty latching on to the breast are those who suck their own tongues. These babies usually slide off the nipple after one or two sucks, and their cheeks dimple with each suck. They may also make clicking noises. When the baby opens her mouth to root or to cry, you may notice that her tongue is far back in her mouth or is curled toward the roof of her mouth.

Attempt to get the baby to latch on only when she opens wide with her tongue down. Stimulating the lower lip or slightly depressing the chin may help the tongue to drop. Pull the baby in very close. The cross-over or football hold is best when you are working alone, and side-lying will give more control and visibility when someone is assisting you.

When refusal persists. If you have followed the preceding suggestions and your baby still has not latched on, try the following measures.

Treatment Measures for Refusal to Nurse

1. Continue working with the baby. Short, frequent sessions may be less upsetting for both of you. If someone is working with you, the side-lying position may give her the greatest control and visibility. These sessions can become intense and sometimes upsetting, so let your helper know if you or the baby needs a break. If you are in the hospital, let several nurses work with you; you may find one or two who are exceptionally skilled and sensitive.

2. Refuse any offers from nurses of rubber nipple shields or bottle nipples to place over your own nipple for nursing. Your baby will latch on and suck, but the shield may not allow for adequate nipple stimulation or for the necessary compression of the sinuses beneath the areola. This can seriously hamper the let-down of milk and adequate emptying of the breast, which may lead to a poor milk supply and insufficient intake for the baby. In addition, some babies will refuse ever to nurse without the shield. Use a nipple shield for entire feedings only if (1) a lactation professional is making sure that the baby is getting enough milk during feedings with the shield, or (2) you use a fully automatic electric pump after each nursing to guarantee that your breasts are being well emptied, and you have the baby weighed every few days to make sure he is gaining at least an ounce daily.

3. If after 24 hours your baby has not latched on, supplementary feedings should begin. Express your milk at least eight times a day, and feed the expressed milk to your baby.

4. If you are discharged from the hospital and your baby is still not nursing, use a fully automatic electric pump (see Appendix A) and keep giving pumped milk to the baby (see Chapter 3 for guidelines on pumping). Refer to Appendix B for the approximate amounts a baby needs at each feeding.

5. Continue short practice sessions several times a day. Some babies do better on a soft or empty breast.

6. Get lots of support and encouragement. If possible, see a lactation professional.

7. Be patient and persistent. Many babies with latch-on problems do overcome them sometime during the first ten days, but a significant number first latch on at about one month of age.

Sucking Problems

Some babies can latch on to the breast but have a faulty sucking pattern. With some the suction is so poor that they easily slide off the breast or can be taken off effortlessly. When they are nursing their cheeks dimple with each suck, and frequent clicking noises may be audible. Most of these babies are sucking not on the nipple but on their tongues, which may perhaps be a habit developed in the uterus. These babies receive only the milk that drips into their mouths.

Although most babies with this problem have it from birth, others may develop it if they lose much weight, usually close to a pound, by the end of the first week. If this happens, and the baby cannot correct her suck after several good attempts at latching on, pump your milk and bottle-feed for 24 to 72 hours, supplementing breast milk with formula as necessary. After the baby is rehydrated and has regained a few ounces, she will probably correct her suck on her own.

A baby may have difficulty sucking at one or both breasts because she is tongue-tied. No matter how hard she tries, she may fail to get milk from the breast, and the mother's nipples may hurt even when the baby is correctly positioned. Sometimes a clicking

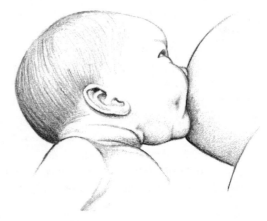

Dimpling of the baby's cheeks during nursing may signify an inadequate suck.

sound can be heard as the baby sucks. To correct such a problem have your doctor or dentist clip the baby's frenulum. (See the section on tongue-tied babies under "Difficult Latch-On: Refusal to Nurse.")

Another group of babies who have difficulty sucking and getting enough milk are those with very high palates. When the roof of the mouth is very high, the baby has trouble compressing the breast against the palate to express the milk into her mouth. Many babies with high, arched palates do little swallowing at the breast and fail to gain weight well. Few health professionals, including pediatricians, yet recognize high palates as a potential problem for nursing babies. If it is difficult to see the very top of a baby's palate without placing your head close to the baby's chest, or if the shape of the roof looks much deeper than the curve of a teaspoon, the palate may be too high. If you can get the baby to suck on your little finger (nail side down), and you feel a frequent loss of suction between your finger and his tongue, or your finger isn't in firm contact with the roof of his mouth, the palate may be too high. Some babies with high palates are also tongue-tied.

In the case of a high palate, the only remedy I know of is for the mother to use an electric pump right after each nursing to bolster her milk supply. After a few days the baby will usually start to swallow more at the breast and gain weight better, but as soon as the pumping stops the baby begins to take less milk and will again fail to gain sufficient weight. Usually supplemental pumping is necessary for several weeks, until the baby has grown enough to suck more efficiently. Using the football hold may help the baby suck better.

Treatment Measures for the Baby with Poor Suction

1. Remove the baby from the breast as soon as this pattern is evident.

2. Observe the position of the tongue when the baby's mouth is wide open. If it is curled against the roof of the mouth, try to lower it with your finger. Sometimes touching the lower lip or pressing slightly on the chin will help.

3. Using the cross-over or football hold, pull the baby in as close as possible for latch-on.

4. Continue working with the baby. Short, frequent sessions may be less upsetting for both of you. If someone is working with you, the side-lying position may give her the greatest control and visibility.

These sessions can become intense and upsetting, so let your helper know if you or the baby needs a break. If you are in the hospital, have several nurses work with you; you may find one or two who are exceptionally skilled and sensitive.

5. Refuse any offers from nurses of rubber nipple shields or bottle nipples to place over your own nipple for nursing. Your baby will latch on and suck, but the shield may not allow for adequate nipple stimulation or for the necessary compression of the sinuses beneath the areola. This can seriously hamper the let-down of milk and adequate emptying of the breast, which may lead to a poor milk supply and insufficient intake for the baby. In addition, some babies will refuse ever to nurse without the shield. Use a nipple shield for entire feedings only if (1) a lactation professional makes sure that the baby is getting enough milk while you're wearing the shield, or (2) you use a fully automatic electric pump after each nursing to guarantee that your breasts are being well emptied, and you have the baby weighed every few days to make sure he is gaining at least an ounce a day.

6. If after 24 hours your baby still has not latched on with strong suction, supplementary feedings should begin. Express your milk at least eight times a day, and feed the baby the expressed milk.

7. If you are discharged from the hospital and your baby still is not nursing, use a fully automatic electric pump (see Appendix A) and keep giving your milk to the baby (see Chapter 3 for guidelines on pumping, and Appendix B for the approximate amount of milk your baby needs at each feeding).

8. Continue short practice sessions several times a day. Some babies do better on a soft or empty breast.

9. Get lots of support and encouragement. If possible, see a lactation professional.

10. Be patient and persist. Many babies with sucking problems do overcome them sometime during the first ten days, but a significant number improve at about one month of age.

Fussiness and Excessive Night Waking

It can come as a surprise when your baby suddenly becomes fussy after spending most of his first few days sleeping. It is difficult to listen to your baby's cry; it may feel like an alarm going off in your body. Sometimes parents are told it is healthy for babies to cry, or that they will become spoiled if tended to every time they fuss.

Letting others take over chores while you rest and enjoy the baby may help you avoid early breastfeeding problems.

Comforting your infant and responding to her needs is very important to her well-being and her development of trust. Babies are really unspoilable.

Newborns cry for a variety of reasons. Often they are fussy their first night home from the hospital. They may be hungry as often as every hour, especially when the milk is just starting to come in, or when feedings have been limited because of their sleepiness or for other reasons. Some babies seem to need more sucking time than others. Some seem to pass a lot of gas, which causes them discomfort. Many newborns become upset when they are not kept snugly wrapped. Perhaps they miss the close, secure feeling of the womb.

Then there are the babies who sleep most of the day and wake frequently during the night. These babies are said to have their days and nights mixed up.

Coping Measures for Fussiness

1. Nurse your baby on demand, or at least every two to three hours for at least 15 to 20 minutes at each breast.

2. Massage your breasts while you nurse to encourage the milk to let down.

3. Burp the baby after he finishes at each breast. This will help prevent swallowed air from passing through the intestines and encourage him to nurse longer. If your baby is passing a lot of gas, you may need to burp him a few times during each feeding. See Chapter 2 if you are having difficulty burping the baby.

4. Burp your baby after he uses a pacifier. Avoid using stuffed bottle nipples as pacifiers as these cause excessive air swallowing.

5. Wrap the baby snugly in a light blanket after feeding.

6. Avoid water or formula supplements. Perhaps you have nursed your baby but he acts as if he is still hungry. You can, certainly, offer him the breast again. But sometimes newborn babies will stay awake after a feeding and behave as if they need to suck longer even though their bellies are full. If the baby frequently seems unsatisfied, refer to "Underfeeding and Weight Loss." Most young infants will take water or formula if it is offered, even when they have had enough breast milk, but supplementing often leads to problems.

If your baby does not seem content after nursing, feel free to nurse him some more, or try comforting him next to your body. Rocking or walking with the baby for a while will probably keep him content. In an hour or two, nurse him again.

Coping Measures for Excessive Night Waking

1. Nurse your baby every two to two and a half hours during the daytime and evening. If the baby is sleeping through feeding times, see "Sleepy Baby."

2. Tuck your baby in with you for at least a few nights; she may sleep better.

Underfeeding and Weight Loss

During the first week, you may wonder if your baby is getting enough to eat. You may worry about whether the milk is adequate—especially if the baby seems to be nursing all the time or is fussy after feedings. Some mothers wonder if their milk has dried up when they observe the normal softening of the breast that occurs as the initial engorgement recedes.

Seeing if the baby will take a bottle of water or formula after nursing is not a reliable method of determining if he is getting enough breast milk. Most babies will take a couple of ounces of water or formula if it is offered, even when they have had enough milk from the breast.

A baby can lose too much weight, though, when the milk doesn't come in by the third or fourth day, when nursing is infrequent, or when he has had trouble latching on and nursing well during the period of initial engorgement. Excessive weight loss can also occur when a mother uses a nipple shield over her nipple for nursing, when a newborn has a faulty suck, and, certainly, when a baby is sick. Sometimes laxatives the mother has taken can cause a baby to have excessive bowel movements and to lose weight or gain too slowly.

Most newborns want to nurse eight to twelve times in each 24-hour period after the first day or two post partum. This frequent nursing is normal; it seldom reflects a poor milk supply and it never reflects "weak milk." The baby is probably getting enough milk if—

- *Your milk has come in by the third or fourth day post partum.* When milk production begins, the breasts become firmer and heavier. The firmness may be less apparent with large breasts, but the breasts should still feel heavier.
- *Your baby is nursing at least eight times in a 24-hour period.* This means your baby is nursing every two to three hours (measured from the start of one feeding to the start of the next) during the day, with a sleep stretch of up to five hours at night. If your baby isn't nursing this often, you may have to wake her for feedings.
- *Your baby is nursing 10 to 45 minutes at each feeding and seems content after feedings.* Babies vary in the length of time they nurse, but they typically need 10 to 45 minutes to complete a feeding. Although babies don't always fall asleep after nursing, they should usually seem satisfied after feedings.
- *Your baby has several periods of swallowing during each feeding.* When babies are getting milk, they take long, drawing sucks and can be heard swallowing or gulping. (When they are not swallowing milk, they take short, choppy sucks.) These

long, drawing sucks usually occur in bursts of five to ten continuous sucks followed by a pause. Babies who are taking enough milk usually have several bursts of continuous sucking and swallowing during a feeding.

■ *Your breasts feel softer or lighter after the baby has nursed.* You should be able to feel a difference in fullness or heaviness in your breasts before and after your baby has fed.

■ *Your baby is having bowel movements every day, and by the fifth day they have turned yellow.* This is the clearest sign that a baby is getting enough colostrum, first, and, later, breast milk. Most newborns have at least three bowel movements each day during the first month. Only after the first month is it normal for breastfed babies to go several days without a bowel movement.

■ *Your baby is wetting more diapers by the fifth day after birth.* Before your milk comes in, your baby will urinate infrequently, but by the fifth day you should notice more frequent and wetter diapers. Be aware that the more absorbent disposable diapers can make wetness difficult to detect.

If not all of the points just listed hold true for you and your baby, you should have him weighed and examined. In the first four to five days after birth, a baby loses weight. After the fifth day, a baby should gain an ounce every day. An initial loss of 10 percent or more of a baby's birth weight suggests the baby is underfed (see the chart in Appendix B). Even if your baby has lost less than 10 percent of his birth weight, have him weighed again in a couple of days to see if he has started gaining an ounce per day. In the meantime, take the following measures.

Treatment Measures for Underfeeding

1. If possible, see a lactation professional.

2. To estimate the amount of milk you are producing and to increase your milk supply, obtain a fully automatic electric breast pump (see Appendix A). Any other pump would be inadequate for accurately estimating milk production, and would be less helpful in increasing a low milk supply.

3. Estimate your milk production by pumping your breasts instead of nursing. If you are pumping one breast at a time, pump each breast twice, for a total pumping time of 20 to 25 minutes. If you have a double-pump kit (see Chapter 5) use it for a total of 12 to 15 minutes. Feed this milk and any necessary formula to your baby (see Appen-

dix A to determine how much milk your baby needs at each feeding). Exactly two hours after the completion of this pumping, pump again. You may very well get less milk at this second pumping than at the first. Multiply the number of ounces collected at the *second* pumping by 12. This will give you an estimate of how much milk you are producing over a 24-hour period; if you collected 1½ ounces, for example, you are producing about 18 ounces per day.

4. Now you can compare the baby's milk requirement in Appendix B with your actual milk production. If you have determined that your baby needs approximately 21.4 ounces per day and your milk production is 18 ounces per day, the baby needs an additional 3½ ounces of formula per day. If you determine that you have enough milk for your baby and yet she has not been gaining well, it may be that she is not taking all of the milk available at some or many of her feedings. This can happen with newborns who were born prematurely, who tend to drift off to sleep while nursing, or who have sucking difficulties.

5. After you have estimated your milk production, go back to nursing your baby. Be sure to nurse her at least eight times in every 24 hours. This may mean waking her for feedings. Wake a sleepy baby every two and a half hours (measured from the start of one nursing to the start of the next) during the day and evening, and every three to four hours in the night. Nurse your baby for 10 to 15 minutes at each breast. Frequent nursings of moderate duration are more effective in increasing milk production than lengthy but infrequent nursings.

6. Pump your breasts right after each nursing to stimulate further milk production. Unless you have a double-pump kit (see Chapter 5), pump each breast for five minutes, then return to each breast a second time for a few more minutes. Pumping both breasts at the same time is more effective in stimulating increased milk production, and also takes less time. Use a double-pump kit for 5 to 10 minutes after nursing.

7. After pumping, feed the baby whatever breast milk you've collected along with any necessary formula. If the baby needs supplemental formula, divide the amount of supplement needed daily by the number of feedings the baby is getting each day (usually eight). A baby who needs 3½ ounces of formula, for example, should get about ½ ounce after each of her eight daily nursings. The goal is to offer about the same amount of breast milk and formula at each feeding so that the baby wants to nurse at regular intervals.

8. You may find fenugreek very helpful in stimulating further milk production. Fenugreek is a fragrant seed that is used as the flavoring ingredient in artificial maple syrup. You can make a tea from the seeds, but it is more convenient to take fenugreek in the capsule form, available in most health-food stores. Mothers who take two to three capsules three times a day typically notice an increase in the milk supply within one to three days. Fenugreek is harmless, although you will probably notice that your sweat and urine take on a distinct odor of maple. Rarely, mothers taking fenugreek report having diarrhea that quickly subsides when the fenugreek is stopped. Although fenugreek is usually used for just several days to boost a low milk supply, some mothers have continued to use it for weeks or months without any difficulties. Fenugreek capsules cost about seven dollars for a bottle of 100.

9. How to feed supplemental breast milk and formula is rather controversial. Many lactation professionals, fearing bottle feeding would interfere with the baby's ability at the breast, suggest using a nursing supplementer (see Appendix A), a cup, a soft tube, a finger, or an eye dropper. If one of these methods is recommended to you and it works well, terrific. But if you find it too frustrating or time consuming, use a bottle. After the first few days of breastfeeding, supplementing by bottle rarely causes "nipple confusion."

10. Weigh your baby every few days to make sure that she is gaining well. After each weighing, re-estimate her milk needs, because as she gains weight her milk needs will increase. Two hours after your last pumping, express your milk instead of nursing, then re-estimate your milk production. Hopefully it will also have increased, so that you can decrease or even eliminate any formula supplementation.

11. Once your baby is gaining well, her nursing seems more vigorous, and you are supplementing nursings only with your breast milk, you might try eliminating some of the supplement. For a few days, offer the baby only half of the milk that you are expressing, and freeze the rest. If the baby gains well over these few days, continue pumping, but don't offer her any of the expressed milk. If the baby continues to gain an ounce a day without any supplement, gradually stop pumping. Continue to have your baby weighed weekly.

If treatment fails. Although the technique just outlined will normally reverse a case of underfeeding right away, sometimes, when breast engorgement has been severe and little milk has been removed during this critical period, the decline in milk production can be difficult to reverse. In unusual instances, a mother fails to produce enough milk. This sometimes happens to women who have had breast surgery, particularly if the surgical incision was made around the areola (see "Nursing after Breast Surgery" in Chapter 3). Other women who cannot produce much milk have insufficient glandular (milk-producing) tissue, or "hypoplastic" breasts (see "Insuring Your Milk Supply" in Chapter 2).

In any of these situations, lack of support from family, friends, and health professionals can only make matters worse. But even with all of the best information and support, things sometimes don't turn out as we hope. If after giving breastfeeding your best effort you end up having to bottle-feed, you have not failed as a mother. Be proud of your efforts to nurse, and concentrate on providing your baby with all of the cuddling and loving that you can. Detailed information about formula and bottle feeding can be found in *The Nursing Mother's Guide to Weaning* (see "Suggested Supplemental Reading").

Some mothers with insufficient milk production have found that continuing to nurse with a nursing supplementer has been a rewarding experience. Others have found nursing supplementers to be cumbersome and frustrating. Another option, particularly if the baby has become frustrated at the breast, is to bottle-feed and then nurse. "Comfort nursing"—nursing just after bottle feedings, in between bottle feedings, or during the night—may be a pleasant experience for both mother and baby.

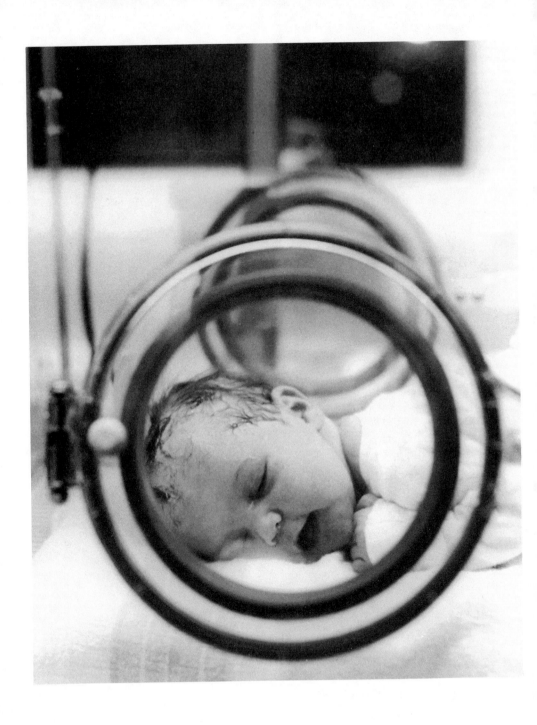

CHAPTER THREE

Special Mothers, Special Babies

Special Mothers

Medical Reasons for Not Breastfeeding
Medications and Environmental Pollutants
Nursing after Breast Surgery
Nursing an Adopted Baby
Relactation
The Diabetic Mother
The Mother with Herpes
The Mother with Epilepsy
Nursing and Thyroid Conditions

Special Babies

Medical Reasons for Not Breastfeeding
The Premature Baby
Nursing More than One
The Baby with a Birth Defect
Developmental and Neurological Problems

NURSING CAN BE A SPECIAL CHALLENGE IN CERTAIN CIRCUM-
stances—that may result from a longstanding condition or that
may take you completely by surprise. Either way, you may be
tempted to give up the idea of breastfeeding altogether. The specific guidelines in this chapter should help you make a realistic
appraisal of your situation and find, I hope, the happiest solution
for you and your baby.

Special Mothers

Medical Reasons for Not Breastfeeding

Although most medical conditions a mother might have pose no
harm to her nursing infant, a few are reasons to delay or even
forego breastfeeding.

A mother with active tuberculosis should not breastfeed—or
have any physical contact with her baby—until antibiotic treatment has been administered for one to three weeks, after which
she can no longer transmit the infection. During this period, she
can express her milk to maintain her supply, but she should discard the milk she expresses. Afterward she can safely be reunited
with her infant, and she can breastfeed.

A woman with hepatitis can generally breastfeed safely. If she
has viral hepatitis, also known as infectious hepatitis or hepatitis
A, her baby should be immunized with gamma globulin. If she has
an active case of hepatitis B or persistent hepatitis B surface anti-
gen (HBsAg), her baby should receive hepatitis B–specific immu-
noglobulin (HBIG) immediately after delivery. She can begin
breastfeeding as soon as the shot is given, but her baby should also
receive the first in a series of hepatitis B vaccines within 24 hours
of birth. If a woman has hepatitis C, she can breastfeed without
any special precautions; according to the National Institute of
Health, this virus cannot be transmitted through breast milk.

Mothers with the human immunodeficiency virus (HIV) are discouraged from breastfeeding until more is known about transmission of the virus.

A woman infected with cytomegalovirus (CMV) can safely
breastfeed her baby if he was born at full term. If the baby was
born prematurely, he may be CMV-negative; that is, he may not

have received antibodies against the disease during pregnancy and so may be vulnerable to the infection. The virus can be destroyed, however, by freezing the breast milk at 0 degrees F. for at least three days.

A mother with herpes simplex, in the form of either cold sores on or near the mouth or genital lesions, can nurse her baby. It is important, however, that anyone with a herpes sore take certain precautions in handling a baby to avoid transmitting the infection. (See "The Mother with Herpes," later in this chapter.)

Breastfeeding is also safe when a woman is infected with toxoplasmosis.

A mother infected with Lyme disease should be immediately treated, and so should her baby. The mother can breastfeed if she has begun antibiotic treatment and her baby is healthy.

Because human T-cell leukemia virus type 1 (HTLV-1) can be transmitted through breast milk, a woman infected with this virus should forego breastfeeding. (HTLV-1 is rare in North America, but it is increasingly common in other parts of the world. It is associated with the development of leukemia and lymphoma.)

A woman who develops chicken pox within the six days before delivery should be isolated from her baby, although someone else can feed the baby the mother's expressed milk. The mother and baby can be reunited after she becomes noninfectious, typically after seven days.

Although the overwhelming majority of women can produce a full supply of milk for their infants, even after a setback due to infrequent nursing or inadequate sucking (see "Survival Guide for the First Week"), a few mothers are unable to produce enough milk. A low milk supply can occur when a mother has had extensive breast surgery (see "Nursing after Breast Surgery"). A relatively uncommon condition is that of breast hypoplasia, in which the breasts are widely spaced and appear underdeveloped; frequently one breast is significantly smaller than the other. Hypoplastic breasts grow little during pregnancy, and, during the first week after delivery, they may not become heavier or fuller or leak milk. About half of women with hypoplastic breasts, however, can develop a full milk supply by six weeks post partum. Those who cannot produce enough milk can still nurse their babies by using a nursing supplementation device designed to provide the extra milk or formula needed.

Medications and Environmental Pollutants

A mother may occasionally wonder if her milk is entirely safe for her child. Most frequently, this concern arises because she needs to take medication. Although most medications pass into the breast milk, the majority are considered safe for the nursing infant. A comprehensive guide to drugs in breast milk can be found in Appendix C. If you can't find the information you're looking for there, call the University of California, San Diego, Drug Information Service at 900-288-8273 (consultation costs $3.00 for the first minute and $2.00 for each additional minute; calls average one to three minutes each).

More and more questions have arisen about the environmental pollutants we are exposed to, such as insecticides and other toxic chemicals. Many of these substances are stored in fatty tissues of the body, and, as a result, small amounts may be detected in breast milk. Experts on the subject, however, have been unable to identify any risks to the baby from such amounts, and most believe that the nutritional and immunological benefits of breast milk far outweigh the possible risks of environmental pollutants. Sadly, our children receive even greater exposure to some of these chemicals in the womb than they do at the breast.

Some women have been exposed to high concentrations of polychlorinated biphenyl (PCB) or polybrominated biphenyl (PBB), both toxic chemicals. Mothers who for many years have eaten more than one meal a week of fish from the Great Lakes or certain of its tributaries, who live on PCB-silo farms, or who have been employed for years handling PCB, should consider having their milk tested for this toxin. Information about analyzing breast milk can be obtained from state health department laboratories. PBB is less frequently found in the food chain; however, it was accidentally added to cattle feed in Michigan during 1973. Mothers in Michigan's general population were subsequently found to have low levels of PBB in their breast milk—levels determined to pose no threat to nursing infants. Women on quarantined farms had higher levels, but their children, many of whom were breastfed, showed no signs of illness or any effect on their growth and development.

Nursing mothers who want to reduce their babies' exposure to toxic chemicals should certainly stop using pesticides in the home, avoid eating fish caught in contaminated waters, stay away from permanently moth-proofed garments, carefully wash or peel fresh fruits and vegetables, and avoid crash diets, which are likely to increase the excretion of toxic substances into breast milk.

Processed infant formulas are not without their own potential hazards. Besides lacking the immunological properties of breast milk that keep the infant healthy, they can easily become contaminated when the person preparing the baby's bottle does not take proper care in handling and storing the formula and equipment. Parents frequently don't pay close attention when diluting powdered and liquid formula concentrates. From time to time, too, manufacturing errors in the production of infant formulas have had serious consequences. High levels of aluminum have been identified in most formulas (Weintraub et al., 1986). And babies have suffered lead poisoning when their formulas have been mixed with tap water high in lead content.

Nursing after Breast Surgery

When performed prior to a woman's giving birth, minor breast surgery such as a biopsy or removal of a lump seldom affects the woman's ability to nurse unless the incision was made on the nipple or areola. A woman who has undergone a mastectomy can nurse on the remaining breast, and by nursing frequently she may be able to provide most or all of the milk that her baby needs. A breast that has been subject to radiation therapy produces little or no milk, but, again, the other breast should produce milk normally.

When a surgical implantation has been performed to alter the size and shape of the breasts, milk production is usually not affected unless the milk ducts have been severed (this may be the case if the incision was made along the edge of the areola). In the case of a breast reduction, milk production depends on the extensiveness of the surgery. When the nipples have been relocated on the breasts, some or all of the ducts have usually been severed, and so the milk supply is often deficient.

When a mother's milk ducts may have been severed, her baby should be observed closely for signs of low milk intake. I recommend a weight check by three to four days of age and every couple of days thereafter. A weight loss of 10 percent or more, or failure to gain an ounce a day after five days of age, indicates a baby needs supplemental feedings.

If you have had breast surgery involving an incision around the areola, you may benefit from renting a fully automatic electric breast pump and using it starting on the third day post partum. Pump for five minutes on each breast right after each daytime and evening nursing; pump both breasts at once, if possible. This can help in bringing in a more plentiful milk supply.

Recently I've worked with several women who have had breast reduction surgery yet have successfully brought in a full supply of milk. For some of these women, using an electric pump after each nursing helped a great deal in building an initially low milk supply. Some of the mothers found that using a nursing supplementer device helped to increase production as well (see Appendix A). In all of these cases, however, two to eight weeks' effort was required before milk production totally met the baby's milk needs.

When the milk supply is clearly insufficient and shows no signs of increasing, a mother can still continue breastfeeding indefinitely, if she wishes. A nursing supplementation device may help to keep the baby from preferring the bottle.

Nursing an Adopted Baby

More and more mothers who are planning to adopt babies are considering breastfeeding them. An infant's suck can stimulate milk production whether or not the mother has ever had or nursed a baby before. Most adoptive mothers, however, need to supplement their breast milk, many for the entire time they are nursing. Probably the safest and most convenient way to supplement breastfeeding is with a nursing supplementation device, which is specifically designed for this situation (see Appendix A).

Some women's enthusiastic claims of producing abundant milk for their adopted babies may set up other adoptive mothers for disappointment. It is impossible to predict whether an adoptive mother will be able to produce milk, or how much she will produce, even if she is currently nursing or has recently nursed another baby. Adoptive nursing will be most successful if you focus on the baby and your relationship rather than on milk production. Measure your success by whether the experience truly helps make the baby yours.

Before the baby arrives, it is wise to learn as much as possible about breastfeeding and adoptive nursing. Be sure to talk with a pediatrician who will be supportive of your efforts. A lactation

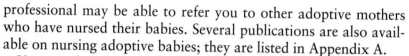

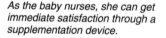
As the baby nurses, she can get immediate satisfaction through a supplementation device.

professional may be able to refer you to other adoptive mothers who have nursed their babies. Several publications are also available on nursing adoptive babies; they are listed in Appendix A.

You may be told you should try to initiate milk production before the baby's arrival by expressing or pumping the breasts several times a day. There is debate over whether this is really beneficial.

Recently, a researcher has developed an eight-week-long hormonal regimen to stimulate milk production in women who are anticipating adoption. This method is still experimental, it requires a physician's close supervision, and it involves very expensive hormones and medications ($500 to $700 worth). The hormones frequently have unpleasant side effects, and one medication must be taken throughout the breastfeeding period. Women with low blood pressure or a history of depression should not undertake this course of medications.

Your baby may be easily persuaded to begin nursing, or he may require a great deal of patience and persistence. In general, the younger the baby is, the easier the transition from the bottle to the breast will be. See "Survival Guide for the First Week" for assistance in getting the baby to nurse.

Most adoptive mothers need to supplement their milk with formula. Some women try to increase their milk production by using formula in only minimal amounts or by overdiluting it. But these practices often result in stressed, underfed babies.

If you've decided to use a supplementation device, you may be hoping for donations of breast milk to use in it, and perhaps you've already received offers of donated milk. But don't expect others to continue donations indefinitely. It can be a real effort for nursing mothers to collect extra milk. There is also a possibility that infectious diseases, including HIV and hepatitis, could be transmitted through donated milk.

Women who have breastfed adopted children often say that it has been one of the most memorable and rewarding experiences of their lives. You may especially enjoy nursing your adopted baby when she is older and you needn't concern yourself so much about milk production. Moments spent soothing a tired, hurt, or frustrated baby or toddler at the breast are priceless for any nursing mother.

Relactation

For a variety of reasons, a mother may want to begin nursing after initially starting her baby on the bottle, or to resume nursing after weaning her baby.

In general, the less time that has elapsed since weaning, the more likely bringing back a full milk supply will be. A mother with a five-day-old baby who has never nursed, or a six-week-old who has been weaned for just a few days, should be able to bring in a full milk supply within several days. After longer periods without nursing or expressing milk, the ability to re-establish full milk production will vary from woman to woman.

Always critical to milk production is frequent and regular stimulation and emptying of the breasts. This means that either a vigorous nursing baby or a fully automatic electric breast pump should be draining both breasts at least every two and a half hours during the day and evening and twice at night. Even when a baby is willing to nurse, using a fully automatic pump with a double-pump kit for 5 to 10 minutes right after nursing can be very helpful in collecting any residual milk the baby leaves behind and stimulating further milk production.

The spice fenugreek is also very helpful in stimulating increased milk production. You can make tea from fenugreek seeds, but more effective are the concentrated capsules sold in health-food stores. If you take two to three capsules three times a day, you should notice an increase in milk supply within one to three days.

For more information, see "Treatment Measures for Underfeeding" in "Survival Guide for the First Week."

A medication that has been used to stimulate milk production is Reglan (metoclopramide). Available only by prescription and commonly used for gastric reflux, Reglan also increases prolactin, the hormone that stimulates milk production. The usual dose is 10 milligrams every eight hours for 10 to 14 days. Mothers usually notice increased breast fullness 48 to 72 hours after starting on the drug. The medication works best with frequent breast stimulation and emptying, and is most effective during the first 12 weeks post partum. If no change is observed after five days, the medication probably will not be helpful.

Although the U.S. Food and Drug Administration has not approved Reglan for the purpose of stimulating milk production, several studies have shown the drug to be effective and safe for increasing milk supplies. Although Reglan has not been shown to cause any problems for a nursing baby—in fact, it is occasionally prescribed for infants—it may make the mother sleepy. More worrisome side effects, such as agitation, are uncommon; when they occur, the drug should be discontinued. Although some mothers find a second two-week course helpful, I would discourage the drug's long-term use, which sometimes causes depression. Compared with other drugs, Reglan is fairly inexpensive for a two-week course.

Regardless of the time that has elapsed between weaning and attempting relactation, a baby will need supplemental feedings until full milk production has been established. You could continue bottle feeding, but offer the bottle only after nursing and give slightly less formula than before. Or you could use a nursing supplementer system, which would allow you to feed your baby the supplement while he sucks at the breast. This option may be most helpful if your baby acts frustrated while nursing. See Appendix A for information on nursing supplementers.

Knowing how much supplemental milk and formula to give a baby can be a bit of a guessing game. If you have a fully automatic breast pump, you can use the method described in "Underfeeding and Weight Loss" in "Survival Guide for the First Week" to estimate your milk production and your baby's supplemental milk needs. Without this type of pump, you will need to rely solely on weight checks.

Whether or not you're using an automatic pump, have your

baby weighed every day or two during the first week or so after you start trying to relactate. Until your baby is three or four months old, he should gain an ounce a day. Gaining less than this amount indicates that he needs more supplemental milk or formula; gaining more may mean that the supplement should be cut back a little. Always weigh your baby naked, on the same scale, at about the same time of day, and just before a feeding.

Recently, a very accurate electronic baby scale for home use has become available for rent. This scale can also be used before and after feedings to determine how much milk the baby takes from the breast. See Appendix A for information on renting a scale.

The Diabetic Mother

Many diabetic mothers enjoy the advantages of nursing. For them breastfeeding often stimulates a remission-like response, resulting in a decreased need for insulin and an increased need for calories. Babies of diabetic mothers are less likely to develop the disease themselves later in life if they are breastfed rather than formula-fed.

If you are diabetic, your requirements for insulin and calories will need to be closely monitored—especially during the early hours after delivery, when your insulin needs will drop dramatically.

For the first day or two, your newborn's blood sugar must be closely watched as her body adjusts to receiving less glucose than it did during pregnancy. She may need frequent nursing, and possibly supplemental glucose by nipple or IV, until her glucose levels stabilize. Because the infant of the diabetic mother is commonly delivered a few weeks early, she may also have respiratory problems, and she is more prone to becoming jaundiced.

Throughout the months of breastfeeding, careful monitoring of your glucose level, insulin dose, and caloric requirements must continue. As the baby stimulates increased milk production, you and your doctor will need to adjust your insulin dosage and caloric intake to prevent insulin reactions.

You should take particular care to avoid sore nipples and breast infections. This means giving careful attention to correct positioning of the baby, watching for signs of thrush (yeast) in the baby's mouth and on the nipples (see "Survival Guide for the First Week"), and getting plenty of rest. Yeast infections are very common in the diabetic mother and her infant. Plugged ducts and other early signs of breast infection (see "Survival Guide for the First Two Months") should be treated promptly.

When weaning begins and milk production declines, you'll need to readjust your insulin dosage and diet again. This will be easier if you wean the baby slowly.

The Mother with Herpes

If you have an active genital herpes lesion or a positive culture near your due date, and you therefore deliver by cesarean, you will most likely be given a private hospital room. So long as the lesion is well covered and you wash your hands thoroughly before feedings, you can nurse the baby safely without gloves. There is no reason that you cannot share a room with the baby as long as you maintain these basic precautions. Should you have a herpes outbreak at home, the same principles apply.

Herpes Type I lesions are generally those that develop above the waist, usually on the mouth. Frequently they appear as cold sores or fever blisters. It is important for you, or any other person with an active lesion, to wash your hands thoroughly before touching the baby, and, of course, to avoid placing her in contact with the sores.

Occasionally a mother will develop a herpes lesion on her breast, nipple, or areola. Should you have such an outbreak, express your milk until the lesion is gone.

The Mother with Epilepsy

Most medications to control the occurrence of epileptic seizures are considered safe for nursing; however, it is best to check out any drug with your doctor. Major anticonvulsant medications are listed in Appendix C, where their safety is discussed.

A nursing mother with epilepsy offers these suggestions for others (Brewster, 1979):

- Have cribs or playpens available in various areas of the house; place gates across stairways and doorways.
- Nurse in a large upholstered chair, or pad the arms of a rocking chair.
- Use guard rails and pillows around the bed for night nursing.
- When alone on outings with the baby, tag the stroller or carrier

with the name of the baby and the name of a person to contact in the event that you have a seizure.

Nursing and Thyroid Conditions

Hypothyroidism. Symptoms of an underactive thyroid gland may include extreme fatigue, poor appetite, and sometimes a low milk supply. Thyroid replacement quickly reverses these symptoms. The mother who is taking medication for hypothyroidism can breast-feed, as these drugs do not affect the baby.

Hyperthyroidism. Occasionally a doctor will discover that a nursing mother has an enlarged thyroid gland. Signs of hyperthyroidism include weight loss, increased appetite, nervousness, rapid heart rate, and palpitations. Nursing must be discontinued for at least 48 hours when radioactive iodine is used for diagnostic testing; however, other tests are available that do not require this interruption. If radioactive iodine is used, express or pump your milk and dispose of it.

If you are taking medication for an overactive thyroid gland, you can breastfeed as long as the specific medication is considered safe for the nursing baby. PTU (propylthiouracil) is the drug of choice, since it has the least effect on a baby's thyroid gland. The baby's thyroid level should be monitored by a pediatrician.

Special Babies

Medical Reasons for Not Breastfeeding

Infants born with galactosemia, a rare inherited disorder, lack the enzyme necessary to break down the sugar found in all milk, including breast milk. They must be fed a special lactose-free formula.

Infants with phenylketonuria (PKU), another rare metabolic disorder, require a diet with little phenylalanine, an amino acid. Because breast milk is low in phenylalanine, a baby with PKU may be breastfed part time provided she is also fed phenylalanine-free formula. Her blood level of phenylalanine must be monitored to be sure that it remains between 5 and 10 milligrams per deciliter.

The Premature Baby

The days after giving birth to a premature baby can be overwhelming, particularly if the baby is sick or very immature. The mother of a premie may have doubts about many things, including her ability to nurse the baby.

If your baby is born prematurely, it is especially important that he receive your milk. Your milk is particularly suited for his special growth needs and is easier for him to digest than formula. Premature infants are at greater risk for developing infections and are less able to cope with them when they arise. The antibodies in your milk will provide your baby with protection against many of these infections. Your milk may also reduce your premature baby's risk of developing cerebral palsy (Lucas, 1992). By providing breast milk, many mothers of premature infants have felt that they were able to contribute something special to their baby's well-being.

If your baby is three to five weeks early, you may be able to begin breastfeeding right away. The sick or very small premie may be unable to nurse for a while, but you can express your milk for him until he is well or mature enough to begin nursing. In this way he can still receive your milk, and you will have established your milk supply by the time he is ready to begin breastfeeding.

Nursing the baby born three to five weeks early. Usually babies who are born a few weeks before their due date are encouraged to begin breastfeeding within the first hours or days of birth. Barring any health complications, most physicians and nurses treat these babies like other newborns and encourage parents to do the same.

Generally, babies who are born a few weeks too soon tend to be rather sleepy; they may or may not start out as vigorous nursers. Many fall asleep at the breast before they have had an adequate feeding. For this reason, they often fail to gain weight. A few days of a baby's sluggish nursing and limited milk removal can also have a devastating effect on milk production.

An effective preventive is the use of a fully automatic electric breast pump. Starting on the third day post partum, a mother should pump for five minutes on each breast right after each daytime and evening nursing. This insures an abundant milk supply for the baby even if his sucking is sluggish. The residual milk collected can be frozen for later use.

The baby should be watched closely for the reassuring signs of adequate milk intake. She should be weighed at 10 to 12 days, or sooner if suspicions arise that she may not be taking enough milk. If the baby is back to her birth weight at 10 to 12 days, the pumping can be gradually discontinued over a few days. Weighing the baby once again before returning the pump to the rental station will give further reassurance that nursing is going well, providing the baby has gained an ounce a day since the tenth day.

If the baby loses 10 percent or more of her birth weight, she should be offered the residual milk being collected.

Expressing milk for your baby. If your baby is unable to nurse, start expressing your colostrum as soon after delivery as possible. Colostrum is especially beneficial for him as it is highly concentrated with protective antibodies. The nursing staff should provide you with a suitable pump and instructions for collecting and storing your milk. Most maternity units have an electric breast pump available. A fully automatic electric breast pump is most suited for a mother who is pumping around the clock for a premie (see Appendix A). If your baby is being transferred to another hospital for care, ask the transport team about their procedures for collecting, storing, and transporting your milk. If you will be following the baby to a special care nursery in another city, try to get a pump to take along with you.

You may receive differing bits of advice on how often and how long to pump your breasts. Keep in mind that your supply of milk depends on the frequent stimulation of your breasts. You should plan on expressing milk as often as your baby would nurse, or at least eight times in 24 hours. Many nursery staffs suggest that women pump every three to four hours during the day and sleep all night. With this limited stimulation, most mothers find that after a while their milk supplies dwindle. Determine a reasonable schedule for yourself that includes eight pumpings in 24 hours. Some mothers prefer to express their milk every three hours around the clock, whereas others would rather pump more often during the day so they can sleep for longer periods at night.

When you first begin to express milk you will probably start out getting just a few drops of colostrum. Until your milk is in, pump each breast for about five minutes, then return to each breast a second time for a few more minutes.

After your milk is in, pump each breast until the flow subsides. Return to each breast a second or third time for a few more min-

utes. Gently massaging each breast for a minute or so before you begin and while you are pumping will help your milk to let down. The whole process should take no more than 20 to 30 minutes. If you can get a double collection kit, pump for 10 to 15 minutes. Double-pumping not only decreases the time needed to pump but maximizes milk production.

Ideally, you should pump more milk than your baby requires. Building and maintaining a volume of at least 24 ounces per day will allow you to have extra milk on reserve should you experience a temporary decline (due to stress or illness, for example) during your baby's hospitalization. Having an abundant supply will also help your baby get milk more easily once she is able to nurse.

Take special care when expressing and storing your milk. Wash your hands before handling your breasts or any of the pump equipment. All pump parts that come in contact with the milk or your breasts must be thoroughly scrubbed with hot soapy water after each use and sterilized in boiling water or a dishwasher twice a day. Your daily bath or shower will cleanse your breasts sufficiently.

After collecting your milk, pour it into a sterile container, according to your nursery staff's preference. Check with your baby's nurses on how much to put in each container to avoid wasting milk. Milk cannot be refrozen or refrigerated after it has been thawed or warmed; whatever is left over after the feeding must be thrown out.

Whenever possible, provide freshly expressed or refrigerated milk for your baby. Freezing the milk preserves many, but not all, of its protective substances. You can keep your milk for 24 to 48 hours in the refrigerator or for up to three months in the freezer.

When transporting your refrigerated or frozen milk to the hospital, pack the containers in ice inside a small ice chest or cooler. Some families use refreezable ice packs to keep the milk cold, or, if they're traveling a long distance, dry ice to keep the milk frozen.

Be sure to let the hospital staff know about any medications you take, including any over-the-counter medicines, such as pain relievers or cold remedies. Although most medications are safe to take while nursing, a few could harm a sick or premature infant.

Expressing milk longer than two weeks. Depending on your baby's maturity and general progress, you may find yourself expressing milk for a while. It is important that you eat well, get plenty to drink, and rest enough to maintain your own energy as well as your milk supply.

If you notice that your milk supply is declining a few days in a row, you will need to assess the situation and make whatever adjustments are necessary. The most common cause of a decreasing milk supply is infrequent expression—fewer than eight times in 24 hours. Although a few mothers can maintain a good milk supply expressing less often than this, most are not able to keep up their supply after a few weeks. If you have been using a hand pump, rent an electric pump. Most mothers find an electric pump requires less effort and is more efficient as well as convenient.

Besides increasing the number of pumpings per day, switch from one breast to the other as soon as you notice the flow slowing down; do this several times during each feeding. This technique is very effective for increasing milk production. Pumping both breasts simultaneously, using one of the double collection kits manufactured by the makers of electric breast pumps, is also a very effective way to increase your milk production and decrease your pumping time. With these kits most mothers can express their milk in 10 to 15 minutes.

Fenugreek capsules also help stimulate increased milk production. See "Underfeeding and Weight Loss," in "Survival Guide for the First Week," or "Relactation," in this chapter.

Occasionally you may notice that your milk supply drops when you and your baby have a difficult day. This is normal and usually temporary. Stress can temporarily decrease your milk supply. The following suggestions have proved helpful when this occurs:

- Pump regularly, every two to three hours.
- Take a short nap or a warm bath just before expressing.
- Apply moist heat to your breasts before expressing.
- Massage each breast as you are pumping, or stimulate the opposite nipple.
- Ask someone to rub your back between the shoulder blades while you are pumping.
- If possible, hold the baby while you are pumping at the hospital, or keep a photo of your baby with your pump.

Supplementing breast milk. Many premature infants need extra nutrients, such as calcium and phosphorus, in addition to breast milk. Although breast milk alone is the perfect food for a full-term infant, a premie's nutritional needs, because of her small size and immaturity, may be somewhat different. Commercially prepared fortifiers can be mixed with breast milk to provide for these special needs. Usually, the fortifiers are discontinued before the baby leaves the hospital.

Some premature babies need a more concentrated source of calories. If this is the case with your baby, ask about feeding hind milk. This is the fattier milk produced after the first few minutes of pumping. To collect hind milk separately from foremilk, pump for about two minutes after the milk lets down, then stop pumping and switch collection bottles. Pump again until the breast is completely drained. Label the first bottle as foremilk, the second as hind milk. Provide the hind milk for the baby's immediate needs, and freeze the foremilk for the future (for use during separations or for supplementation). Feeding hind milk for a week or two can be very helpful in achieving good weight gain in a premie.

When breastfeeding begins. When the time arrives to begin nursing the premature infant, most mothers have very high expectations.

Premies' abilities at the breast vary greatly, but most are unable to complete an entire feeding at first.

Have a nurse help you during the first few sessions. Your goal is to position the baby well for nursing and to encourage her to latch on to the breast. These early practice sessions go best when the baby is awake and alert and the breast is not overly full. Keeping the baby wrapped in a blanket will usually discourage her interest. A premie will usually stay warm undressed next to her mother's body. Lay a blanket over your shoulder and the baby to limit heat loss. The nurse can check the baby's skin temperature after 5 to 10 minutes.

The cross-over hold and the football hold (see Chapter 2) are the positions of choice for nursing a premature baby. Both of these positions support the baby's head. Place your hand around the baby's head with your fingers behind and below her ears. Support her neck and shoulders with the palm of your hand and your wrist. With your thumb at the point where the baby's nose will touch the breast, compress the breast with your fingers. Lightly stroke the baby's upper lip with your nipple to signal her to open her mouth wide. As soon as she does, pull her head and shoulders toward you so that the nipple is on top of her tongue and far back in her mouth.

Again, premies' abilities at the breast vary greatly, so be patient. As long as you have positioned your baby correctly and are encouraging her to open her mouth, you have been successful.

Once latched on to the breast and sucking, a premie may fall asleep after just a few minutes. She may need a supplement after nursing until she is feeding more vigorously at the breast. Most hospitals give nursing premies supplements by bottle; others give them by passing a soft tube through the nose or mouth into the stomach, to avoid "nipple confusion."

While you are nursing your baby, you should be able to hear her swallowing. This means she is sucking effectively and getting your milk. If you do not hear swallowing, make sure the baby is actually latched on to the breast. Her suction should be so strong that it is hard to pull her off. You should not see dimples in her cheeks or hear clicking noises as she sucks. These signs would indicate she was sucking on her tongue and not on your breast.

When the baby seems interested in the second breast, you can simply pass her head and body over to the other side, or you can reposition her entirely in the opposite arm using the football hold.

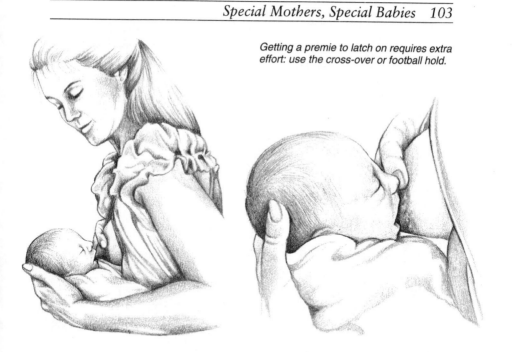

Getting a premie to latch on requires extra effort: use the cross-over or football hold.

To maintain your milk supply, be sure to pump after these feeding sessions with the baby. The collected milk can be used for supplemental feedings.

Difficult latch-on. Many premature infants have difficulty latching on, due to their own immaturity as well as having received rubber nipples as pacifiers or for feedings. Some babies have trouble learning to lower their tongue to latch on, whereas others seem unable to identify their mothers' nipples in their mouths.

If your baby has not been able to latch on to the breast, refer to "Difficult Latch-on: Refusal to Nurse," in "Survival Guide for the First Week." In my experience, most premature infants learn to nurse after a period of daily practice sessions.

The transition to full-time nursing. While you and the baby are establishing nursing, you may wonder how much milk the baby is taking. Although mothers and health professionals often try to gauge the baby's milk intake by how long he nurses, how much swallowing can be heard, or whether the baby will take supplemental milk, none of these methods are accurate. The best way to determine the baby's milk intake is to weigh him before and after nursing, in the same diaper and clothing, on an electronic gram scale. Each gram of weight gain equals 1 milliliter of milk intake. Recent studies have shown that these pre- and post-feeding weights are extremely accurate in indicating how much milk a baby has taken.

How much breast milk a baby should take at each feeding can be calculated by multiplying the baby's weight in kilograms by 22.5 (a pounds-to-kilogram conversion chart is in Appendix B). This will give you in milliliters the amount of milk a baby needs at each of eight daily feedings. For example, if a baby weighs 2.2 kilograms he will need 49.5, or approximately 50, milliliters of milk eight times per day. If the baby takes 30 milliliters during the nursing session, he will need an additional 20 milliliters after nursing to gain an adequate amount of weight.

While you are in the hospital, have your baby weighed on the nursery's scale before and after nursings. If you do this at each nursing, you should begin to develop a sense of how much milk the baby is taking at any feeding. Once at home, you may need weight checks only every two days or so to help you judge how much supplement the baby needs. If you want to continue pre- and post-feeding weight checks at home, rent a highly accurate electronic scale (see Appendix A).

Until your baby is nursing without any supplemental feedings, you will need to continue expressing milk after each nursing to maintain your milk supply.

Nursing More Than One

Needless to say, caring for two babies takes a tremendous amount of time and energy. Breastfeeding multiples is not only more healthful and economical than giving them formula, but in many ways it is more convenient. Mothers of twins often say that nursing is easier and less time-consuming than preparing and feeding bottles, particularly when a woman has mastered the skill of nursing two babies at the same time.

Although many mothers worry about being able to produce enough milk for more than one baby, most women are capable of producing plenty of milk for two and even three babies.

As soon as you become aware of the twins during pregnancy, you should begin some special preparations. You will want to arrange for as much help as possible, of course, for the first several weeks after the birth. It's also a good idea to get to know other mothers who have successfully nursed their twins. Many communities have organizations for mothers of twins. You might also contact your local breastfeeding support group; such a group usually provides literature on caring for and nursing twins.

Approximately half of all twins are born prematurely. During pregnancy you can do much to lessen the risk of premature delivery and other complications by maintaining a diet high in calories—at least 2,900 a day—and protein—at least 110 grams a day. Talk with your health-care provider about monitoring yourself for signs of preterm labor.

Establishing an abundant milk supply. Making enough milk for two or more babies depends on the frequent and complete drainage of the breasts. Multiples who are born early or of low birth weight may not consistently nurse effectively enough to stimulate abundant milk production. For this reason I recommend using a fully automatic breast pump, with a double-pump kit, whenever multiples are born three or more weeks before the due date or weighing less than six pounds. Even if your babies are healthy and latching on to the breast frequently, pump for five to ten minutes after each nursing to insure complete drainage of the breasts and to stimulate abundant milk production. Read "The Premature Baby," in this chapter, for more information on nursing premature babies and pumping after feedings.

If the babies are in a special-care nursery and are unable to nurse, use the electric pump at least eight times in every 24 hours. Be sure to review the information on expressing milk in "The Premature Baby." You should aim to produce at least 16 ounces of milk per day for each of your babies.

Breastfeeding two or more. You should nurse each of your babies at least eight times in every 24 hours. This may mean waking smaller babies every three hours during the day and evening for feedings, and every four to five hours in the night, until they are gaining weight well without any supplementation.

Some mothers prefer nursing their babies together as much as possible, whereas others choose to nurse them separately. Nursing two at once certainly saves time, and it may be necessary when both of the babies are hungry. If you want to nurse the babies together, there are three basic positions you can try:

- both babies in the cuddle hold with their legs side by side or crossed over each other,
- one baby in the cuddle hold and the other in the football hold, or
- both babies in the football hold.

During the early weeks, you may need assistance getting the babies on the breast at the same time. You will also probably need a few pillows for positioning. (A special pillow is available for nursing twins. See Appendix A for ordering information.) It may be easier to position the baby who nurses less vigorously first, and then put the vigorous nurser to the breast. Nursing the twins simultaneously should get easier as they get older and need less head support and assistance latching on.

*You can nurse twins simultaneously using the cradle hold,
the football hold, or a combination of the two.*

Nursing the babies separately, each baby on one breast only, may be easier to manage and will allow you more time with each individually. You may decide to feed each baby whenever she seems hungry or you may prefer to encourage the babies to eat and sleep on approximately the same schedule. To maintain a similar routine for both babies, simply offer the breast to the second baby, waking her if necessary, after nursing the first. Although most twins eventually develop a preference for one breast over the other, it is wise to alternate the babies at each feeding during the early weeks so the breasts will be evenly stimulated; this is particularly important when one baby is more active than the other. Keeping a simple written record may be helpful at first.

Mothers of triplets generally nurse two babies simultaneously and then the third baby from both breasts, or else another caregiver gives the third baby a bottle. Again, alternate the babies from one feeding to the next.

During the early weeks, if the babies are gaining weight adequately, substituting bottle feedings for nursings is best avoided. You want to be sure your breasts are stimulated by the babies' sucking so that milk production remains adequate. Foregoing the bottle also helps to minimize the occurrence of plugged ducts and breast infections.

Caring for yourself. For the mother who is nursing two or more babies, plenty of rest, food, and drink is essential. Most nursing mothers are naturally more hungry and thirsty than usual, but if you take on too much and become fatigued, you may lose your appetite and too much weight. Nutritionists recommend that a mother nursing twins consume at least 3,000 calories daily. Your diet should include high-protein foods and a quart or more of milk a day, the equivalent in other dairy products, or a calcium supplement. Vitamin C, and B-complex supplements or brewer's yeast, may also be beneficial.

The Baby with a Birth Defect

It may be that the baby with a birth defect needs his mother's milk, and the comfort and security of the breast, even more than other infants. Nursing such a baby is usually possible, but it is important that the mother is supported in her efforts. Although some mothers of babies with birth defects have been discouraged from attempting breastfeeding, many have gone on to nurse their babies successfully.

Depending on your baby's problem, you may be able to begin nursing right after birth, or you may need to express milk for a while (see "Expressing Milk for Your Baby"). Whatever the circumstances, it may be helpful to seek guidance from a lactation professional. Some helpful publications are listed at the end of the book.

Heart defect. Infants with heart defects generally have little trouble breastfeeding. The exception is the baby with a severe defect, who may become easily fatigued or stressed during feedings; he will start breathing rapidly, his heart will beat faster, and his overall color may change. His growth may be greatly affected due to the abnormality of his heart. He may also be more prone to infections, and therefore in greater need of breast milk than other babies.

The baby who becomes stressed during feedings needs to be nursed more frequently for shorter periods of time. He may also be more comfortable when held upright for nursing, as in the football hold.

Cleft lip and palate. The baby born with a cleft lip, palate, or both may have difficulty latching on and sucking effectively, so feeding her may present special challenges. Breastfeeding may be possible, depending on the location and extent of the cleft, but most of these babies, particularly those with cleft palates, are unable to get enough milk from nursing alone. Yet breast milk helps reduce the number and severity of ear and respiratory infections, which are more common in these babies than others. Many mothers, therefore, pump their milk and feed it to their babies with whatever method works best for the baby.

The baby born with a cleft lip alone may have little difficulty nursing. Until the lip is repaired, usually when the baby is several weeks old, she will need to be positioned with the cleft sealed, to permit suction. You may insure a complete seal just by pulling the baby close against your breast, so that your breast occludes the cleft, or you may need to place your finger or thumb over the cleft. If you find that your baby has more difficulty nursing on one side than the other, try using the football hold on that side.

Whether a baby with a cleft palate can nurse usually depends on the location and extent of the cleft. When it is in the soft palate only, the baby may or may not be able to nurse without much difficulty. It's best to position her so her head is raised; milk may come out of her nose if she is fed while lying flat. Ask the baby's doctor or a lactation professional about techniques to help babies with cleft palates to breastfeed. An infant may be fitted with a plastic dental appliance, an obturator, that covers the cleft and allows for adequate sucking. Some lactation professionals have reported success with the use of a nursing supplementation device (see Appendix A) and certain positioning techniques.

If your baby has a cleft lip or palate, try to get her to latch on and suck as soon as possible after birth. If she can't latch on, use a fully automatic electric breast pump after every nursing, or every two to three hours around the clock, to stimulate and maintain an abundant milk supply. An electric breast pump, ideally a lightweight model with a double-pump kit, is most efficient and requires the least amount of pumping time.

Bottle-feeding a baby with a cleft lip or palate can also be challenging. The nursing staff should have special feeders of various types that you can try while you are in the hospital. The Haberman Feeder, a new device for feeding babies with cleft palates, has worked well for some of my clients. See Appendix A for ordering information.

When a baby has an extensive cleft palate or a cleft palate and lip, nursing can be difficult or even impossible. In this case you will probably need to express milk for some time. Although long-term pump rental is far cheaper than purchasing infant formula, you may eventually decide to use formula anyway, since a cleft palate is generally not repaired until the baby is one to two years old.

Whether your baby has a cleft lip, a cleft palate, or both, closely monitor her weight to make sure that she is getting enough to eat. If you are exclusively bottle-feeding, see Appendix B to determine how much milk she needs at each feeding. If your baby is able to latch on and suck, you may be unsure how effective she is at getting milk and whether she needs supplemental milk, or how much she needs, to gain weight. In this case, weigh the baby every couple of days, and adjust the amount of supplement according to how much she is gaining. Renting an electronic scale for a few weeks may be helpful. You can use the scale before and after nursings to determine how much milk the baby is getting, or use it simply to get an accurate daily weight. See Appendix A to locate a scale.

Developmental and Neurological Problems

Babies with Down syndrome, hydrocephalus, spina bifida, and other neurological problems benefit greatly from breastfeeding. Because nursing provides frequent physical contact, it may be especially valuable to such a baby's development.

If the baby's sucking ability is affected, teaching him to nurse will require a great deal of patience. Professional guidance from a lactation professional experienced with such problems and a physical therapist may be necessary. When a baby is unable to suck, some mothers have been able to nurse with a nursing supplementation device (see Appendix A) or have provided their expressed milk in a bottle. Sources of additional information are listed at the end of the book.

Down syndrome. Not only will nursing further the development of the infant with Down syndrome, but it may also provide him with much needed protection from illness, as he is at greater risk than most babies for developing infections. Although many infants with Down syndrome are able to nurse, some have difficulty learning how to latch on and suck effectively. The baby may have weak muscle tone and may act sleepy and uninterested in the breast. He will need to be roused frequently for nursing (see "Sleepy Baby," in "Survival Guide for the First Week").

Typically, the baby with Down syndrome grows slowly. If his suck is weak and inefficient, you may need to pump out the milk he leaves in the breast. Regular pumping will allow you to maintain sufficient milk production and provide the baby extra milk, which you can feed as a supplement after each nursing.

Hydrocephalus and spina bifida. These birth defects are usually corrected surgically as soon as possible. Until the baby can begin to nurse, the mother must express milk (see "Expressing Milk for Your Baby"). For many such babies, positioning at the breast requires special attention so that they are protected and comfortable.

Cerebral palsy. Babies with cerebral palsy may also be able to nurse, depending on the severity of their conditions. Breastfeeding problems that occur are usually related to either (1) poor muscle tone and a weak suck or (2) excessive muscle tone (rigidity and abnormal posture), tongue thrusting, clenching of the jaw, and difficulty swallowing. Both of these situations usually lead to slow weight gain. Some infants with cerebral palsy are able to breastfeed successfully with a nursing supplementation device.

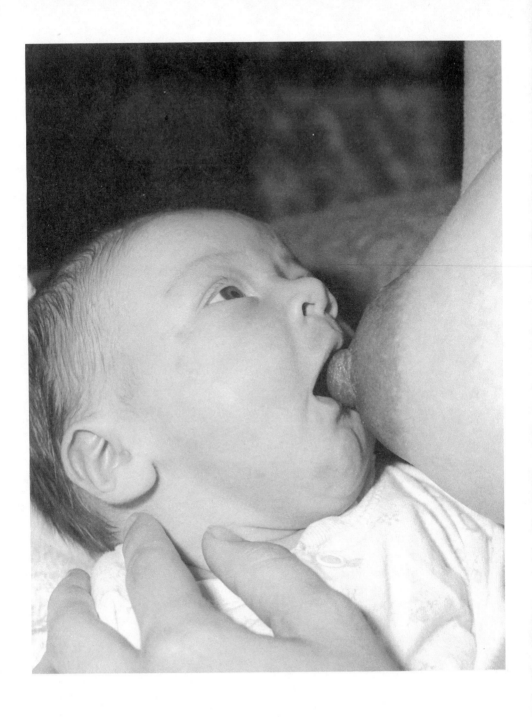

CHAPTER FOUR

The Learning Period: The First Two Months

Now that You Are Post Partum

Caring for Yourself

Nutritional Needs

Nursing Your Baby

Your Nursing Style

Your Milk Supply

Scheduled Feedings

Infant Dietary Supplements

Illnesses: Yours and the Baby's

The First Two Months: What's Normal?

AFTER THE FIRST WEEK, YOU MAY ALREADY BE FEELING ENERGETIC and confident in your abilities as a new mother—or you may be exhausted, overwhelmed, and perhaps troubled with some aspect of breastfeeding. In any case, it is important to realize that the first two months after giving birth are a time for adjustment and learning. Mothers normally have questions and concerns about themselves, their babies, and nursing during this period.

Now that You Are Post Partum

Caring for Yourself

The postpartum period is the six weeks after birth in which all of the many changes of pregnancy are reversed. Virtually every system in your body will go through some readjustment. As your uterus shrinks in size and the inner lining is shed, a new layer is formed. The vaginal flow, or lochia, decreases in amount and progresses to pink or brown and then to white. Many women continue bleeding throughout the first month. Intermittent spotting is common. Too much activity may cause the lochia to become heavier and turn red again—a signal that you should slow down.

If you have had a vaginal birth, your vagina, perineum, urethra, and rectum have undergone considerable stress. Frequent warm baths will speed healing and help relieve discomfort—unless you have hemorrhoids, in which case ice packs may be preferable. Menstrual pads soaked with witch hazel and then frozen are very soothing for hemorrhoids.

Kegel's exercises will help this area return to normal by strengthening the entire pelvic floor. These exercises are simple and can be done anytime, anywhere. Several times a day, tightly squeeze the muscles around your anus, then around your vagina and urethra. Gradually work up to 100 "kegels" a day.

If you have had a cesarean birth, keep in mind you are recovering from major abdominal surgery. Most likely, you will need to take pain medication during the first week or so at home. You may perhaps be bothered by an uncomfortable feeling that your abdomen may fall out. A lightweight girdle can provide some welcome support.

Constipation is a common complaint after giving birth. It can best be prevented by drinking plenty of fluids, adding fiber to your diet, and getting regular exercise. Be aware that some laxatives could affect the baby through your milk, causing cramping, excessive stools, and even weight loss.

Night sweats are very common in the first few days after birth, and they sometimes continue for several weeks.

Starting at approximately six to twelve weeks after birth, some women experience generalized hair loss *(telogenefffluvium)*. Because of the hormonal changes following birth, hair follicles simultaneously move from the growing phase (which they were in during pregnancy) to the resting phase of their development. Postpartum hair loss is seldom severe, and women never go bald because of it. The period of hair loss lasts about three to six months. It has no relationship to breastfeeding.

Most women experience emotional changes during the postpartum period. Anxiety, moodiness, and irritability are common responses to the hormonal changes that occur after giving birth, as well as to the tremendous responsibility of caring for a new baby. Some mothers notice other postpartum "symptoms" such as forgetfulness, inability to concentrate, and difficulty expressing thoughts. These problems seem to pass with time. If you fall prey, though, to exhaustion, poor nutrition, and isolation from other adults, depression may be the result.

Because of the rapid physical changes of the postpartum period and the tremendous amount of time and energy needed to care for and nurse a baby, rest should continue to take high priority for all new mothers. Lack of rest can slow your recovery from the birth and may lead to tension, inability to cope, poor appetite, and depression. Be sure to take at least one nap every day during these important first weeks. Do essential household chores and activities while the baby is awake so that you can nap together. Tucking the baby in with you at nap time and bedtime may help you both sleep better. Getting plenty of rest now will contribute greatly to your sense of well-being and your breastfeeding success.

After a couple of weeks some light exercise can do much to renew your energy. A brisk twenty-minute walk with the baby can be invigorating; the fresh air will do you both good. Many community centers offer exercise programs for new mothers. Often the babies are included in the exercises, and sometimes infant care is provided. Despite recent claims that exercise causes lactic acid to build up in breast milk, and babies therefore to refuse to nurse, moderate exercise has little or no effect on the composition or volume of breast milk. With whatever activity you choose, however, you will want to start out slowly.

You may feel isolated as a new mother, especially if you have left work or school—and most of your friends—to care for the baby. You need adult companionship. Check with your childbirth educator or public-health nurse about groups for new mothers. Attending La Leche League meetings, taking a mother-baby exercise class, or socializing with women from your childbirth class are excellent ways of getting out with the baby and getting to know other new mothers.

Nutritional Needs

Drinking enough. Maintaining an adequate intake of fluids is usually not a problem for the nursing mother. Most women are naturally more thirsty while they are breastfeeding. Contrary to popular belief, forcing fluids beyond satisfying natural thirst does not increase milk production. But when a nursing mother does not drink at least six to eight glasses of fluids every day, dark,

New mothers' groups provide opportunities for socializing as well as learning about infant development.

concentrated urine and constipation usually result. She may need to make a conscious effort to increase her fluid intake.

Eating well. Provided you established good eating habits during pregnancy and gained an adequate amount of weight, you probably won't need to change your diet much at all. Nursing mothers are often told to add about five hundred calories, including 65 grams of protein, to their pre-pregnancy diets. Recent research, however, indicates that many mothers may not need this much food, so don't feel you must eat more than you want. You can get extra nutrients in between-meal snacks, perhaps during nursings: half a sandwich and a glass of milk, three glasses of juice, or one-half cup of shelled peanuts will supply about five hundred calories.

Some mothers experience a temporary loss of appetite during the first couple of weeks after delivery. Eating smaller, more frequent meals or snacks may be more appealing than three big meals each day.

You may feel discouraged that your shape is not back to normal. The clothes in your closet may seem as if they belonged to someone else. Although you lost some weight when you delivered, you

Don't expect to be able to get into your jeans for several weeks, at least.

are probably still pounds away from your usual weight. During the early months of breastfeeding, this extra fat is a useful energy store. If you let your appetite guide you as you continue nursing, you will probably lose the excess weight gradually and feel good while doing it. Dieting during the early weeks is not a good idea.

If you like, you can estimate your daily caloric needs by multiplying your current weight by 15. Add 500 to your total to meet the caloric needs of nursing (if you are nursing twins, add 1,000 calories).

$$
\begin{array}{r}
\textit{Example:} \quad 135 \text{ pounds} \\
\times\ 15 \\
\hline
2{,}025 \text{ calories} \\
+\ 500 \text{ calories} \\
\hline
2{,}525 \text{ calories}
\end{array}
$$

If you are a moderately active woman, you can expect to lose a pound every two to three weeks on this diet. If you are very active and have no problem controlling your weight, or if you burn calories slowly, you will need to adjust the figures somewhat: multiply your weight by 17 (high activity) or 13 (low activity). The minimal safe food intake for a nursing mother of average size is about 1,800 calories per day.

Milk production is largely independent of nutritional intake during the first few months of breastfeeding. This is partly because the fat accumulated in pregnancy is available as a ready supply of calories. When a mother's diet is inadequate, however, milk production usually continues at her expense—leading to fatigue, listlessness, and rapid weight loss.

Some women have trouble finding time to fix nutritious meals for themselves when they are at home alone with the baby. If you find yourself in this situation, start the day with a good breakfast, and then snack throughout the day on nutritious foods such as hard-boiled eggs, leftover chicken or beef, cheese, peanut butter, yogurt, seeds, and nuts. Don't forget the fiber: whole-wheat bread, whole-grain crackers, and fruits and raw vegetables will provide it. Some mothers have developed their own favorite recipes for high-energy blender drinks using ingredients such as milk, yogurt, nuts, and bananas or other fruits.

Avoid snacking on foods or drinks that are high in sugar. Refined sugar provides only "empty" calories—empty, that is, of vitamins and minerals. Soda, cookies, and candy will not provide sustaining energy and may diminish your desire for more nutritious foods.

Mothers who are vegetarians can certainly maintain a diet to support their nutritional needs. But since vitamin B_{12} is found only in the animal kingdom, deficiencies may occur when a mother maintains a "vegan" diet, excluding eggs and milk products as well as meat. Supplementation with up to 4 milligrams of vitamin B_{12} per day is recommended.

Although most nutritionists recommend that a nursing mother drink three 8-ounce glasses of milk a day, there is no need to drink milk if you don't like it or can't tolerate it. A woman's bone density tends to decrease somewhat during lactation even when her calcium intake is relatively high. This causes no long-term harm. The bones grow denser again after weaning, and some studies suggest that women who breastfeed actually reduce their risk of developing osteoporosis later in life.

Still, nutritionists recommend that breastfeeding women consume 1,000 milligrams of calcium per day. If you don't drink milk, make sure you're getting enough calcium from other sources, such as those listed in the table.

Serving	Milligrams calcium
yogurt (8 oz.)	288
cheeses (1 oz. cheddar or swiss)	213
cottage cheese (½ cup)	106
ice cream (½ cup)	110
tofu (½ lb.)	290
salmon (3 oz.)	207
sardines (3 oz.)	272
mackerel (3 oz.)	321
broccoli (½ cup)	68
corn tortilla (1)	42

Although dark green vegetables in general are rich in calcium (100 milligrams per half cup), the calcium they provide is poorly absorbed by the body. Broccoli is the one exception to this rule. If you do not use dairy products at all, then, calcium supplements may be necessary. The least expensive supplement, with the highest concentration of calcium, is calcium carbonate. Avoid bone meal and dolomite, as some types have been found to be contaminated with lead.

Dietary supplements. If you are well nourished, vitamin supplements are unnecessary while you are nursing, although you may need iron supplements if you are anemic after birth. Also, some nursing mothers develop vitamin B deficiencies, experiencing depression, irritability, impaired concentration, loss of appetite, and tingling or burning feet. A daily B-complex supplement is often prescribed to reverse these symptoms. Sometimes nursing mothers are advised to take brewer's yeast, a natural source of B vitamins, iron, and protein. Some mothers feel it has improved their milk supply or has increased their overall energy level. Health-food stores carry brewer's yeast in a powdered form that can be mixed with juice or milk.

If you decide to take vitamin supplements or brewer's yeast, remember that they are no substitute for a varied diet of nutritious foods, and in large quantities they can sometimes be dangerous. There have been reports of fussiness in babies whose mothers take brewer's yeast or large doses of vitamin C. Vitamin B_6 supplements in large doses have been reported to reduce milk production.

Foods and substances you may be wondering about. There are no foods that should be routinely avoided by nursing mothers, but occasionally a baby will be bothered by something the mother has eaten. Some babies fuss for up to 24 hours after their mothers have eaten garlic, onions, cabbage, broccoli, brussels sprouts, cauliflower, or beans. Citrus fruits and their juices, chocolate, and cinnamon can also bother young nursing babies. If your baby has unusual and persistent symptoms such as sudden refusal to nurse, vomiting, diarrhea or green stools, gassiness, redness around the anus, fussiness at the breast, or colic symptoms, see "Survival Guide for the First Two Months."

Caffeine taken by the mother has been known to cause irritability and colic symptoms in some babies. Caffeine is present in coffee, tea, and many soft drinks. You may want to limit your intake of these beverages.

An occasional glass of wine or beer is not believed to harm a nursing infant. Because alcohol passes through the breast milk, however, moderation is essential.

Mothers who smoke have lower levels of vitamin C in their milk than nonsmokers. Breathing cigarette fumes increases a baby's risk of contracting bronchitis and pneumonia, and perhaps of succumbing to crib death. If you smoke, try to limit the amount, and don't do it around the baby.

Nursing Your Baby

Your Nursing Style

During the early weeks, each mother develops her own style of nursing. Many women feel comfortable putting their babies to breast whenever they signal the desire to nurse. Others expect their babies to fall into a predictable feeding schedule. They may be troubled when their babies nurse irregularly or want to nurse again soon after being fed. These mothers may worry that perhaps they have too little milk or that it is somehow inadequate. Sometimes they feel they must hold the baby off until a certain number of hours have passed since the last feeding. But the breasts do not need to rest for any period of time to build up a supply for the next feeding; they produce milk constantly. The expectation that a baby should nurse on some type of a schedule usually leads to frustration for both mother and baby—and not uncommonly to breastfeeding failure.

The typical newborn infant nurses between eight and twelve times in a 24-hour period, or about every one to three hours. Because of the ease with which breast milk is digested, nursing infants have been described as continuous feeders. Not only must a baby nurse often to satisfy her hunger and stimulate an adequate milk supply, but she also seeks out the breast to satisfy her needs for sucking, security, and comforting.

It is a common misconception that the breast empties in a certain number of minutes, and that a baby should be taken from the breast after those minutes have elapsed. In fact, most mothers experience the release of milk several times during a feeding. The length of time required to complete a feeding varies from baby to baby. The "all-business" nurser, who swallows continuously with few pauses, may be done in 10 minutes, whereas the "dawdler" may take up to 45 minutes. The length of nursing time may vary in the same baby from feeding to feeding. Before long, most mothers can tell when their babies have had enough.

Some babies nurse from only one breast at a feeding some or most of the time. This is fine so long as the baby seems satisfied and is gaining weight adequately. You may prefer to offer only one breast per feeding, in fact, if you have an abundant milk supply. Your baby is more likely to drain the breast completely this way, and complete drainage helps prevent plugged milk ducts and breast infections. Your baby will also be sure to get the rich hind milk, which is produced near the end of a feeding.

I strongly recommend that your baby be weighed at 10 to 14 days of age. Although many infants are not scheduled for a routine well-baby exam until three to four weeks of age, a weight check at two weeks can be very beneficial. If the baby is back to her birth weight or beyond, you can be reassured early on that your nursing relationship is progressing well. On the contrary, if the baby has not yet regained her birth weight, you can usually correct this. When a poor weight gain is not discovered until three or four weeks, it is more likely to upset everyone and may be harder to correct than it would have been at two weeks.

You may find that nursing is the most enjoyable part of your day—a time to sit back, relax, and simply enjoy being with your baby. But it may be difficult at times for you to break away from what you are doing or sit still long enough for the baby to have a leisurely nursing. It may help to make a special little nursing area for yourself—or two or three nooks in different parts of the house. You might want to include a book, some magazines, or a note pad within reach. Having the phone nearby may also be handy. Some mothers make a point of getting a snack or something to drink just before sitting down to nurse.

Many babies seem to get hungry whenever food is served. If you usually find yourself nursing while trying to eat dinner, you may find a baby swing handy. Some parents have found that taking the baby for a walk just before dinner lulls her to sleep so that they can eat without interruption.

Your Milk Supply

During these early weeks your milk production may seem somewhat erratic. At times your breasts may feel as if they are bursting with milk. At other times you may worry there is not enough milk, especially if your breasts seem empty and your baby wants to nurse all the time. Many mothers notice this happening around two to three weeks and then again at six weeks, when a baby normally experiences appetite spurts and nurses more often to stimulate increased milk production. You can expect fluctuations in your milk supply as production becomes regulated according to the baby's demands.

By six to eight weeks after birth, many mothers notice that their breasts seem smaller or feel less full. This does not usually mean that less milk is being produced, but only that the breasts are adjusting to the large amount of milk within and the baby's feeding pattern.

Some mothers misinterpret their babies' increased demands and their own softer breasts, and begin offering supplemental bottles. For most mothers and babies, this marks the beginning of the end of breastfeeding. The mother begins to assume that she cannot make enough milk for her baby, and she offers more and more formula instead of allowing the baby to increase her own supply of milk. After receiving formula the baby sleeps longer and nurses less often. He becomes increasingly frustrated at the breast as his mother's milk supply dwindles. For these mothers and babies, breastfeeding is soon over.

Some mothers try to satisfy their babies' hunger with solid foods. Introducing solids during these early weeks is also inappropriate, since young infants are both physiologically and developmentally unable to manage them. Their digestive systems and kidneys are not mature enough to handle cereals and other baby foods. Infants may develop allergies to solid foods given during this period because their immune systems are still immature.

Fluctuations in the fullness of your breasts and in your milk supply will probably pass by the end of the second month. In the meantime you can be reassured your milk supply is probably fine so long as you are nursing at least eight times in each 24-hour period and allowing the baby to nurse as long as he needs, and he is gaining an ounce a day. If you have additional concerns about your milk supply, see "Survival Guide for the First Two Months."

Scheduled Feedings

In recent years, some parenting books and classes have promoted a philosophy of scheduled breastfeeding. Called Parent Directed Feeding, the program teaches parents to feed babies on a rigid three- to four-hour schedule and to eliminate nighttime feedings at an early age. The purpose is to relieve parental anxiety and instill a sense of order and discipline in the infant. Although most parents like the idea of predictable, widely spaced nursings and full nights' sleep from the early weeks on, these practices are often associated with low milk production, poor weight gain in the baby, and early weaning. Some babies subjected to the method have become dangerously thin and dehydrated.

Babies do best if they are nursed when they seem hungry. Parent Directed Feeding fails to take into account two important facts about breast milk and breastfeeding. First, nature has designed breast milk to be taken frequently. Low in protein, it is easily and quickly digested. Second, a mother's milk supply depends on frequent, complete drainage of the breasts. If she nurses fewer than seven times in a 24-hour period, her milk production generally declines. Although some mothers can meet their babies' needs with fewer than seven daily feedings, most cannot.

The American Academy of Pediatrics, and every other organization that supports breastfeeding, recommends that babies be fed whenever they show signs of hunger.

Infant Dietary Supplements

Vitamins. It is generally agreed that vitamin supplements are unnecessary for the healthy, full-term infant who is breastfed. Although it was previously thought that breast milk contained little vitamin D, a water-soluble variant that appears in milk was recently discovered. Vitamin D is important for the formation of teeth and bones, and a deficiency can cause rickets. This disease, though, is rarely seen in breastfed babies. Babies who may be at risk include those with low birth weights, those with dark skin, those who are rarely exposed to the sun, and those whose mothers do not eat meat, fish, or dairy products. The recommended dose of vitamin D for these infants is 400 units per day. Twice this daily dose can be toxic.

Iron. The full-term newborn has sufficient stores of iron for the first six months after birth. The small amounts of iron in breast milk are very well utilized by the nursing infant, so iron supplementation is unnecessary. Furthermore, iron supplements can interfere with the protective properties of breast milk. The premature infant, however, is likely to use up her iron stores earlier than the full-term infant. Supplemental iron is recommended for the premature infant beginning at two months of age or earlier.

Fluoride. Fluoride given from infancy is believed to reduce cavities 50 to 65 percent during childhood. Even though a mother may drink fluoridated water, little fluoride reaches the baby through the breast milk. The American Academy of Pediatrics therefore recommends that a baby receive fluoride supplements of 0.25 milligram per day, unless she is being fed formula mixed with fluoridated water.

Some authorities, however, believe fluoride supplementation is unnecessary for the breastfed infant, and point out that too much fluoride can cause spotting of the tooth enamel. Additionally, some infants are reported to become fussy and irritable and to have gastrointestinal upsets after being given fluoride.

For these reasons, the American Academy of Pediatrics now recommends delaying fluoride supplements until a baby is six months old. Fluoride is available by prescription, either alone or in combination with vitamins A, C, and D (which most breastfed infants do not require).

Illnesses: Yours and the Baby's

When you come down with a minor illness such as a cold or flu, you need not interrupt breastfeeding. Most likely your baby will have already been exposed to the virus that causes you to get sick. In fact, the antibodies you produce against the illness will reach the baby through the milk and may protect him from getting the same sickness. Even though you may not feel much like eating, try to drink extra fluids to keep from getting dehydrated. Should you need to take a medication, even an over-the-counter drug, be sure to check on its safety for the baby (see Appendix C).

Temporary weaning is also unnecessary if you suspect you have a case of food poisoning, provided your only symptoms are vomiting, diarrhea, or both.

Your milk supply may seem low during or just after an illness, but a few days of frequent nursing will usually bring milk production back to normal.

Should your baby become ill, nursing should certainly continue. Breast milk is the best source of fluids and nourishment for recovery and nursing the best source of comfort. But sickness often changes a baby's nursing pattern. He may nurse more than usual, or he may lose interest in feeding.

Ear infections, sore throats, and fever blisters may make nursing painful for the baby. As long as he is nursing infrequently or is refusing to nurse, be sure to express your milk every couple of hours to keep up your supply. Colds and stuffy noses may make nursing difficult for him. Holding him upright while feeding, using a humidifier in the room, or administering saline nose drops and using a bulb syringe may make nursing more comfortable.

Fever is a sign of infection. During the first four months, a temperature above 99°F., if taken in the armpit, or 101°F., if taken rectally, should be reported to the baby's doctor. If, besides having an elevated temperature, the baby doesn't act like his usual self or he nurses poorly, he should be checked by your doctor. The severity of a fever does not always correspond with the seriousness of an illness; a high fever may appear with a minor infection and a low fever may accompany a serious infection. Because a fever may lead to dehydration, frequent nursing is very important.

Diarrhea in the breastfed baby, although less common and usually less severe than in the formula-fed baby, is characterized by frequent (12 or more per day), extremely loose or watery bowel movements. Often the stools are foul-smelling, and they may contain mucus or blood. Since babies lose a great deal of fluid with diarrhea, they can easily become dehydrated, making frequent nursing important. With its high water content, breast milk helps replace the lost fluids. Diarrhea generally improves within three to five days. Fever, infrequent feedings, or signs of dehydration (dry mouth, few wet diapers, listlessness) are signs to notify your doctor. In cases of severe diarrhea, doctors occasionally recommend supplements of an electrolyte solution, such as Pedialyte, in conjunction with nursing.

The First Two Months: What's Normal?

During the first two months you can expect your baby will nurse between 8 and 12 times a day, including at least once at night. If your baby sleeps four to six hours at a stretch at night or takes a three- to four-hour nap during the day, she will probably want to nurse often during the next few hours to make up for the meal she missed. The baby who is nursing less than eight times in a 24-hour period or who is sleeping longer than six hours at a stretch at night is typically the infant who fails to gain enough weight during the early weeks of nursing.

Generally, eight or more wet diapers a day are a sign the baby is getting enough milk. By two weeks, most nursing infants have regained their birth weight. A gain of at least an ounce a day is normal.

The breastfed baby typically has loose, watery, or seedy stools. During the first month most infants have at least one bowel movement daily. After the first month it is not uncommon for a baby to go several days without a bowel movement. As long as the baby seems comfortable there is probably no need for concern; your baby is unlikely to be constipated or underfed. The baby who is not getting enough to eat typically has small, and usually infrequent, brown or greenish stools.

Many mothers continue to experience dripping or spraying milk during or between nursings. But some women stop leaking altogether after the first several weeks, and most gradually notice less leakage.

At some point during the first two months you will probably start to experience the sensations of milk let-down. You may notice this tingling, pins-and-needles feeling in your breasts just before or during a feeding or at any time your baby signals you with his cry.

Occasionally babies spit up after a feeding. Some babies spit up after every nursing. This is usually due to an immature digestive system; what comes up is normally just a few teaspoons. If your baby spits up more, the cause may be certain foods or beverages in your diet (see "Something in Your Diet" in "Survival Guide for the First Two Months"). In any case, spitting up passes with time; until it does, keep a diaper or small towel handy.

A baby cries for any of a number of reasons. She may be hungry or tired, or she may just want to suck and be held. Sucking at the breast is soothing and comforting for her. Babies usually have a fussy period in the evening. Although many theories have been suggested to explain why this is, most babies are comforted by extra nursing. Try not to assume your milk is somehow lacking. Many mothers who interpret their babies' cries this way begin supplementing with formula and soon find the babies weaned. See "Survival Guide for the First Two Months" for more on why babies cry and how to cope with crying.

During the appetite spurts at about two to three weeks and six weeks of age, your baby may act more fussy than usual and want to nurse more often. After a few days of frequent nursing, your milk supply will increase to meet her needs and she will return to her usual nursing pattern.

Some babies cry hard, as if they were in pain, for prolonged periods every day. They are said to have *colic*, which is just a name for extreme irritability that continues day after day—for any of a number of reasons. Some cry at the breast or refuse nursing entirely. If your baby has colic symptoms, see "Survival Guide for the First Two Months."

You may have heard that tending to your baby each time she cries will spoil her or will reinforce her behavior and cause her to cry more often. Nothing could be further from the truth. Babies do not cry to exercise their lungs, but because they are in need of something. If your baby's needs are met in infancy she will develop a sense of security, and she will grow to trust in you and others as well.

During these early weeks, while you are learning about your baby, caring for his needs, and learning to breastfeed, you are apt to experience some feelings of concern, confusion, and perhaps even inadequacy regarding your mothering abilities. Motherhood and breastfeeding may not be exactly what you expected. Your baby's crying and the unpredictability of his sleeping and wakeful periods may be upsetting. The baby's nursing schedule (or lack thereof) and his many needs may make it impossible to feel organized or productive. Perhaps you are disappointed by the lack of help from your health-care providers. Early motherhood may also bring feelings of loneliness and isolation.

It is normal to have mixed feelings about nursing. Try to keep in mind that new motherhood brings a period of uncertainty and adjustment and that nursing, and mothering, gets easier with time.

SURVIVAL GUIDE
for the First Two Months

Concerns about Yourself

Sore Nipples

Breast Pain

Plugged Ducts

Breast Infection (Mastitis)

Breast Abscess

Breast Lumps

Leaking Milk

Overabundant Milk

Lopsided Breasts

Depression and Anxiety

Concerns about the Baby

Spitting Up and Vomiting

Pulling Away from the Breast

Refusal to Nurse

Fussiness and Colic

Underfeeding

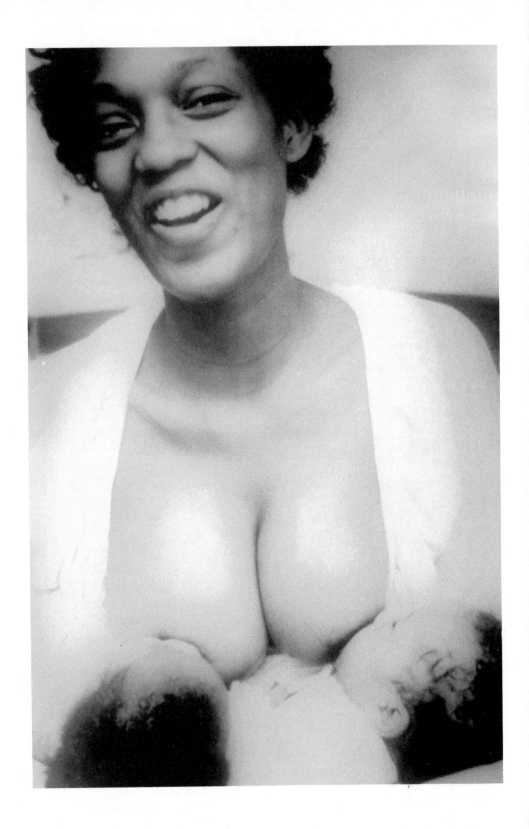

Concerns about Yourself

Sore Nipples

It can certainly be discouraging when sore nipples persist beyond the first week. If this happens to you, review the information in "Survival Guide for the First Week." It may be helpful to have your partner, friend, or lactation professional observe your latch-on technique and compare it with the descriptions of latch-on in Chapter 2. Don't discount the possibility that your nipples are irritated due to thrush or another dermatologic condition, as these are frequent causes of sore nipples.

If you have suddenly developed sore nipples after a period of comfortable nursing, the most likely cause is thrush. See "Survival Guide for the First Week."

Breast Pain

For a variety of reasons, your breasts may begin to hurt during nursing or become perpetually tender or sore. If this happens, it is important to identify the cause so that any necessary action can be taken.

Engorgement can occur any time the breasts become overly full—when the baby misses a feeding, for example, or when he begins to sleep longer at night.

Most mothers begin noticing normal let-down sensations during these early weeks. Let-down may be experienced as a mild ache at the start of nursing or a tingling, pins-and-needles sensation.

A deep pain, often described as "shooting," that occurs just after nursing is thought to be related to the sudden refilling of the breast. These pains disappear after the first few weeks of nursing.

Pain during nursing, often described as burning or stinging, is usually associated with thrush. The nipples may be pinker than usual. Sometimes a rash may be visible. See "Thrush Nipples," in "Survival Guide for the First Week," for additional information on causes and treatment.

Plugged Ducts

If you can feel a tender area or painful lump in your breast, the cause is probably a plugged milk duct. A plugged duct may be small or it may involve a large area of the breast that feels overly full and does not soften with nursing. The skin over the area may be reddened.

Occasionally a plug in one of the nipple openings blocks the milk flow and causes a backup of milk in the breast. If the nipple looks normal in color but you can see a white spot on the tip, particularly right after the baby comes off the breast, the problem may be a plugged nipple pore.

Plugged ducts are most common during the early weeks of nursing, but they can occur at any time during breastfeeding. They occur for a variety of reasons. During the early weeks and months of nursing, they frequently seem due to incomplete drainage of the breast. Mothers with high milk production, including those nursing twins, tend to be more prone to plugged ducts. Interrupting the baby's nursing to switch to the other breast before the baby signals that he is finished may lead to a plugged duct. A plugged duct may follow a missed feeding or a long stretch at night without nursing. Overly tight bras, especially underwire types, may obstruct milk flow and lead to plugged ducts. Baby carriers with tight straps can also cause this to happen.

For unknown reasons, plugged ducts seem to be more common during the winter months. Some breastfeeding specialists feel that mothers who drink an insufficient amount of fluids, who become slightly dehydrated due to a cold or flu, or who are overly fatigued may also be more susceptible to developing plugged milk ducts.

Any breast lump that does not get significantly smaller within a week should be examined by a doctor.

Treatment Measures for Plugged Ducts

1. Remove your bra if there is any question that it may be too tight or may be pressing into part of your breast.

2. Apply moist heat to the breast for 15 to 20 minutes before nursing.

3. Nurse frequently, at least every two hours. Begin each nursing on the affected breast.

4. Gently massage the breast just behind the sore area while nursing.

5. If you are following the preceding recommendations but notice no change in your breast after a feeding or two, try positioning the baby with his chin close to the plugged duct, if possible, to promote better drainage. If this doesn't work, get into the shower. With your

breast well soaped, apply steady but gentle pressure behind the plugged area, pressing toward the nipple.

6. Increase your fluid intake so that you urinate more frequently.

7. When the blockage seems to be in the nipple, look for dried milk secretions or a clogged nipple pore, which may resemble a white-head. If necessary, you can gently remove a visible plug from a nipple opening with a sterile needle. This may cause a little bleeding, but you probably won't feel any pain.

8. Be alert for signs of a developing breast infection—fever, chills, and achiness—so you can treat it promptly.

Breast Infection (Mastitis)

Up to 30 percent of all nursing women develop mastitis, or infection of the breast. It occurs most commonly in the first three months after birth.

Mastitis causes flu-like symptoms, including fever, chills, achiness, headache, and sometimes nausea and vomiting. Usually only one breast is affected; it typically becomes swollen, tender, and reddened in a limited area.

A breast infection may follow a cracked nipple or a plugged milk duct. Other possible causes are a tight bra, skipped feedings, infrequent changing of wet breast pads, anemia, stress, and fatigue. Although doctors usually prescribe antibiotics for mastitis, many women recover quickly without them. In one study of women with mastitis, half used no antibiotic, and none of them suffered complications (Riordan and Nichols, 1990). However, an antibiotic may be necessary if your symptoms do not resolve after you've followed the treatment measures specified here, or if you are anemic. Otherwise you may prefer to avoid antibiotics, as they can lead to yeast infections in both mother and baby.

With prompt and proper treatment the symptoms usually subside within 24 hours. It is most important to continue nursing frequently during this period; discontinuing nursing would slow healing and might lead to the development of a breast abscess. You don't need to worry that the baby will get ill, since the infection involves only the breast tissue, not the milk. Try to identify the probable cause of the infection so you can prevent a recurrence in the future.

Mastitis in both breasts, though rare, is sometimes a sign of B-streptococcal infection, which is transmitted by the infant to the breasts. When both breasts are affected the baby's doctor should be promptly notified so that any necessary treatment of the infant can begin.

Treatment Measures for Mastitis

1. Go to bed, if you haven't already.

2. Remove your bra if you are more comfortable without it or if there is any question that it may be too tight or pressing into part of your breast.

3. Nurse frequently, at least every two hours, and begin each nursing on the affected breast. Advice to wean or temporarily discontinue nursing is based on disproven theories. Giving up nursing may slow healing and lead to a breast abscess.

4. Increase your fluid intake so you notice an increase in urination.

5. Apply moist heat to the breast for 15 to 20 minutes before nursing and intermittently between feedings.

6. Monitor your temperature. Acetaminophen tablets (such as Tylenol) or ibuprofin (such as Advil or Motrin) may help reduce your fever and discomfort.

7. Some mothers report that taking 1,000 milligrams of vitamin C four times a day speeds healing and recovery.

8. If after 24 hours you feel no better, call your doctor, who will probably prescribe antibiotics. Antibiotics should be taken for the entire time they are prescribed, even though the symptoms may disappear.

9. After you have completed a course of antibiotics, watch for symptoms of yeast growth—thrush, diaper rash, or sore nipples (see "Survival Guide for the First Week").

10. See "Survival Guide for Months Two through Six" if you have a recurrence.

Breast Abscess

On very rare occasions, a breast infection may develop into an abscess. A breast abscess is an accumulation of pus walled off within the breast. It may occur when a mother stops nursing during a breast infection, when treatment for mastitis is delayed, or when a mother has trouble fighting off a breast infection because she is severely anemic.

A breast abscess should be suspected whenever mastitis symptoms are prolonged beyond a couple of days and a lump persists.

The lump may be hard or soft but does not change with nursing. An abscess must usually be drained by a physician, either in an office or a hospital. After it is drained, recovery is rapid.

The development and treatment of an abscess is usually a rather traumatic experience. You may be advised to stop nursing entirely, or you may doubt yourself whether you should continue. Although you need not abandon nursing completely, it may be suggested that you not nurse on the affected breast for the first few days after it is drained. In the meantime, you can use an electric pump to maintain your milk flow until the baby resumes nursing on both sides. The incision may leak milk for a short while, but it will heal and close over. I developed an abscess at six weeks after birth and went on to nurse successfully without any further difficulties.

Breast Lumps

Lumps in the breast are very common during the early weeks and are usually related to lactation.

The breast may feel generally lumpy when it is overly full or engorged. A sudden tender lump is usually a sign of a plugged milk duct or, when accompanied with fever and flu-like symptoms, a breast infection. A lump that appears just before nursing and seems to get smaller or disappear afterward is probably a small cyst that fills with milk.

Whenever a lump shows no change in size for longer than a week, it should be examined by a doctor. It is probably a harmless cyst or benign tumor; cancer is rarely the cause. But breastfeeding women with persistent lumps have been found to have breast cancer, so see your doctor for a thorough breast exam as soon as possible. If further diagnosis is recommended, you don't need to wean your baby, although a doctor unfamiliar with the lactating breast may recommend weaning. Many women have undergone mammography, ultrasound, breast biopsy, and lump removal without any interruption of nursing. Feel free to get a second opinion whenever drastic measures are recommended.

Leaking Milk

See "Survival Guide for the First Week" for basic information on leaking, dripping, and spraying milk.

After a few weeks of nursing you may notice that leaking diminishes or stops entirely. This need not be a cause for concern so long as the baby is continuing to nurse frequently and is gaining weight.

But, if continuing leakage is becoming bothersome, you might want to try to stop it by pressing your wrist or the heel of your hand against your nipples whenever they start to drip.

If leaking at night continues to be troublesome, you might try nursing the baby just before you go to sleep.

Overabundant Milk

Some mothers seem to produce too much milk. Besides feeling weary of the jokes about being able to nurse twins, you may feel uncomfortably engorged much of the time. Leaking and spraying may be bothersome. Your baby may gasp and choke as the milk lets down.

Most women find this less of a problem after the first two months of breastfeeding. In the meantime, nursing your baby on just one side at each feeding should make your breasts feel more comfortable. When your baby is draining your breasts more completely they will feel less engorged, even though each is nursed on less often. Decreasing your fluid intake is not recommended. Nor is wearing plastic breast shells or pumping after or between feedings, either of which would probably increase, not decrease, milk production.

If your baby has difficulty nursing because the milk lets down forcefully, see "Pulling Away from the Breast." Refer to "Survival Guide for Months Two through Six" if you continue to produce milk in overabundance after two months.

Lopsided Breasts

When one breast receives more stimulation than the other, milk production in that breast increases, commonly resulting in a lopsided appearance.

Providing more stimulation to the smaller breast will usually even out the size difference between the two. Start each feeding on the smaller side for a day or so. If your baby nurses there only a few minutes, encourage her to take the smaller breast again after she has nursed at the fuller one. As soon as your breasts become closer in size, you can begin alternating the breast at which the baby begins each feeding.

Depression and Anxiety

Most women go through emotional changes after giving birth. Many new mothers experience moodiness, mild anxiety, or an occasional "blue" day during the first two weeks after delivery. These feelings are due to the sudden hormonal changes that follow birth, to fatigue from labor and lost sleep, and to the stress that becoming a mother entails. But when emotional symptoms are severe, when they continue beyond the first two weeks after birth, or when they start later and last more than two weeks, they may indicate postpartum depression or anxiety. Many new mothers who complain that they are depressed or anxious are told that their feelings are normal and to be expected. This is not true. Postpartum emotional disorders are often misunderstood or unrecognized by family, friends, and health professionals.

As many as one out of every nine or ten new mothers experiences postpartum depression, postpartum anxiety, or both. Much rarer is postpartum psychosis, characterized by delusions, hallucinations, or extreme mental confusion. Postpartum emotional disorders are more common in women who have had a stressful pregnancy or difficult birth, previous psychological problems, or relationship difficulties. Occasionally, a thyroid disorder may mimic postpartum depression.

Symptoms of postpartum depression or anxiety usually include several of the following:

- Change in eating habits (poor appetite or overeating);
- Change in sleep pattern (difficulty falling or staying asleep, oversleeping);
- Tenseness, nervousness;
- Panic attacks with physical symptoms such as shakiness, palpitations, shortness of breath, or lightheadedness;
- Fatigue or lack of energy;
- Poor concentration, forgetfulness, or confusion;
- Crying every day;
- Feelings of hopelessness;
- Withdrawal, lack of interest in usual activities;

- Excessive worry or guilt feelings;
- Recurrent disturbing thoughts or compulsive behaviors that cause distress or take up a great deal of time; and
- Failure to keep appointments.

Symptoms that call for immediate assistance from a mental-health professional include—

- Thoughts of suicide,
- Fears of harming the baby,
- Sounds and voices heard when no one is around,
- Thoughts that seem not your own or out of your control,
- Sleeplessness lasting 48 hours or longer,
- Inability to eat, and
- Inability to care for the baby.

For any woman suffering with postpartum depression or anxiety, I strongly recommend the book *This Isn't What I Expected: Recognizing and Recovering from Depression and Anxiety after Childbirth*, by Karen Kleiman and Valerie Raskin (see "Suggested Supplemental Reading"). Many women with mild cases have helped themselves without professional assistance. Try the coping measures that follow.

Coping Measures for Depression and Anxiety

1. Tell your partner, a supportive friend, or a relative how you are feeling. Although some people may not understand, you may find valuable support close by.

2. Talk to your doctor or midwife about how you are feeling. Ask about having blood tests done to make sure something else, such as a thyroid disorder, isn't the problem.

3. Call Depression After Delivery (800-944-4PPD) to find out whether there is a postpartum support group in your area.

4. Make getting extra rest a priority; being tired makes depression and anxiety worse. Nap when your baby naps. Maximize your baby's sleep stretches at night by feeding him every two to two and a half hours during the day and evening.

5. Enlist the help of others to relieve you of some mothering and household duties. Eliminate or lessen your daily chores until you are feeling better. If you want to do some chores, set minimal goals for yourself.

6. Eat a well-balanced diet. If you have little appetite, fix small, nutritious snacks for yourself throughout the day. Avoid all caffeine and sugary foods and beverages; these are associated with worsening symptoms. Increase your intake of foods made up of complex carbohydrates, such as whole-grain breads and cereals, potatoes, rice, and pasta. Eat more fruits and vegetables. Using powdered milk or yogurt, wheat germ, and fruit or juice concentrate, you can make nutritious blender drinks. If you find it difficult to prepare food for yourself throughout the day, your pharmacist can recommend a high-calorie nutritional supplement such as Ensure or Sustacal.

7. Take time with your appearance every day. When you get up, make a point of getting dressed, fixing your hair, and putting on a little makeup, if you like it. Pamper yourself with a facial, a new hair style, or something new to wear. Looking good helps you feel better about yourself.

8. Get some exercise every day. Many people find that exercise has an antidepressant effect. Join an exercise or dance class; many offer free child care. Take a brisk walk every day with or without the baby.

9. Nurture yourself as much as possible. Take long bubble baths, get a massage, ask your partner to hold you, spend the afternoon watching a video or reading a light novel.

10. Make an effort to spend time with other adults. Invite friends over, join a postpartum group, or make friends with other mothers from your childbirth class. Your childbirth instructor may have additional suggestions. If you have just moved to the area, ask your pediatrician's or family practitioner's nurse for other resources.

If your distress is severe or unrelieved by these measures, consider seeking professional help. Low-cost mental-health care is available in most communities. If cost isn't an issue, ask your doctor, midwife, or childbirth educator to refer you to a therapist, ideally one who has a special interest in postpartum illness.

Depending on your symptoms, a therapist may recommend medication. Some antidepressants are safe to use during nursing. One safe antidepressant is sertraline, which is sold under the trade name Zoloft; when nursing mothers take this drug, it is undetectable in their babies' blood. You may be tempted to try St. John's wort, now a popular remedy for depression. This herb, however, has not yet been proven safe to use during breastfeeding.

Unfortunately, many doctors who recommend that women

wean their babies before taking antidepressants do so because they don't know about recent studies on the safety of particular drugs during breastfeeding. In Appendix C you'll find what information is available about the safety of various antidepressants. You may need to share this information with your doctor before coming to an agreement about what is best for you and your baby.

Concerns about the Baby

Spitting Up and Vomiting

Spitting up small amounts of breast milk is common; some babies do this after almost every nursing. Occasionally a baby may vomit what seems like an entire feeding. Although there may be no apparent cause, this can sometimes be traced to something the mother recently ate. Vomiting can also be a sign of infection. You will want to notify your doctor if the baby has a fever or if the vomiting continues.

When a baby continues vomiting forcefully after most feedings, you should suspect that either he is sensitive to something in your diet (see "Something in Your Diet") or he has pyloric stenosis. *Pyloric stenosis* is an obstruction of the stomach that typically develops at about two to four weeks of age. Although this condition is most common in first-born males, it can occur in females. Typically the vomiting becomes progressively worse; the baby eventually stops gaining weight, or loses weight, and may become dehydrated. In the breastfed infant the condition may go undiagnosed longer than in the bottle-fed infant, since breast milk is digested much more easily than formula. The baby's weight may not be affected until the obstruction becomes nearly complete. Frequently waves can be seen moving across the baby's lower abdomen from the left side to the right just after a feeding and prior to vomiting. X-rays confirm the diagnosis. The obstruction is corrected with a relatively simple surgical procedure.

Breastfeeding can resume within a few hours after the obstruction is removed. At this time breast milk is especially good for the baby because of its digestibility. Some mothers notice a temporary reduction in the milk supply after the baby's surgery. Rest, frequent nursing, and switching the baby from side to side during the feeding usually reverse this situation.

Pulling Away from the Breast

Babies pull off the breast while nursing for a variety of reasons. Often it is because they have had enough to eat or they need to be burped. If your baby has a cold, she may pull away because she is having trouble breathing through her nose. Try to position her so her head is elevated more during nursing. A cool-mist vaporizer may help to thin the nasal secretions so she will breathe easier.

Some babies pull away from the breast gasping and choking as the milk suddenly lets down. This is usually a temporary problem; the baby gradually learns to keep up with the rapid flow of milk. In the meantime, positioning the baby differently may help. Try sitting the baby up, using the football hold, or lying on your back with the baby's head over you. Some mothers manually express or pump milk until the initial spray has subsided. If your baby pulls away from the breast and cries or refuses to nurse, see "Refusal to Nurse," as follows.

Refusal to Nurse

If your baby pulls away from the breast crying or refuses to nurse, don't assume he is ready to wean. There are a number of possible reasons for such behavior, but when it persists, it can frequently be traced to certain foods in the mother's diet to which the baby is sensitive. Typically this starts around two weeks of age. The baby usually acts fussy and colicky; he may have greenish stools, or he may spit up or vomit. Other symptoms may include gassiness, redness around the rectum, a mild rash anywhere on the body, or a stuffy nose. Fussiness while nursing and refusal to nurse may increase as the day goes on. Although the baby refuses the breast, he may eagerly take the breast milk from a bottle. The reason for this is unclear.

A baby who has developed a yeast infection (thrush) may also become fussy at the breast and refuse to nurse. Besides the characteristic white coating in the baby's mouth, you may notice he is gassy and somewhat cranky. You may also notice a bright red, dotted or peeling rash on his bottom or on your nipples. Your nipples may burn or itch.

Occasionally a baby will refuse to nurse if the mother's milk has developed a strong and unpleasant taste due to a particularly spicy food he has recently eaten. Deodorant and perfume sprays have also been identified as causing some babies to refuse the breast.

When a baby has been fed supplemental formula and the milk supply has lessened, he may lose interest in the breast, preferring the bottle.

Finally, a baby may refuse to nurse any time he is not feeling well. Ear infections and other discomforts commonly cause this behavior.

Treatment Measures When the Baby Refuses to Nurse

1. As long as your baby refuses to nurse, express your milk every two to three hours so your supply will not be affected. Feed the baby by bottle.

2. Taste your milk a few times to determine if a food you have recently eaten has flavored the milk. If you notice a strong peppery aftertaste, try to identify a spicy food you may have eaten. In the meantime, pump until the baby resumes nursing (usually within 12 hours).

3. Check your baby's mouth and your nipples for signs of thrush. See "Survival Guide for the First Week."

4. If you think your baby may have a food sensitivity, see "Something in Your Diet."

5. If your baby is irritable and refuses to nurse, and you can find no reason for it, have the baby examined by your doctor. An ear infection or other discomfort may be causing your baby to act this way.

Fussiness and Colic

You may be surprised to learn how much crying a baby can do and how uncomfortable it can make you feel. The sound of a baby's cry is intended to be distressing, so adults will be alerted to his needs and answer them.

All babies have fussy periods during their early weeks. You will probably notice that your baby is more fussy at around two to three weeks and again at around six weeks, when most babies experience appetite spurts. Fussiness in the late afternoon or evening is typical.

Many mothers tend to blame themselves for their babies' crying, wondering if their inexperience, nervous feelings, or milk supply is somehow responsible. Keep in mind that most babies fuss and seek out the comfort of the breast when they are tired, bored, lonely, or uncomfortable as well as when they are hungry. For unknown reasons, some babies simply need to suck more than others. When babies are having appetite spurts, they increase their nursing frequency for a few days to stimulate increased milk production. If you are worried that the baby is not getting enough milk, have him weighed. A weight gain of an ounce a day or more means your baby is getting enough milk (see "Underfeeding").

Coping Measures for Fussiness

1. Offer your breast—it is a source of comfort as well as nourishment for your baby.

2. Pacifiers are soothing to many babies who need a lot of extra sucking, who are fussy, or who have difficulty calming themselves. If your baby doesn't take a pacifier at first, try different kinds.

3. Be sure to burp your baby frequently while he nurses or sucks on a pacifier.

4. Some babies are comforted by being swaddled tightly in a light blanket.

5. Warm baths with the baby may be soothing to both of you.

6. Most babies love motion. Try walking, using a baby pack, sling, or stroller. Rocking can also be comforting—borrow a rocking chair if you don't already have one. You can put a small baby in a baby swing if you bolster him with towels or blankets. Most babies are lulled to sleep by car rides.

7. Noise may calm a crying baby. A radio in the baby's room, a tape recording of a humming car or vacuum cleaner, or an aquarium near the baby's bed may help him sleep.

8. Consider sleeping with the baby, if you aren't doing so already.

9. Take a short break from the baby each day. Your partner might play with the baby while you take a bath, go for a walk, or visit a friend.

10. Find another mother who has a fussy baby. There's nothing like a friend who really understands.

More serious crying. Some babies are extremely irritable and fussy during the early weeks. They have periods of intense crying, when it seems something must be terribly wrong. Such babies are said to have colic—but this is only a catch-all term for an unidentifiable discomfort.

If your baby's crying makes you feel that something is wrong, trust your instincts. By all means have your baby examined by your doctor. Outlined below are common reasons I have identified for periods of intense crying in infants. I highly recommend the book *Crying Baby, Sleepless Nights* by Sandy Jones (see "Suggested Supplemental Reading") as an excellent resource for parents of fussy babies.

Swallowing excessive air. Some babies swallow a great deal of air when nursing or sucking on a pacifier. When this air passes through the intestines the baby can be quite uncomfortable. If your baby is passing a lot of gas, make an effort to burp her more frequently. Try to get a burp at the start of each feeding as well as several times during it. If you give the baby a pacifier, she will need extra burping. Do not allow the baby to suck on a bottle nipple in place of a pacifier, even if the open end is taped or stuffed with cotton.

Diaper rash. A baby may fuss a lot if she has a diaper rash. For an entire day, apply a zinc oxide ointment (such as Desitin); expose the baby's bottom to the air as much as possible, and leave off disposable diapers or plastic pants. The rash should improve dramatically, unless it is caused by yeast. A yeast diaper rash is a dotty, red rash or a peeling rash that resembles a mild burn, typically in the genital area.

Yeast infection. Although they are common in infants, yeast infections are frequently overlooked as the cause of excessive fussiness. A baby with a yeast infection usually shows signs in his mouth—on his inner lips or cheeks, and sometimes also on the tongue. This is known as thrush. The baby is typically very gassy, as the yeast is frequently present in the intestinal tract as well. The yeast may also cause a diaper rash, as just described. The mother's nipples are often reddened; they may show a rash, and they may itch or burn. One nipple may be more affected than the other.

Nystatin suspension (Mycostatin) is usually the drug of choice when a baby has a yeast infection. Because the nystatin is swallowed, the yeast in the bowel will be eliminated. Treatment with gentian violet kills only yeast in the mouth and therefore is not recommended for the baby who is fussy and gassy unless the nystatin seems ineffective after several days of treatment. See "Thrush Nipples," in "Survival Guide for the First Week," for a complete discussion of treatment measures.

Nystatin ointment can be used to treat the baby's diaper rash; it can also be used on your nipples. If your baby has no rash it would not be unusual for one to appear shortly after treatment with the oral medication. If the baby does have a rash, don't be surprised if it gets worse during the first few days of treatment.

If the baby's stools are green, he may also be reacting to certain foods in his mother's diet. See "Something in Your Diet," as follows.

Something in your diet. Occasionally foods or beverages in a mother's diet cause colic symptoms in her baby. Certain medications and dietary supplements can produce such symptoms, too. The baby may want to nurse all the time, cry and fuss a lot, or have other symptoms, such as spitting up and vomiting, a stuffy nose, frequent, watery stools that may be green, mucousy, or bloody, redness around the anus, and excessive gas. Some babies have rashes on the face and upper body. Some pull off the breast crying or simply refuse to nurse but may take expressed milk from a bottle. Colic symptoms usually resolve after the baby reaches three months, but in the meantime the baby is unhappy, and her mother may wonder if breastfeeding is to blame.

Your colicky baby should be examined to rule out any other illness, but don't be surprised if the doctor has no other specific diagnosis, even if you've asked whether something in your diet could be to blame. Some doctors are aware of two or three foods that can cause colic symptoms, but most doctors think colicky behavior does not have any connection to a mother's diet.

If your baby exhibits colic symptoms every day or nearly every day, try writing down everything you have eaten and drunk during the past three days. Make notes, too, of any particularly difficult periods the baby has had during the past three days. If you are producing a lot of milk, also have your baby weighed to see how fast she is gaining. A baby who is gaining much more than an ounce a day may be having symptoms of what I call hyperlactation syndrome, which is described later.

Most foods that bother breastfeeding babies, as either intestinal irritants or allergens, fall into one of several major food categories. When a baby has been fussy at particular times, a suspect food can often be identified by looking back one to two meal periods. If eating chocolate, say, seems to cause your baby's symptoms, you can try giving up chocolate and see if she does better. But because more than one food may be making your baby fussy, you might be

Thursday

8:30 A.M.
Grapefruit juice
Prenatal vitamin
Granola with milk
Toast with butter

12:15 P.M.
Roast beef and cheese
  sandwich, with mayonnaise
  and lettuce
Potato chips
Milk

3:00 P.M.
Pineapple juice

6:45 P.M.
Chicken-green pepper stir-fry
Spinach and mushroom salad,
  Italian dressing
Rice
Milk

8:15 P.M.
Chocolate frozen yogurt

10:30 A.M.–12:00 noon
Fussy, spitting up

2:00 P.M.–5:00 P.M.
Crying

11:30 P.M.–2:00 A.M.
Very fussy, vomited

Sample chart of a mother's diet and her baby's reactions.

wise to avoid all of the commonly offending foods for a while, then reintroduce them to your diet one by one. This way, you'll know exactly what bothers your baby.

Completely eliminating all of the following foods for three days may bring speedy relief to your fussy baby. Be sure to check the ingredients in any commercially processed food before eating or drinking it.

■ *Chocolate and spices.* The major offender in chocolate is theobromide, even in small amounts a potent irritant in the digestive tract of many infants. In the example given, the chocolate frozen yogurt was probably responsible for this baby's (and mother's) difficult night. Many flavorful spices, including cinnamon, garlic, and curry, can also bother young infants.

- *Citrus.* A frequently overlooked cause of digestive disturbances are the citrus fruits and their juices. Oranges, lemons, limes, tangerines, and grapefruits can all bother a baby's intestines. Other strongly acidic fruits, such as pineapples, kiwis, and strawberries, affect many babies similarly. In the chart, the mother had grapefruit juice at breakfast and pineapple juice in the afternoon. Her baby may have been bothered by these.
- *Gas-producing vegetables.* Certain vegetables can also cause temporary digestive problems for young babies. These include onions, broccoli, cauliflower, brussels sprouts, cabbage, bell peppers, and cucumbers. Prepared mustard can cause a similar reaction. Onions, an ingredient in so many dishes, can cause gastric upset for a baby even when they are cooked, ingested in small amounts, or eaten as onion powder. The stir-fry dish in the chart contained one of these offending foods.
- *Cow's milk.* Some infants are allergic to cow's milk and cow's milk products, including cheese, yogurt, sour cream, cottage cheese, and ice cream. If a baby is truly allergic to cow's milk products, cutting back on how much you have will probably not eliminate the baby's symptoms. You must eliminate from your diet all dairy products, including those in commercially processed foods like creamed soups, certain types of salad dressings, and puddings; cow's milk may be identified as "casein" or "whey" on the label. (Don't worry if milk is a minor ingredient in a baked product such as bread.) Many infant formulas are made from cow's milk. The baby in the chart may or may not be reacting to dairy products.

If possible, do without medications and dietary supplements while you're avoiding these four food categories. Laxatives taken by a nursing mother can disturb her baby's intestinal tract. Aspirin and the chemical phenylpropanolamine, a decongestant, can make a baby fussy; both of these drugs are in many headache and cold remedies. Certain dietary supplements taken by the mother or given directly to the baby, such as Vitamin C, brewer's yeast, and fluoride, have been known to cause colic symptoms. Fluoride is very helpful in preventing cavities, but is best delayed until the baby is six months old.

During the three days of eliminating all the commonly offending foods from your diet, write down what you eat and drink along with observations of your baby. If the baby has particularly difficult times, look back one to two meal periods, or about two to eight hours before the symptoms began, and try to identify any suspect foods. You may find that you ate something forbidden without realizing it, or perhaps another food seems to be at fault. Other foods that can cause reactions include eggs, peanuts and peanut butter, corn and corn syrup, wheat (in breads, crackers, cookies, cakes, and noodles), soy (the basis of some infant formulas and an ingredient in many processed foods), apples, and bananas. If you decide to eliminate any one of these foods, you should continue to avoid the original four food categories, too. More than one food group may be affecting your baby.

If your baby is much better after the three days, and having very few fussy periods or other symptoms, try adding milk products back into your diet. Have a lot of milk products early in the day and then watch the baby for 24 hours. If the baby reacts, avoid milk products completely for the next couple of days. After this you might experiment with small amounts of milk, cheese, yogurt, or ice cream to see which of these, if any, your baby can tolerate, and in what quantity. Although some babies cannot tolerate any milk products, others do fine when their mothers have hard cheese, and some can tolerate small amounts of any milk products as long as their mothers take them only once every few days. (If you must cut dairy products from your diet completely, be sure you are taking sufficient calcium in another form; see Chapter 4). Every few days thereafter, add another food category to your diet, eating a lot at a time. If the fussiness recurs, eliminate the offending food category from your diet again. Continue adding food categories until you have tested all the foods that you had eliminated. Again, more than one food may be a problem for a very sensitive baby.

Hyperlactation syndrome. Recently researchers have identified a kind of colic that is characterized by gassiness, frequent stools, spitting up, and general discomfort and fussiness (Woolridge and Fisher, 1988). Although these babies may seem to be allergic to something in their mother's diet, they show little or no improvement with the elimination of common allergens. Typically these babies nurse frequently from both breasts and are gaining more than an ounce per day. Their mothers often have overabundant milk supplies.

The underlying cause of the colic is thought to be the baby's disproportionate intake of the low-fat foremilk, the milk that is available early in the feeding. When a baby consumes large amounts of foremilk and little of the fatty hind milk, his stomach rapidly empties, dumping excess lactose into the bowel. This results in increased fermentation and colic symptoms.

Relief of the colic is achieved by getting the baby to empty one breast at each feeding so that he receives not only the foremilk but the fatty hind milk too. The baby should be allowed to nurse from the first breast until he spontaneously pulls away satisfied. He should not be interrupted at any point to be switched over to the second breast. Some authorities feel that until the colic subsides the baby should be offered just one breast per feeding and should be limited to that side for one and a half to two hours before nursing on the other side.

The baby's temperament. Every baby is born with her own distinct personality. Some babies tend to be quiet, whereas others are more active. Some babies are highly sensitive to their surroundings, overreacting to any sudden stimulation. They are tense and jumpy, and often fussy. They may go almost instantly from sleep to calm to full-blown crying. Once crying, they may be difficult to soothe. Although some of these babies need to be carried around or entertained continually, others actually resist being held or cuddled.

Learning how to mother a highly sensitive baby takes time and patience. You will soon develop a sense of what your baby enjoys and what she does not, how much stimulation she can tolerate and how to help her settle down. If your baby does not enjoy touching, try not to take it personally. With time and a gradual increase in physical closeness, she will eventually be able to tolerate and enjoy being held. Most babies outgrow their early fussy months and grow to be happy children.

Underfeeding

For any number of reasons, you may wonder if your baby is getting enough to eat. It may be that he seems to be nursing all the time or is especially fussy. Most young infants want to nurse eight to twelve times in each 24-hour period. Nursing this often is normal and seldom reflects a poor milk supply. You can't tell whether your baby is getting enough breast milk by offering him a supplemental bottle of water or formula after nursing. Most babies will take one to two ounces if it is offered, even when they have had enough milk from the breasts. The baby is probably getting enough milk if—

- he is nursing at least eight times in a 24-hour period,
- he is nursing 10 to 45 minutes at each feeding and seems content after feedings,
- he has several periods of swallowing during each feeding,
- your breasts feel softer or lighter after the baby has nursed, and
- your baby is having bowel movements every day during the first month.

If any of these statements is false, have your baby weighed. Even if all are true, have your baby weighed if you need the reassurance. The nurse in your baby's doctor's office should be happy to do this for you.

Between the fifth day and the end of the third or fourth month after birth, a baby should gain an ounce every day. A weight gain of an ounce a day reflects an adequate milk intake. If your baby was weighed at any time after the fifth day, you can see whether he has gained enough by weighing him again now. If he hasn't

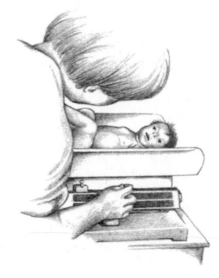

been weighed since the fifth day, consider that by 10 to 14 days of age most babies have regained their birth weight. If your baby is two weeks old and weighs less than his birth weight, he probably needs more milk. If your baby is two weeks old and weighs more than his birth weight, he is probably getting plenty of milk. If you have any doubt about how much the baby is gaining, weigh him again in a couple of days.

Inadequate weight gain usually occurs when a baby has had trouble latching on or nursing vigorously during the period of initial engorgement in the first week, or when nursing has been infrequent. Underfeeding often occurs to the group of mothers and babies listed in Chapter 2 under "Babies Who May Not Get Enough." This problem can also occur when a newborn has a faulty suck, when a mother has used a nipple shield over her nipple for nursing, and, certainly, when a baby is sick. Some laxatives, when taken by the mother, can cause a baby to have excessive bowel movements and to lose weight or gain too slowly even if he is taking enough milk.

Usually a baby's failure to latch on or suck well during the early weeks quickly leads to low milk production. The solution is to build the milk supply by pumping after nursing, and to feed the baby the expressed milk along with any necessary formula.

Treatment Measures for Underfeeding

1. If possible, see a lactation professional.

2. To estimate the amount of milk you are producing and to increase your milk supply, rent a fully automatic electric breast pump (see Appendix A). Any other pump would be inadequate for accurately estimating milk production and would be less helpful in increasing your milk supply.

3. Estimate your milk production by pumping your breasts instead of nursing. If you are pumping one breast at a time, pump each twice, for a total pumping time of 20 to 25 minutes. If you have a double-pump kit (see Chapter 5) use it for a total of 12 to 15 minutes. Feed this milk and any necessary formula to your baby. (See Appendix B to determine how much milk your baby needs at each feeding.)

Exactly two hours after completing the first pumping, pump again. This time you may get less milk than in the first pumping. Multiply the number of ounces collected at this *second* pumping by 12. This will give you an estimate of how much milk you are producing over a 24-

hour period; if you collected 1½ ounces, for example, you are producing about 18 ounces per day.

Now you can compare the baby's daily milk requirement, as listed in Appendix B, with your milk production. For example, if you estimate that your baby needs 21.4 ounces per day and your milk production is 18 ounces per day, the baby needs about 3½ ounces of formula per day until your milk production increases.

If you determine that you have enough milk for your baby and yet he has not been gaining well, it may be that he is not taking all of the milk available at some or many of his feedings. This can happen with newborns who were born prematurely, who tend to drift off to sleep while nursing, or who have sucking difficulties. In such a case, you'll still want to take the steps that follow, feeding your baby expressed breast milk (rather than formula) after nursing until his feeding skill improves.

4. After you have estimated your milk production, go back to nursing your baby at least eight times in every 24 hours. This may mean waking him for feedings. Nurse him every two and a half hours during the day and evening (counting from the start of one nursing to the start of the next) and every three to four hours in the night, for 10 to 15 minutes on each breast. (I suggest limiting the nursing to this period so that the entire nursing-pumping-supplementing session can be completed in 40 to 50 minutes.) Frequent short nursings are more effective in increasing milk production than infrequent lengthy ones.

5. Pump your breasts right after each nursing to stimulate further milk production. If you're pumping one breast at a time, pump for five minutes on each side, and then pump each breast a second time for a few minutes. Pumping both breasts at once not only takes less time but increases milk production faster. Use a double-pump kit for 5 to 10 minutes after nursing.

6. Right after pumping, offer the baby whatever breast milk you've collected along with any necessary formula. If the baby needs supplemental formula, divide the total amount needed by the number of feedings the baby is getting each day (usually eight). For example, the baby needing 3½ ounces of formula could take about ½ ounce after each of his eight daily nursings. The goal is to offer about the same amount of milk and formula at each feeding so that he wants to nurse at regular intervals.

Many lactation consultants, fearing the bottle would interfere with the baby's ability at the breast, suggest that a baby be supplemented with a nursing supplementer, cup, eye dropper, or soft tube taped onto the feeder's finger. If one of these methods is recommended to you and it works well, then continue with it. But if you find it too frustrating or time-consuming, use a bottle. After the first few days of nursing, using a bottle for supplemental feedings rarely causes latch-on or sucking problems.

7. To stimulate even greater milk production, try fenugreek. Take fenugreek capsules, which are sold in health-food stores, two or three at a time, three times a day. See "Treatment Measures for Underfeeding" in "Survival Guide for the First Week."

8. Weigh your baby every few days to be sure that he is gaining well. After each weighing, re-estimate his milk needs, since as he gains weight his milk needs will increase. Re-estimate your milk production, too. Two hours after your last pumping, use the breast pump instead of nursing, and figure your milk production as explained in item 3. Hopefully your milk production will have increased enough that you can decrease or even eliminate any formula supplementation.

9. Once your baby is gaining well, his nursing seems more vigorous, and he is receiving supplements only of your breast milk, try eliminating some of the supplement. For a few days, offer half of the milk that you are expressing to the baby, and freeze the rest. If the baby continues to gain well, keep pumping, but don't offer the baby any of the pumped milk. Once the baby is gaining an ounce a day without any supplement, you can gradually stop pumping. Continue to have your baby weighed weekly.

If treatment fails. It is frightening to realize that your baby is not getting enough to eat. Although the technique just described usually ensures a gaining baby and higher milk production within several days, occasionally these measures won't work. Sometimes, when breast engorgement has been severe and little milk has been removed during the first week, the decline in milk production is difficult to reverse.

In unusual instances, a mother fails to produce milk. This sometimes happens to women who have had breast surgery, particularly when the surgical incision is around the areola (see "Nursing after Breast Surgery," in Chapter 3), or who have insufficient glandular (milk-producing) tissue, or "hypoplastic" breasts (see "Insuring Your Milk Supply," in Chapter 2).

In any of these situations, lack of support from family, friends, and health professionals can only make matters worse. But even with all of the best information and support, things sometimes don't turn out as we hope. If you have given nursing your best but finally end up having to bottle-feed, you have not failed as a mother. Be proud of your efforts to nurse, and concentrate on providing your baby with all of the cuddling and loving that you can. Detailed information about formula and bottle feeding can be found in *The Nursing Mother's Guide to Weaning* (see "Suggested Supplemental Reading").

Some mothers who can't produce enough milk have found that continuing to nurse with a nursing supplementer has been a rewarding, worthwhile experience. Others have found nursing supplementers to be cumbersome and frustrating. Another option, particularly if the baby has become frustrated at the breast, is to first bottle-feed and then nurse. "Comfort nursing"—nursing after or between bottle feedings, or during the night—may be a pleasant experience for both mother and baby.

CHAPTER FIVE

Traveling Together, Being Apart

Taking the Baby Along

Being Apart

Occasional Separations

Returning to Work or School

Work Options

Choosing a Caregiver

Expressing Milk

Introducing a Bottle

Collecting and Storing Your Milk

Back at Work

TODAY'S NURSING MOTHER IS OUT AND ABOUT, TAKING CARE OF business, enjoying the company of friends, returning to work or school, taking time out for fun. In many ways, nursing simplifies life considerably. With the increasing acceptance and popularity of breastfeeding, more and more mothers are able to nurse their babies while participating in a wide variety of activities.

Taking the Baby Along

Your nursing baby can go with you almost anywhere—and with a lot less hassle than you would face if you were fussing with formula and bottles.

You may feel comfortable nursing in the presence of family or friends you are visiting, or you may be a bit uneasy. You can always retreat to the bedroom, of course, but that's not much fun. Learning to nurse discreetly and without embarrassment will put most people at ease. You might want to practice ahead of time getting the baby on your breast with a blanket or shawl draped over your shoulder and the baby's head. If you wear a shirt or a sweater you can pull up, or if you unbutton your blouse from the bottom, you will expose less of yourself. Most maternity shops carry a line of attractive tops and dresses designed for discreet nursing. Try nursing in front of your partner or in front of a mirror so you'll know what others will see.

If you are going out for the day or spending a few hours in town, you may want to nurse just before you leave. A couple of diapers and a few moist wipes in a sandwich bag, and you're off. If you are using a cloth baby carrier, you may find it easier to put it on before you go.

After a couple of hours out, look around for a comfortable place to sit with your baby. Many mothers feel comfortable nursing in public places and are hardly noticed when they do so. Some stores and restaurants have dressing rooms or pleasant restrooms where you may prefer to feed the baby.

Mothers appreciate the ease of taking long trips with their nursing babies. Most young infants travel well in a car. (Of course, the baby should always ride in a car seat approved for safety, no matter how short the trip.) You will want to stop every few hours for nursing and a diaper change. If the baby's car seat faces backward, you may be able to manage nursing while sitting in the back seat next to her.

The older baby may be less happy in the car seat for long periods. Whenever possible try to start long stretches in the car just before nap time. Try hanging some of the baby's toys on her car seat or keeping a bag of toys and other fun things in the back seat.

If you are planning to fly, you might try to reserve bulkhead seating; this will give you extra space. Try to choose a flight that is lightly booked. This way you are more likely to get an empty seat next to you for more room and privacy. Nursing during takeoff and landing will help the baby's ears adjust to the changing air pressure. If you must fly when the baby has a cold, give her a safe decongestant an hour before takeoff.

Being Apart

Occasional Separations

Any number of situations may come up in which you must be separated from your baby—an evening out, perhaps, a family or career obligation, or a stay in the hospital.

When you plan to be away from the baby for just a few hours, you can manually express or pump some milk for him ahead of time. The best time to collect milk is just after nursing, especially if the baby has nursed from just one breast. In this way you will not lessen the amount of milk available for the baby at his next feeding. Getting an ounce or so after the baby nurses is typical. You will need to collect milk several times for each feeding you'll miss, as most young babies take about three to four ounces at a bottle feeding. If you will be away longer than four to five hours, bring the pump along; you will need it to prevent engorgement and to keep up milk production (see "Expressing Milk" and "Collecting and Storing Your Milk," in this chapter).

If you will be separated from the baby for a day or longer, you may be able to store enough milk for him ahead of time. If not, you can substitute a commercially prepared formula. While you are away, try to pump at least every two and a half to three hours. A rental electric pump may be more convenient than other kinds, and also most effective for keeping up your milk supply. If possible, freeze the milk you pump while you are apart so that it can be used later.

Hospitalization of a nursing mother rarely necessitates weaning, even though some doctors advise it. Some hospitals have electric breast pumps available for nursing mothers. If your hospital doesn't, you can rent a pump and take it with you, or have one brought in. You may be able to arrange for the baby to be brought in for nursing visits, or even for the baby to stay with you (providing you, a family member, or a friend can care for him). Try to express your milk frequently to maintain your milk supply. Ask the nursing staff to refrigerate your milk so that it can be taken home for your baby.

Questions may arise about the safety of medications you need to take in the hospital. Although most medications pass through the breast milk, the majority are safe for nursing babies. Occasionally a doctor may be unsure whether a given medication is safe for a baby, and so recommends weaning when the question arises. You can check the safety of the drug yourself in Appendix C. If a drug is not considered safe for a nursing baby, you can continue to pump your milk, discarding it until the medication is no longer required.

Returning to Work or School

Not so long ago, a new mother planning to return to work might never have considered nursing her baby or would have decided to wean near the end of her maternity leave. Today, with the growing number of working women and the increasing awareness of the many benefits breastfeeding offers, more and more mothers are choosing to nurse their babies while continuing with their careers.

Your extra efforts to continue nursing are well worthwhile. The cost of formula aside, breastfed babies are generally healthier. The less your baby is sick, the less time you must spend away from work or school. Nursing also saves you time and energy, which is especially important when you are combining the responsibilities of employment and family. Perhaps most important, nursing helps you maintain the close, loving relationship you have with your baby. Many mothers who work outside the home or attend school feel that breastfeeding offers emotional compensation for the hours that must be spent apart. The security of your breast comforts the baby and helps make the time you are together special and rewarding for both of you.

Work Options

Although there may be no question in your mind that you will be returning to work or school after your baby is born, you are lucky if you have some flexibility in determining the length of your maternity leave. Your time at home after giving birth is important for both you and the baby: it is the time in which you will get to know each other and form a special tie between you. It will also be a time for you to rest and recover from the physical stress of the birth process. Some women need a little while, and some need a long while, before they are ready to add to the demands of work or school. Breastfeeding experts have noted that mothers who stay home for 16 weeks or longer experience fewer difficulties maintaining their milk supply once back at work.

Because you cannot know just how you will feel after you deliver, explore what options may be open to you ahead of time. Depending on your financial situation and your work demands, you may be able to arrange for an extended leave, beyond the usual six to eight weeks. Or you may be able to arrange to work at home, return to work part time, take fewer classes, or share your job with another person. Each of these options has worked well for many mothers.

Part-time work offers many advantages to the nursing mother. Fewer hours apart means fewer missed feedings, lower child care costs, and generally less hardship for both mother and baby.

Your employer also benefits by agreeing to shorter hours. Replacing an employee is time consuming and costly, especially if she has special skills that are an asset to the organization. Besides, part-time employees are known to be just as productive as those who work full time, if not more so. They tend to stay out sick less often, and they generally waste less time when they are at work. Part-timers can also help to reduce the overtime hours employers must pay for. You might agree to come in fewer hours each day, or fewer full-hour days. Both arrangements have advantages and drawbacks for the nursing mother.

Of course, part-time work also means part-time pay. Perhaps

the only choice for you is full-time work. Still, a somewhat flexible arrangement may be possible. With a "flextime" schedule, you might work eight hours a day but remain free to start earlier or later than normal. This system could allow you to spend a leisurely morning with the baby and perhaps get a few chores done. You might also be able to reduce the number of hours that the baby must be left with someone else if your partner can pick her up after work.

Some mothers arrange to take their babies to work with them. Although this is not possible for most women, it can be managed in some work settings. Another option is child care at the work site. Some employers and employees have found this to be an ideal arrangement. If you work with other parents of infants or small children, it might be well worth looking into this possibility.

Another possibility is having the baby brought to you for nursings, or going to the baby yourself during your lunch hour. Usually, the major obstacle in having the baby come to your work place is finding someone willing and able to bring her. If you choose to go and spend your lunch hour with the baby, you will need to find child care close to your work place. Combining your coffee breaks with your lunch hour may give you enough time to leisurely manage travel time, nursing, and eating.

Choosing a Caregiver

Finding just the right person to care for your baby can make all the difference in your state of mind while you are away. You may have the good fortune of relying on your partner or another loving relative to provide child care. Although this can be an ideal arrangement that makes the separation easier on both mother and baby, for most of us it is not an option.

If you will be shopping for a caregiver, be sure to start early so you can take your time. You may prefer that the caregiver come to your home, or that you take the baby to her. If you decide on the latter arrangement, try to locate a caregiver who lives close to your place of work or school. This will help you minimize the time you and your baby are apart and will be more convenient if you decide to nurse during your lunch breaks. You may prefer someone who will care for your baby alone, or you may be willing to share the caregiver's services with others.

Let each prospective caregiver know about your nursing relationship and your own particular style of caring for the baby. Be sure to ask for the names and telephone numbers of other families whose children she has cared for in the past or is caring for now. It's also a good idea to try to find out if she can make a long-term commitment to your baby; having to suddenly find a replacement can be upsetting for both you and your baby. If she cares for other children, try to schedule your meeting for when they will be present. This will give you the opportunity to observe firsthand the caregiver's style, and to see whether your baby would receive enough individual love and attention in the setting. In some states, child-care providers are licensed and limited in the number of infants and children they can care for. Feel free to ask about this.

In making your final choice of who will care for your baby, trust your intuition. If something doesn't feel quite right, look elsewhere. Before making a final commitment, be sure to discuss how you will handle illness (either your baby's or the caregiver's), who is to be called in an emergency, how much advance notice is necessary if the baby will be absent or late, fees and when they will be due, and any written agreements.

You may consider having the baby spend several hours or a full day with the caregiver a week or so before you go back to work

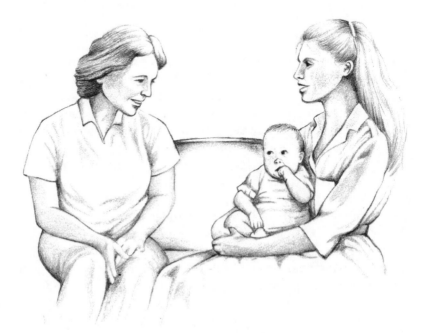

or school. Such a "trial run" may be reassuring for you, or you may feel, as many mothers do, that the first separation should occur only when the situation demands it.

Expressing Milk

If you will be missing one or more feedings while you are away at work or school, you should plan to express your milk. This will help to prevent engorgement and, more important, to maintain your milk supply. The milk you express can be used later to feed your baby while you are away. If you leave your baby for longer than four to five hours three or more times a week and do not express your milk, particularly if your baby is less than eight months old, your milk supply will probably diminish.

How often you should express milk depends on the age of your baby, how long you will be apart, and how often the baby nurses while you are together. Young babies normally nurse at least seven times in 24 hours; emptying the breast this often is necessary to maintain adequate milk production. If your baby is less than four months old, then, plan on expressing milk every two and a half to three hours while away.

Four- to seven-month-old babies typically nurse at least seven times a day. If your baby is this age, express milk often enough so that, with pumping and nursings, your breasts are emptied seven times in each 24 hours. If your five-month-old nurses frequently during the day and twice at night, you may not need to express milk while you work four hours a day, unless you prefer that your baby receive only breast milk when you are apart.

A baby who is eight months old or older may be nursing often or just a few times a day. Whether or not to express milk at this age depends not only on how much time you spend away from your baby, but also on whether he is eating a wide variety of solid foods and how you feel about providing formula instead of breast milk.

If you decide against expressing milk, your baby will need a commercially prepared formula for missed nursings during the first year.

Manual expression. Many mothers feel that expressing milk by hand is more convenient and natural than using a pump. You can learn this technique while nursing, practicing on the free side when the baby stimulates the milk to let down. Place a towel in front of you to catch the spray as you get started. Position your thumb and index finger about one and a half inches behind the nipple, where the milk sinuses are located. Push your fingers straight back toward your chest and then squeeze them together with a slight rolling motion, lifting the nipple outward. Avoid sliding your fingers away from their original position. With several practice sessions most mothers can master manual expression. Once you have the motion down, rotate your fingers around the nipple to empty other milk sinuses.

When you begin expressing milk away from the baby, you will probably find that a few moments of gentle breast massage will stimulate the milk to let down. Catch the milk in any clean container. To get a greater amount, switch back and forth from one side to the other as soon as you notice the flow lessening. You can save time by expressing milk from both breasts at once, into containers on a table in front of you. Once you have learned how, the whole process should take about twenty minutes.

In recent years breast pumps have become increasingly popular with nursing mothers. There are three basic types of pumps: hand- or foot-operated, battery-operated, and plug-in. Since each pump has its own unique features, you will need to find the one that is best suited to your particular needs.

When using hand expression, catch the milk in a cup or any other clean container.

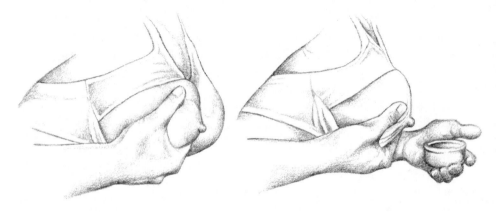

Hand- and foot-operated pumps. These are portable and relatively inexpensive; the best are also comfortable and easy to use. They are ideal for at-home mothers who need to pump only occasionally. Listed as follows are the models most commonly available.

bicycle horn pump

"Bicycle horn" pumps. These are widely available for under ten dollars in most drugstores. A bulb is squeezed for suction, and the milk flows directly into it. Most authorities warn against using milk collected this way, since the bulb is difficult to clean and may harbor harmful bacteria. Many women find, moreover, that these pumps do not work well and can be uncomfortable. When used improperly, they can cause trauma to the breast or the nipple. And since they hold little milk, they must be emptied frequently.

Evenflo Manual Pump

Evenflo Manual Pump. Available for about $20 in many drugstores, this pump creates suction by use of a plunger that is pulled outward.

Ora'lac Pump. Designed by a nursing mother, this pump can be used more discreetly than others. The mother sucks on a tube to create the suction and release. Some mothers have found the device a bit tipsy. The Ora'lac Pump is available through some drugstores and from the company. Send $30 (this amount includes shipping and tax) to Ora'lac Pump, Paradigm, Inc., 204 East A Street #1, Moscow, Idaho 83843. Phone 208-882-4149.

Ora'lac Pump

Ameda One-Hand Breast Pump. With this pump you create suction by squeezing a hand grip. As the name implies, you can operate the pump with just one hand. The pump is available for about $28.00 from Ameda retailers and rental stations and from Hollister, Inc., 2000 Hollister Drive, Libertyville, Illinois 60048. Phone toll free 800-323-4060.

Ameda One-Hand Breast Pump

Avent Isis Pump. A relatively new pump on the market, this one is becoming a favorite among nursing mothers. When you squeeze the handle, a soft silicone insert gently compresses the breast behind the nipple to stimulate milk flow. The Isis is available at baby-goods stores and from the manufacturer for about $37. To find a supplier or to order direct, write Avent America, Inc., 501 Lively Boulevard, Elk Grove Village, Illinois 60007, or call toll free 800-542-8368.

Avent Isis Pump

Loyd-B Pump

Loyd-B Pump. With this pump you create suction by squeezing a hand grip. Suction is released through a valve near the grip. Many mothers have used the Loyd-B Pump successfully, although it sometimes requires practice in maneuvering. Women with small hands may find it more difficult. To order the pump send $40 (this amount includes shipping and tax) to Lopuco, Ltd., 1615 Old Annapolis Road, Woodbine, Maryland 21797. Phone toll free 800-634-7867.

angled-head cylinder pump

Cylinder pumps. Available in many drug and discount stores as well as maternity shops, cylinder pumps are very popular with nursing mothers. They consist of two plastic cylinders. Suction is created by sliding the outer cylinder away from the breast, starting with short, frequent pulls to initiate the milk flow. If the head of the pump is not angled, the mother may need to lean slightly forward. After two or three ounces are collected, it is usually necessary to empty the milk into another container. Cylinder pumps range in price from about $15 to about $25. There are many brands on the market, but the following are tried and true.

straight-head cylinder pump

- *Ameda Cylinder Breast Pump.* This angled-head pump is available from Hollister, Inc., 2000 Hollister Drive, Libertyville, Illinois 60048. Call toll free 800-323-4060.
- *Omron Comfort Plus Breast Pump.* This straight-head pump is available in many drugstores, discount stores, and baby-goods stores. For replacement parts, write or call Omron Healthcare Inc., 300 Lakeview Parkway, Vernon Hills, Illinois 60061. Phone toll free 800-634-4350.

Medela Manualectric Pump

Medela Manualectric Breast Pump. This pump creates a gentle suction when the plunger is pulled outward; a spring in the plunger makes the release automatic. The milk flows into the attached bottle. The pump can be easily adapted for use as a milk receptacle with an electric pump. The Medela pump is available for about $34 from Medela pump rental stations and from Medela, Inc., P.O. Box 660, McHenry, Illinois 60051. Phone toll free 800-435-8316.

Medela PedalPump. This foot-operated pump may be less tiring to use than hand-operated models. And because it permits pumping both breasts at once, it may be the best choice for the mother who must regularly leave her baby but can't afford to rent or buy a fully automatic pump. The PedalPump is used with the Medela single- or double-pump kit (see "Plug-in Pumps"). The PedalPump sells for about $52, the double-pump kit for about $40. Both pump and kits are available from Medela rental stations and from Medela, Inc., P.O. Box 660, McHenry, Illinois 60051. Phone toll free 800-435-8316.

Medela Pedal Pump

Battery-operated pumps. Most of the pumps in this category are powered with AA batteries and are available with an AC adapter. These pumps generate suction automatically; in most cases, you release the suction by pressing a button or bar. The pumps require only one hand to use.

These pumps have several disadvantages. First, most take from eight to ten seconds to build up to a maximum suction, and some of them are slow to completely release the suction. This means that the cycles per minute (usually four to six) are much less frequent than a nursing baby's sucks. For this reason, most battery-operated pumps are less than ideal for mothers who must be away from their babies regularly. These pumps are also more expensive than hand-operated pumps, and unless you use an AC adapter the batteries must be replaced rather often. Finally, these pumps seem to have a high rate of breakdown (most of the manufacturers offer a 90-day warranty).

Five battery-operated pumps are currently available.

Gentle Expressions Pump. Made in Japan, this pump uses two AA batteries; an AC adapter can be purchased separately. The suction is released by pressing a small button on the side of the pump. The pump can be purchased from drugstores and discount stores for about $60 with an AC adapter and about $45 without. Accessory parts are available from Lumiscope, Edison, New Jersey 08837. Call toll free 800-221-5746.

Gentle Expressions Pump

Mag-Mag Pump. This battery-operated pump is available in two models. The "Deluxe" costs between $30 and $40; the "Advanced," which has variable suction strength, costs $40 to $50. For both models, an AC adapter is included. This pump is sold at drugstores and discount stores. Accessory and replacement parts are available from Omron

Mag-Mag Pump

Healthcare, Inc., 300 Lakeview Parkway, Vernon Hills, Illinois 60061. Phone toll free 800-634-4350.

Evenflo Portable Battery/Electric Pump. Available in drugstores and discount stores, this pump has a flexible silicone breast funnel, uses longer-lasting C batteries, and includes an AC adapter. The basic model costs about $40; the deluxe model, which includes a tote baby with a separate compartment for storing milk, costs about $45.

*Evenflo Portable
Battery/Electric Pump*

Gerber Battery/Electric Breast Pump. This pump has a flexible silicone breast funnel and includes an AC adapter. As with other semiautomatic pumps, you release the suction by pressing a button. The pump is available at drugstores and discount stores for about $50.

*Gerber Battery/Electric
Breast Pump*

Medela Mini-Electric Pump. This Swiss-made pump is the only battery-operated breast pump that both sucks and releases automatically. It cycles 32 to 34 times per minute, less often than larger, rental pumps but far more often than other battery-operated pumps. An AC adapter is included. The basic Mini-Electric pump costs about $95; a model that allows pumping both breasts at once costs about $160. Both are available through Medela pump rental stations and from Medela, Inc., P.O. Box 660, McHenry, Illinois, 60051; call toll free 800-435-8316. The double-pumping model is also available at some discount stores, where it is labeled as the Little Hearts Double Deluxe Pump.

*Medela Mini-Electric
Pump*

Plug-in pumps. The final type of breast pump runs on electricity from a wall socket. These pumps have several advantages over hand-held and battery-operated pumps. In addition to requiring only one hand to operate, they require less effort generally. This means you can pump while reading, talking on the phone, or eating lunch. Most mothers find that these pumps work gently yet very efficiently, and faster than both hand- and battery-operated pumps.

automatic pump

Fully automatic pumps create a regular suck-release pattern that, at 48 to 60 cycles per minute, closely approximates the sucking action of a baby, and they promote very efficient letdown. Most fully automatic pumps offer optional double-pump kits so that both breasts can be pumped at the same time. Double pumping can significantly cut the amount of time needed to empty both breasts; also, studies have suggested that more milk is obtained using the double-pump kit. A fully automatic pump is preferable if you are pumping frequently, because your baby isn't nursing, you're working full days, or you're working several days a week. Such a pump is less portable than other kinds, however, and is also more expensive to buy. But you can rent one instead (and long-term rental rates are around a dollar a day, about a third the cost of formula feeding).

Evenflo Dual Electric Breast Pump

Semiautomatic pumps also run on electricity from a wall socket, but the mother uses her finger to create the suction. Most of these pumps are available for purchase only, not for rent. Although semiautomatic pumps are less expensive to buy than fully automatic pumps, they may be less efficient, and therefore less suitable for the mother who is pumping full time.

Evenflo Dual Electric Breast Pump. This semiautomatic pump cycles rather slowly, six to eight times per minute. It does, however, allow for pumping either one or both breasts at a time. The pump is available for about $110 at discount stores.

Nurture III Pump. Also semiautomatic, the Nurture III is about the size of a small aquarium pump. It has variable suction strength, single or double pumping capability, and a two-year warranty. The basic model costs $110 plus $7.50 for shipping; a deluxe model, including a tote bag, a refreezable ice pack, extra bottles, and an instructional video, costs $145 plus $7.50 shipping. Order either model from Bailey Medical Engineering, 2216 Sunset Drive, Los Osos, California 93402. Call toll free 800-413-3216.

Nurture III Pump

DoubleEase Breastpump. Ideal for mothers who are separated from their babies 24 hours a week or less, the DoubleEase is the newest fully automatic pump. It cycles approximately 32 times per minute, somewhat slower than its sister pump the Pump in Style. The DoubleEase allows you to pump either one or both breasts at a time, and it comes in an attractive leather-like bag with an insulated area for milk storage and refreezable ice packs. This pump can run off C batteries as well as electricity from a wall socket. The DoubleEase is available for about $200 from

DoubleEase Breastpump

Medela rental stations and from Medela, Inc., P.O. Box 660, McHenry, Illinois 60051. Call toll free 800-435-8316.

Medela Pump in Style Professional Electric Pump. This was the first fully automatic pump intended for sale to nursing women rather than for rental use. Ideal for working mothers, the Pump in Style cycles quickly—48 to 50 times per minute—and it allows you to pump either one or both breasts at a time and to vary the suction strength. The pump is housed in an attractive leather-like shoulder bag, weighs only four pounds, and comes with a one-year warranty. Included are refreezable ice packs, extra bottles, milk storage bags, and an adapter for a cigarette lighter. The Pump in Style is available for about $280 from Medela rental stations and from Medela, Inc., P.O. Box 660, McHenry, Illinois 60051. Call toll free 800-435-8316.

Medela Pump in Style Professional Electric Pump

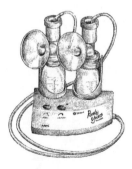

Ameda Purely Yours Breast Pump. This is the second fully automatic pump meant for purchase by working mothers. It allows you to control both the speed—up to 60 cycles per minute—and the strength of suction, and to pump either one or both breasts at a time. When an electric outlet is unavailable, you can operate the pump using six AA batteries. Extra bottles, refreezable ice packs, and a one-year warranty are included, and a tote bag is optional. The Purely Yours pump is available for about $230 with the tote bag or $195 without it from Ameda retailers and rental stations and from Hollister, Inc., 2000 Hollister Drive, Libertyville, Illinois 60048. Call toll free 800-323-4060.

Ameda Purely Yours Breast Pump

Ameda SMB and Lact-E Pumps. These automatic pumps are heavy, hospital-grade machines; the SMB weighs over 20 pounds, the Lact-E about 12 pounds. Although these pumps cost about a thousand dollars each to buy, they are widely available through rental stations for about $2.50 per day, or about a dollar per day long-term. Single- or double-pump kits can be used with either pump. To locate a rental station near you, contact Hollister, Inc., 2000 Hollister Drive, Libertyville, Illinois 60048. The toll-free number is 800-323-4060.

Ameda Elite Pump. Also intended for rental use, the fully automatic Elite weighs only seven pounds, and you can vary both the rate and the strength of its suction. In case you'll be pumping where there's no electric outlet, one model comes with a built-in battery pack. Long-term rental rates are available through most rental stations. To locate a rental station near you, write Hollister, Inc., 2000 Hollister Drive, Libertyville, Illinois 60048, or call toll free 800-323-4060.

Ameda Elite Pump

Medela Classic Electric Pump. This fully automatic pump, a sturdy machine weighing over 20 pounds, is widely available through rental stations. It comes with a single- or double-pump kit. Most rental stations offer reduced rates for long-term rentals. To locate a rental station near you, contact Medela, Inc., P.O. Box 660, McHenry, Illinois 60051. Call toll free 800-TELL-YOU.

Medela Lactina and Lactina Select Electric Pumps. Weighing just four pounds each, these rental pumps are ideal for the working mother. The Lactina Select has a variable speed control, which many mothers prefer. Both pumps can be used with single- or double-pump kits. In case you'll be pumping where no electric outlet is available, a battery pack and an adapter for a cigarette lighter are available separately. Long-term rental rates are available. To locate a rental station near you, contact Medela, Inc., P.O. Box 660, McHenry, Illinois 60051. Call toll free 800-TELL-YOU at any time.

Medela Lactina Electric (016E) Pump

White River Electric Pumps. Each of these models, one fully automatic and one semiautomatic, has a soft silicone breast funnel. The White River pumps are available through rental stations; call 800-342-3906.

Introducing a Bottle

Getting your baby used to a bottle is important if she will be fed by someone else while you are away at work or school. It is best to wait until she is three to four weeks old before introducing a bottle. By this time nursing should be well established, so the bottle will not interfere with the baby's interest in the breast. Some babies refuse the bottle if it is first offered much after they are one month old.

It is generally best if someone other than the mother bottle-feeds the baby. You can manually express or pump your milk instead of nursing, then have your partner or someone else feed the milk to the baby. Most infants will continue to accept a bottle if it is offered about twice a week. Offering a bottle periodically will also give you the opportunity to practice manual expression or become proficient with your pump.

If you have waited longer than a month and the baby refuses to take a bottle, be sure to have someone else try. Frequently a baby is more confused and upset by the bottle when her mother tries to persuade her. Trying to force the baby is upsetting for everyone, and rarely successful. Some parents have succeeded by offering the bottle while walking with the baby. Hold the baby facing away from you and bounce her gently as you walk. Some babies dislike the taste of formula; try breast milk instead. Tasteless silicone nipples may be more readily accepted than rubber types. Recently I've been successful in getting babies to take a bottle fitted with the Avent Fast-Flow nipple or the Evenflo HealthFlow nipple. Another technique that has been successful for some mothers is to nurse the baby for just a few minutes, then unlatch the baby and slip the

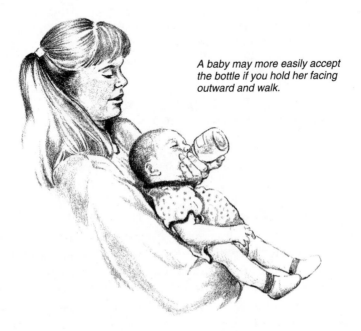

A baby may more easily accept the bottle if you hold her facing outward and walk.

bottle into her mouth. If she objects, you can try again after a few minutes more.

The baby who refuses a bottle may do surprisingly well with an ordinary cup, particularly if she is about six months or older.

Collecting and Storing Your Milk

Most mothers who will be manually expressing or pumping their milk while away feel more secure if they collect and store a backup supply of milk ahead of time. You can safely store breast milk in the freezer compartment of your refrigerator for up to three months. If you have access to a deep freezer (maintained at 0 degrees F.), you can store it there for six months or longer.

If you plan to store your milk in the freezer compartment, collect it in clean plastic containers; you can use small plastic baby bottles or disposable plastic bottle liners. More durable plastic bags, designed for milk storage, are also available (see Appendix A). For storing milk in a deep freezer, hard plastic or glass bottles are preferable. Because the entire amount must be used once breast milk is thawed, you will want to store small amounts in each container to prevent waste. If you are not sure how much milk your baby will want at each feeding, put about 3 ounces in each bag or bottle. Leave some room at the top of the container to allow for the expansion that occurs with freezing. Secure bottle liners by twisting the tops, bending them over, and closing the ends with rubber bands or twist ties. Be sure to label each container with the date you collected the milk.

If you wish to add more milk to some that is already frozen, chill it first in the refrigerator for about half an hour to keep the top layer of frozen milk from defrosting.

Occasionally a mother finds that her expressed milk has an unpleasant smell or taste. Certain vitamin or mineral supplements can cause this; so can steroidal nasal sprays. In either case, the affected milk is harmless.

Breast milk can take on a soapy smell if the fat has broken down, freeing fatty acids. Apparently, some women have an excess of lipase, the enzyme that breaks down the fat in milk. Usually they notice the soapy smell after the milk has been refrigerated or frozen, but in some cases the smell develops immediately after expression. Most babies will take such milk without complaint, but the peculiar odor and taste can usually be lessened or eliminated either by chilling the milk before freezing it, or by putting it directly into the freezer, then thawing it in the refrigerator before warming it in a hot water bath. If these methods fail for you, you can inactivate the enzyme by scalding the milk on the stove—that is, by bringing the milk almost to a boil—and then immediately refrigerating or freezing it.

Frozen breast milk often takes on a yellow color. This does not mean that it has gone bad.

The best time to collect milk for storage depends on your baby's routine. You may need to pump after a few feedings each day if he nurses frequently around the clock; you may get only an ounce or two each time. But if your baby sleeps for five or six hours at night you may be able to collect a few ounces of milk just before you go to bed or early in the morning, depending on what time he begins his sleep stretch.

While you are collecting milk at home you will also be becoming more proficient at hand expression or pumping. Occasionally a mother finds that the pump she has purchased does not work well for her. If this happens to you, be sure to review the manufacturer's instructions and check to see that all the parts are present and properly connected. Most pumps require some practice. If you are not happy with yours, though, try a different style.

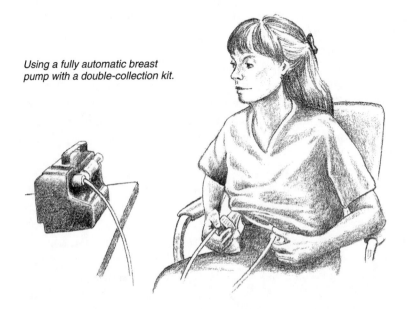

Using a fully automatic breast pump with a double-collection kit.

When expressing your milk either by hand or with a pump, switch from one breast to the other as soon as the flow starts to diminish. This is the most effective way to stimulate more milk flow. Massaging the breasts just before and during expression encourages milk let-down and also increases milk flow.

A small proportion of women have trouble getting their milk to let down while they are pumping. A more efficient pump usually improves the situation; a fully automatic electric pump with double-pumping capability is best.

At work or school, you will need a time and a place to collect your milk. Almost any private place will do—an empty office, an unused room, or a women's lounge, locker room, or health center. Talk to your supervisor if you need to make special arrangements for regular or extended breaks from work. You may need to deduct the time from your usual hours or make it up at the end of the day.

You will also need a place to store your milk. Investigate whether a refrigerator is available. If there is no refrigerator, you can take a small cooler with refreezable plastic ice packs inside. Milk stays cold for several hours in these coolers, which are also handy for transporting milk home or to the caregiver's. Coolers specially made for storing and transporting breast milk are commercially available (see Appendix A).

When you pick up the baby at the caregiver's house, you can leave milk in the refrigerator for the next day. Fresh refrigerated milk is best for the baby, since it retains more antibodies than frozen milk. If the milk will not be used the following day, however, it should be labeled with the date and frozen.

You will want to thoroughly instruct whoever is caring for the baby on how the milk is to be stored and prepared. Specific written guidelines, like those that follow, are most helpful.

Refrigerated Milk

Use refrigerated milk within 72 hours. Take the milk out of the refrigerator just before using. Gradually, over 5 to 10 minutes, warm the milk to room temperature in a container of warm water. Do not warm the milk in a microwave or on the stove.

Frozen Milk

Use milk within three months if it has been stored in the freezer compartment of a refrigerator. Milk stored in a deep freezer is good for six months or longer. Always use the oldest milk first. Thaw the milk either in the refrigerator, where it can remain up to 24 hours, or in water just before feeding, gradually increasing the temperature to warm. Do not defrost the milk in a microwave or over the stove. Whatever milk the baby does not take must be discarded. Breast milk should not be refrozen.

Occasionally, some caregivers express concern about the safety of handling breast milk; they apparently fear that diseases might be transmitted through it. You can assure your caregiver that breast milk is not a "biohazardous material." The U.S. Centers for Disease Control and the Occupational Safety and Health Administration (OSHA) agree that people handling and feeding breast milk need not wear rubber gloves nor store the milk in a refrigerator where no other foods are kept.

Back at Work

Once you are back at work, you will discover what routines work best for you, the baby, and your milk supply. Nursing twice in the morning before you leave the baby is ideal. Some mothers find that bringing the baby to bed with them, if she isn't already there, and nursing an hour or so before getting up works well. You can nurse again just before you leave home or when you get to the caregiver's house. While you are at work, try to express milk about as often as you would be nursing at home. This means at least two expression sessions if you will be gone a full eight hours—three is even better.

After work, you may want to nurse at the caregiver's house before going home. Many mothers find this provides a welcome opportunity to relax and talk with the caregiver about the baby's day. Encourage the caregiver to schedule the baby's feedings so that he will be ready to nurse as soon as you arrive. This generally means the baby should last be fed about two to three hours before you are expected.

When you are at home, of course, you will want to nurse as much as possible. Some mothers encourage their baby to nurse more frequently during the evening and night; they find this helps to keep their milk supply plentiful.

Some mothers find they are unable to express as much milk as the baby needs while they are away. In this situation there are several measures to take. You can try to express milk more frequently while you are at work. This may be easier if you rent an electric pump for a while. You should be sure to switch from one breast to the other frequently as you express if you are pumping with a single collector. Using an electric pump with a double-pump kit may help you to obtain greater milk volumes. While you are nursing, you should switch the baby from one breast to the other whenever you hear her swallows becoming farther apart. You might want to consider spending a weekend in bed with the baby nursing frequently. Some mothers also stimulate increased milk production by pumping for a few minutes after nursing.

Some nursing mothers find that fenugreek is very helpful in stimulating increased milk production. You can make a tea from the fragrant seeds, but it may be more convenient to take fenugreek capsules, which are sold in most health-food stores for around five to seven dollars per 100. Take two to three capsules three times a day, and you'll probably notice an increase in your milk supply within one to three days. The only likely side effect will be maple-scented sweat and urine, although in a few women fenugreek also causes diarrhea. Most of my clients take fenugreek just long enough to boost a low milk supply, but some mothers continue to use it for weeks or months without any difficulties. Keep in mind that fenugreek is less effective if the breast is not completely drained at least seven times in 24 hours.

Even if you follow all the other measures, if you cannot express milk more often at work you may find that the baby needs a supplement when you are away. This may be formula, but if the baby is at least four months old and seems ready for solids, you may want the caregiver to begin introducing them.

Some mothers leak milk while they are at work. You may need to wear thick pads in your bra; keep an extra supply of them with you. Wearing printed blouses or keeping an extra jacket or sweater at work will help hide any wetness. Some mothers prefer to use plastic breast shells to keep their clothes dry. Although this usually serves the purpose, keep in mind that these cups can encourage further leaking. The milk they catch should not be saved for the baby.

If you and your partner are both working, you may be too overwhelmed by chores to cuddle and enjoy the baby as much as you would like during your hours at home. Perhaps you can afford to pay someone to come every week or so to catch up on the house-cleaning.

Combining nursing and working takes a great deal of time and energy. Aside from the responsibilities of your job, the baby, and the rest of your family, it is very important that you take time to care for yourself. Nursing mothers need to eat well. Although it may be tempting to skip breakfast or lunch, most women who do this find they have little energy to meet the many demands of the day. Get up a little earlier, if you must, to fix a nutritious breakfast. Bring snacks such as yogurt, cheese, nuts, and fruit to eat throughout the work day. Some mothers find brewer's yeast gives them an energy boost and helps keep up the milk supply. To avoid constipation and plugged milk ducts, you will also need to drink plenty of fluids while you are at work. Finally, rest is essential. Most working and nursing mothers find they must go to bed earlier every night than they once did. If you can, take an hour's nap just before dinner, and nap on your days at home with the baby.

CHAPTER SIX

The Reward Period: From Two to Six Months

Caring for Yourself
Making Love
Nursing Your Baby
Starting Solid Foods

THE PERIOD BETWEEN THE BABY'S SECOND AND SIXTH MONTHS IS exciting and rewarding. With the newborn stage behind, most mothers feel relaxed and confident. The baby is more predictable, his needs easier to interpret. By three months, his crying lessens considerably. Day by day, the baby becomes more sociable and attuned to the people and things around him. Still, nursings are an important part of his day, intervals for nurture and nourishment at the breast.

Caring for Yourself

During this time, I hope, you are beginning to feel more like your usual self. Napping whenever possible is still important, especially if your baby is waking at night for feedings or if your energy seems low. Your intake of food and drink continues to be essential to your overall well-being. Neglecting your need for fluids could lead to constipation and, possibly, recurrent plugged milk ducts. Skipping meals or substituting "empty-calorie" foods for more nutritious ones could result in fatigue and rapid weight loss. If you are overweight, limit your weight loss to one pound per week; crash dieting could decrease your milk supply. Most nursing mothers lose weight gradually without worrying about snacks or calories, whereas others find that eating three regular, satisfying meals and limiting high-calorie snacks and beverages, such as juices and soft drinks, helps them to achieve their weekly goal.

Making Love

After the birth of a baby most couples need time to readjust to each other sexually. You can probably resume intercourse by the sixth-week postpartum exam. In the meantime, you and your partner can enjoy physical loving such as cuddling, kissing, massage, and fondling. If your perineum feels fine and you want to have intercourse at three or four weeks post partum, there is no reason to wait. But you may not yet feel ready even when your doctor, nurse, or midwife gives you the go-ahead.

You may be worried that intercourse will be painful. If you have had an episiotomy, you may feel some initial tenderness and tightness, but your stitches should be completely healed after one month. Relaxing as much as possible will help make lovemaking more comfortable the first few times. A warm bath, a glass of wine, and extra time with foreplay may be helpful. Be sure to use a generous amount of lubricating gel, such as K-Y Lubricant, Astroglide, or a contraceptive gel, in and around your vagina. You may also want to experiment with different positions, especially if you have had an episiotomy. Some women prefer to be on top so that they control the degree of penetration. Others find that a side-lying position feels best at first.

Most new mothers experience some vaginal dryness during love-making because of the hormonal changes that occur after giving birth. The vaginal secretions increase once regular ovulation resumes. Ovulation is generally delayed during nursing, for a variable period. Until your periods resume, a water-soluble lubricant can make intercourse more comfortable and pleasurable.

The breasts need not be off limits when making love. Some women, however, find them less sensitive to stimulation during the nursing period; they may also feel tender during the early weeks, and later on just after nursing. Breast stimulation and orgasm may cause the milk to let down and leak or spray. If leaking milk is bothersome for you or your partner, you might nurse shortly before you make love, or wear a blouse, a bra, or a nightgown during lovemaking.

For some time after having a baby, many women find they have less interest in making love than formerly. There are a variety of reasons for this. Estrogen, which influences a woman's sex drive as well as the amount of vaginal secretions, is produced in lower levels after she gives birth. Sometimes having so much skin-to-skin contact with the baby all day dampens a woman's desire for more physical contact. A new mother may also fear another pregnancy—whether or not the recent one was planned. At the end of the day, too, a mother may be just too tired for lovemaking.

New fathers also suffer from overwork and night wakings. Like their partners, they may be too exhausted to make love, and they may also worry about having another baby too soon.

It is important that your intimacy as a couple continues. As with most other changes in life, talking over your feelings and making some adjustments will make this period easier.

Finding the time to make love can be difficult, especially when you are tired. You may need to plan times to be together when you are rested and when the baby is likely to be asleep. Making love early in the morning or when the baby is napping may work the best. Perhaps you can take a nap in the afternoon so you will have more energy for your partner in the evening. Having the baby sleep in another room may help you to feel more comfortable.

But if neither you nor your partner is much inclined to have frequent intercourse, don't feel there is something wrong with you—your physical and emotional intimacy can continue without it. Passionate feelings will probably come easier as the baby gets older. Remember, you have a lifetime ahead of you to share your love.

Contraception. If you are concerned about the possibility of getting pregnant again, talk over birth-control options with your partner and your health-care provider. Foam, condoms, IUDs, diaphragms, cervical caps, and surgical sterilization are all considered safe during nursing. (If you used a diaphragm or cervical cap before your pregnancy, you will need a refitting now.)

Many women want reliable and convenient birth control in the form of "the pill." Although hormonal birth control apparently does no direct harm to the nursing baby, pills containing estrogen, even in low doses, often reduce a mother's milk supply and may thereby lead to poor weight gain in the baby. Not all birth-control pills, fortunately, interfere with milk production. The progestin-only pill, also known as the "mini-pill," has no impact on milk supply. Nor do progestin-only injections, which give three months protection against pregnancy, or Norplant subdermal implants. All of these hormonal birth control methods are considered safe during breastfeeding.

Whichever of these birth-control methods you use, its reliability is increased by the fact that you are breastfeeding. For now, in fact, breastfeeding may be the only birth-control method you need. That breastfeeding affects fertility is a truth that has been largely ignored in a century when partial breastfeeding and early weaning have been the norm. But breastfeeding has provided more contraception worldwide than all other methods combined. Frequent nursing, especially during the first several months after birth, suppresses ovulation in most women. If you haven't yet had a period, in fact, exclusive breastfeeding provides more than 98 percent protection against pregnancy in the first six months post partum (Kennedy, 1989). But when the baby is receiving any food or drink besides your milk, when your periods have resumed, or when the baby reaches six months of age, your chance of getting pregnant again increases. If you want to rely on breastfeeding-as-contraception (which medical texts call the Lactational Amenorrhea Method, or LAM), nurse at least eight times in every 24 hours, with no more than six hours between nursings and a cumulative sucking time of at least 60 minutes per day. For best results, don't feed anything else or even use pacifiers.

Once your periods resume, you may prefer to track your natural menstrual cycle, abstaining from intercourse around the time of ovulation instead of relying on birth-control pills or devices. If you want to use the "rhythm method," try to get personal instruction in it. Learn to keep track of all three basic body measures: basal body temperature, cervical mucus, and length of menstrual cycle.

Nursing Your Baby

As your baby quickly grows and develops you will notice her nursing pattern also changes. You can expect two more appetite spurts during this period, the first at about two and a half to three months and the second between four and a half and six months. As with the earlier appetite spurts, the baby will nurse more frequently for a few days to stimulate an increase in milk production. Most mothers produce 30 to 36 ounces of milk or more each day during this period, a 50 to 80 percent increase over the first month.

By three or four months of age, many babies have dropped a feeding or two and are nursing about seven or eight times a day. Nursing less often than seven times a day may result in decreased milk production and slowed weight gain for the baby. This most commonly occurs when a baby spends much of her day sucking on her fingers or on a pacifier, or when she begins sleeping long stretches at night but isn't nursed more often during the day. It can also happen when a working mother does not express milk frequently enough while she is away. Your baby should continue gaining an ounce a day until she is three to four months old. Between three and six months of age, a breastfed baby normally gains one-half ounce or more each day.

Some babies prefer to nurse from just one breast at each feeding. So long as the baby seems content and is continuing to gain enough weight, this is normal.

You may also notice that your baby is nursing for shorter periods. She can now get a large quantity of milk quickly because both she and your breasts have become so efficient. At four to five months, a baby also becomes easily distracted during nursing. At any new, sudden, or interesting sight or sound, she pulls away from the breast to look around. This does not mean she has lost interest in nursing. After several weeks she will no longer have to interrupt herself to check out what's going on around her; she'll turn her head with the nipple still in her mouth. In the meantime, you may find that nursing in a quiet or semi-darkened room helps the baby to complete her feedings.

Most three- to six-month-old babies are chubby; some may be quite plump. Parents and sometimes even doctors may become concerned about the baby who gains weight above the norm. These babies slow their growth during the second half of the first year and typically begin to slim down during toddlerhood. It is not advisable to restrict the baby's nursing because of her weight.

About half of all infants start sleeping through the night—that is, for a six- to seven-hour stretch—by three to four months. A small minority of babies sleep eight to twelve hours, and so need to nurse every two to two and a half hours during the day and evening to get enough milk. Few infants nursing less often than seven times a day can gain well. Most infants, both breastfed and bottle-fed, continue to need night feedings until they are six months or even older. Feeding the baby formula, cereal, or other solid foods in the evening will not help her to sleep longer at night.

Sometimes babies who have been sleeping through the night begin waking again for feedings. This can occur when a baby decreases the number of nursings during the day either because she gets distracted or because she spends too much time sucking her fingers or a pacifier. To encourage your baby to get more of her milk during the day, try offering the breast in a quiet, darkened room or whenever she begins sucking her fingers—and limit the use of a pacifier.

Sudden night waking may be due to the discomfort of teething. Other signs of teething may include general fussiness, drooling, changes in nursing pattern, biting, and finger sucking. Giving the baby a cold washcloth or a chilled water-filled teething ring to bite on may make her more comfortable. Some doctors also recommend the use of gum gels and acetaminophen drops (such as Infants' Tylenol or Tempra). An ear infection may also be the reason for sudden night waking. If your baby has recently had a cold (or a previous ear infection), beware that her ears may be the problem, even if she has no fever and isn't pulling on them.

Starting Solid Foods

Probably no area of infant development attracts as much confusion and range of opinion as the starting of solid foods. Your family, friends, and child-care advisors probably all have different ideas on when and how to begin giving solid foods to your baby. By far the most sensible approach I have found is that of Ellyn Satter, a nutritionist who breastfed her own three children. I highly recommend her book *Child of Mine: Feeding with Love and Good Sense* (1991).

Solid foods are best introduced when a baby becomes developmentally ready for them and is able to benefit from the nutrition they offer. Although this does not happen until a baby is close to six months of age, many mothers feel pressured to begin solids earlier. Some think of feeding solids as a sort of status symbol, something to brag about. But the American Academy of Pediatrics (1998) now recommends that breastfed babies not be fed solid foods until they are at least six months old.

Offering solids prematurely means replacing breast milk, which is nutritionally perfect, with foods that are nutritionally incomplete. Additionally, the early introduction of solids may lead to obesity (perhaps lifelong), allergic reactions, decreased milk production, and early weaning. Rest assured, your milk provides all the nutrients your baby needs for at least the first six months after birth. Besides, holding off on solids is practical: the closer to six months you introduce them, the more likely you will be able to skip the "baby food" stage and start with table foods.

Some mothers go to the opposite extreme: they feel they should delay solids until eight to twelve months to prevent allergies and excessive weight gain. But obesity should not be a problem if a baby is at least six months old and seems ready for solids. You don't need to worry about allergies, either, if you avoid foods that are commonly allergenic—such as wheat, egg white, citrus fruits, and dairy products—and any foods to which members of your family are allergic.

You'll know your baby is developmentally ready for solid foods when he can sit with support, control his head and neck movements, and tell you he is hungry or full by leaning forward with an open mouth or pulling away and turning his head. He may indicate his readiness for solids by grabbing food off your plate or out of your hand.

At this time he will also begin to lose his tongue-thrust reflex, which causes him to push anything in his mouth forward and out. This means he will be better able to eat from a spoon, move the food to the back of his mouth, and swallow. The baby's digestive system will also be mature enough to handle solids at this time. His kidneys will be able to excrete the waste products of solid foods, and he will be less likely to develop allergic reactions from them. His iron stores will lessen, so the iron from solid foods will be beneficial for him.

When your baby is close to six months old, you may begin to notice that he still seems hungry after nursing. If after a few days of stepped-up nursings he still seems unsatisfied, feel free to experiment with solids. Occasionally a four- to five-month-old fails to gain sufficient weight, or stops gaining at all. If normal weight gain doesn't resume after a week or so of more frequent nursings, it may be time to begin solids.

Quite a variety of foods have been recommended as the first solids for infants: fruits, vegetables, meats, yogurt, egg yolks, cottage cheese. But all of these foods contain either too much carbohydrate, protein, or fat, or too little iron.

An iron-fortified baby cereal mixed with breast milk is the ideal first solid food for a baby. It meets both his nutritional and his developmental needs. Cereal meets the baby's increased demand for iron that occurs around six months. Mixing the cereal with milk provides a good proportion of carbohydrate, protein, and fat. The texture of cereal can be adjusted to match the baby's ability with semisoft food.

Rice or barley cereal is less likely to cause an allergic reaction than wheat or a mixed-grain cereal, and is therefore a better first food (be sure to check the label, as some rice cereals do contain other grains). Although they are sometimes recommended for infants, cereals that must be cooked do not contain as much iron as dry baby cereals, and what iron they do contain is not nearly as well absorbed. Ready-made baby cereals in jars also have less iron than the dry versions, and are more expensive. High-protein cereals provide more protein than young infants need.

Mix dry baby cereal with breast milk, formula, or evaporated milk diluted one to one with water. You can use whole cow's milk (less than eight ounces a day) if your baby is six months or older and you are not concerned about an allergic response. Breast milk or a hypoallergenic formula (soy-based or "predigested") is probably the best choice if you are concerned about allergies. Mixing the cereal with water or juice will not provide protein and fat for the baby.

Nurse your baby before offering cereal or another solid food. It is important to do this until he is eating three regular meals of table food, at some time after eight months of age. Until then, breast milk will continue to be his most important food.

Begin with one feeding of cereal a day. At first, mix one teaspoon of cereal with enough milk to make a thin paste. At the first few feedings, don't be surprised if your baby pushes back out almost as much as you have put in. It may take a little time before he learns to move the food to the back of his mouth and then swallow it. Should your baby become upset and refuse to eat, wait a few days before trying again.

Gradually increase the amount of cereal you give at each feeding, and add a second feeding so the baby is getting a total of one-half cup of mixed cereal a day. Thicken the mixture as his eating ability improves. If you are giving supplemental iron, stop when the baby is taking one-third to one-half cup of mixed cereal a day.

For advice on adding fruits, juices, and other foods to the baby's diet, see Chapter 7.

SURVIVAL GUIDE
for Months Two through Six

Concerns about Yourself

Recurrent Plugged Ducts and Breast Infections
Overabundant Milk

Concerns about the Baby

Slow Weight Gain
One-Sided Nursing
Sudden Refusal to Nurse

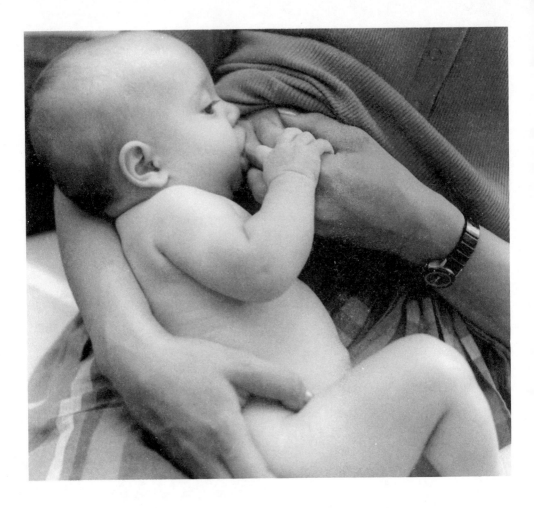

Concerns about Yourself

Recurrent Plugged Ducts and Breast Infections

Many nursing mothers experience recurrent plugged ducts or breast infections. If you are suffering from either at the moment, carefully review the information in "Survival Guide for the First Two Months." If you have had more than two or three episodes, the following suggestions may be helpful in preventing more.

Treatment Measures for Recurrent Plugged Ducts and Breast Infections

1. Be sure that you are nursing the baby frequently, and that at least one breast is emptied well at each feeding. Avoid skipping or delaying feedings. To encourage complete drainage of the milk ducts, massage your breasts gently while nursing. Pick a quiet place to nurse if your baby gets distracted during feedings. Wake the baby at night if your breasts feel too full. If your baby routinely sleeps for long periods at night, consider using an effective breast pump before you go to bed, after the first morning feeding, or both. This way you'll ensure that your breasts are completely drained at least once or twice a day.

2. Change nursing pads whenever they become wet.

3. Get as much rest as possible. Nap whenever you can. Consider sleeping with the baby if you aren't already.

4. Make sure you are getting plenty to drink every day.

5. Check your bra and any other restrictive clothing you may be wearing.

6. If your doctor prescribes antibiotics, take the entire course. A ten-day prescription may be needed; a five- or seven-day course may be insufficient for complete treatment.

7. If an infection recurs in the same part of the breast shortly after antibiotic therapy has ended, the antibiotic may be ineffective. Some antibiotics do not penetrate breast tissue as well as others. Discuss this possibility with your doctor or pharmacist.

8. Take a daily iron supplement if you are anemic.

9. Many lactation professionals believe vitamin C supplements may help prevent recurrences of breast infections. Some suggest that taking supplemental lecithin (three capsules a day) and avoiding saturated fats in the diet may prevent plugged milk ducts.

10. A high salt intake may increase susceptibility to breast infections. Some women seem to be prone to breast infections premenstrually; this may have to do with the fact that they retain water just before their periods. If your periods have resumed, try limiting your salt intake for several days before your period is due.

11. If a plugged duct or breast infection does not go away within three days, consult a physician.

Overabundant Milk

Some mothers continue to be bothered by an oversupply of milk after two months post partum. You are not necessarily producing too much milk, however, if you leak or become engorged during the baby's long sleep stretches. Only if you are still feeling uncomfortably engorged most of the time should you consider taking steps to decrease your milk supply.

Treatment Measures for an Overabundance of Milk

1. Continue drinking plenty of fluids. Decreasing fluids does not decrease milk production.

2. Nurse your baby at just one breast per feeding. Let him suck as long as he likes on one side. If you become uncomfortable, express a small amount of milk from the other breast. Switch breasts with each feeding.

3. Should you be caught in a routine of expressing milk while nursing full time, gradually decrease the amount of milk you take until you are no longer expressing any.

Concerns about the Baby

Slow Weight Gain

A two- to three-month-old baby is considered a slow gainer when he is putting on less than an ounce a day. A slow-gaining three- to six-month-old is gaining less than one-half ounce per day.

A baby who is discovered to be gaining weight slowly, not gaining at all, or losing weight may be nursing too infrequently—that is, fewer than seven times in a 24-hour period. Between three and four months of age, most babies find their fingers or become avid pacifier users. Some babies stop letting their mothers know when they are hungry and instead suck away at fingers or a pacifier, decreasing the number of nursings to fewer than seven a day. The baby who sleeps eight or more hours at a stretch each night may fail to get enough milk if he doesn't nurse at least seven times during his waking hours. A baby may also slow his weight gain after losing some interest in nursing because juices or solid foods have been introduced prematurely, especially if they have replaced nursings.

Slow weight gain may occur, too, when a working mother fails to express her milk often enough while she is away from the baby, causing an overall decrease in her milk supply. Estrogen-containing birth-control pills, even the low-dose kind, often decrease milk production. Occasionally, a baby who has never had normal weight gain suddenly becomes a worry to his physician and parents. This happens because health professionals do not always identify a newborn who gains less than an ounce a day during the early weeks as being underfed. Eventually such a baby may become obviously underweight. This is sad, since a low milk intake can be much more easily remedied if the problem is recognized early on. A milk supply that has been low for two, three, or even four months can be very difficult to improve.

Treatment Measures for Slow Weight Gain

1. Devote at least two to three days to nursing the baby and doing little else. Put the pacifier aside, and each time you notice the baby beginning to suck a finger offer the breast. You may find yourself nursing every hour or so, although increasing feedings to eight or more per 24 hours is usually sufficient to quickly increase milk production. If your baby is sleeping through the night, try to include at least one late evening feeding. You might also consider waking the baby for a feeding after he has slept five or six hours.

2. While the baby is nursing, listen for swallowing. As soon as you notice the swallowing taper off, switch breasts. Continue switching back and forth for as long as the baby is willing to continue, ideally at least 10 minutes. If the baby is easy distracted, nurse in a quiet, darkened room.

3. If your baby has been losing weight or has never gained weight adequately, consider giving him supplemental formula while you work on increasing your milk supply. For instructions on estimating the

amount of milk you are producing and the amount of milk your baby needs, see "Underfeeding and Weight Loss" in "Survival Guide for the First Two Months."

4. Consider taking fenugreek capsules to help increase your milk production. See "Underfeeding and Weight Loss" in "Survival Guide for the First Week."

5. Should your baby refuse to nurse as often as every two hours or resist switching back and forth, you might consider expressing or pumping milk after each nursing to stimulate an increase in milk production. An electric pump may be most convenient. After two or three days of this regime, both the baby's nursing pattern and your milk supply should begin to improve.

6. If you are working, try to spend two or more consecutive days at home following the recommendations just given. While you are at work, express milk as often as possible. If you cannot express milk often enough, you may need to supplement with formula on days you are with the baby.

7. After two or three days of stepped-up nursing, you should notice that your breasts feel fuller and that the baby swallows over a longer period during feedings. Continue nursing frequently, at least eight times a day. Have the baby's weight checked after a week of frequent nursing, and again a week after that. If the baby still isn't gaining well, supplementation with an ounce or two of formula after some of the feedings may be necessary. You can add cereal to his diet, once or twice daily *after* nursing, if the baby is four months or older.

One-Sided Nursing

Occasionally a baby develops a preference for one breast over the other. Perhaps the favored breast produces more milk or lets it down more rapidly. Sometimes there is no apparent reason—the baby simply prefers one side. Twins usually choose opposite sides.

Sometimes a mother unknowingly nurses the baby more at one breast than the other, increasing milk production on the favored side. Some mothers prefer nursing on one side only; in certain cultures one-sided nursing is common.

One breast can fully support a baby's nutritional needs. But if a single baby nurses substantially more at one breast than at the other, the less used breast may become noticeably smaller. After weaning, the breasts will equal out in size.

Treatment Measures for One-Sided Nursing

1. Offer the baby her least favorite side first. After she has nursed on both sides, encourage her to nurse on the first side again.

2. Should the baby totally refuse one side, try changing positions. Use the football hold, or nurse while lying on your side. The baby may be more willing when she is sleepy or actually asleep, or when you nurse in a darkened room.

3. Increase the milk supply in the less used breast by manually expressing or pumping milk after each nursing for a few days.

4. If all else fails, simply accept your baby's preference to be a one-sided nurser.

Sudden Refusal to Nurse

Occasionally a baby under six months suddenly refuses to nurse. A "nursing strike" usually lasts for a few days, but sometimes for as long as two weeks. It rarely means the baby is ready to wean. Weaning seldom occurs this suddenly. See "Nursing Strike," in "Survival Guide for the Later Months," for the reasons behind this problem and suggestions for coping with it.

If your baby suddenly refuses one breast but is happy to nurse at the other, see "One-Sided Nursing."

CHAPTER SEVEN

Nursing the Older Baby and Toddler

Nursing Your Six- to Twelve-Month-Old

The Transition to Table Food

Nursing Your Toddler

The Toddler's Diet

Nursing during Pregnancy

Tandem Nursing

Weaning

As BREASTFEEDING PROGRESSES PAST SIX MONTHS, THE NURSING relationship continues to change. Although the baby is busy exploring the world around him and has shortened most of his feedings, breast milk continues to be his primary source of nutrients until he is well established on table foods. Breastfeeding also continues to provide protective antibodies against illness.

Nursing Your Six- to Twelve-Month-Old

The typical baby of this age is venturing out on his own and seemingly becoming more independent, but he often scampers back to the safety and reassurance of his mother's arms. By eight to ten months, in fact, he probably cannot bear to have his mother out of his sight for even a minute. This is known as separation anxiety. Until the baby learns to trust that his mother will return, out of sight means gone forever.

It is during this time that many mothers experience a change in their babies' interest in nursing. One baby may become so intent on exploring that she has days when she is simply too busy to nurse. Another is more secure having his mother close by while he creeps about, turning to her often for comfort and the breast. In either case, nursing now starts to become mainly a break for a snack and a bit of love and reassurance. For many mothers, nursing becomes the main tool to help a tired baby fall off to sleep at naptime and bedtime.

Some older babies sleep from bedtime until dawn, but most wake more often. Very frequent waking may be due to teething, illness (especially ear infections), separation anxiety, or a chill from kicking off the covers. But babies normally wake two or three times a night.

Many mothers notice that it takes longer for their milk to let down in these months. This may be a response to the lessening milk supply, and perhaps it is the reason some infants seem to lose interest in nursing at around nine or ten months.

A woman's menstrual periods may return as the baby begins eating regular meals at the table. (Some women start menstruating earlier, however, and others do not start until 12 to 24 months post partum. Generally, mothers who are nursing frequently find their periods resume much later.) These initial periods may be heavy and irregular. Some mothers report that their babies are fussy for a couple of days, or even refuse to nurse for a short time, when menstruation resumes. You may experience sore nipples for a few days between ovulation and the start of your period.

You may sometimes feel tired and run-down during this time. Becoming more active and getting overtired seems to be especially common around six months post partum. Certainly, eating poorly and losing too much weight can contribute to a loss of energy. Taking it a bit easier, getting some extra rest, and paying attention to your diet can do a lot to improve your overall well-being. Taking brewer's yeast or a B-complex preparation may also be helpful.

The Transition to Table Food

From six to eight months. Sometime after her sixth month, when your baby is taking a total of a half cup of cereal in two feedings a day, she is ready for other foods. She should still nurse before eating, however, until she is well established on table foods and is having three meals a day. The nutrients in breast milk are the ones that she needs most.

Because fruits and vegetables offer vitamins A and C, they become important in the baby's diet as her intake of breast milk drops. They also accustom her to different tastes and textures and encourage the development of tongue control and chewing ability. Although puréed fruits and vegetables, whether commercially prepared or homemade, are nutritionally adequate, they do not accustom the baby to different textures or help her learn chewing skills. Commercial baby food in jars may be appropriate when you are eating out or traveling, but at other times mashed soft fruits and vegetables are best.

The order in which fruits and vegetables are introduced isn't all that important. Some nutritionists and others feel that vegetables may be more readily accepted if they are introduced before fruits, whose sweeter flavor many babies prefer. Fresh or canned fruits can be mashed, scraped, diced, or chunked according to your baby's ability. Fresh or frozen cooked vegetables are preferable to those that are commercially canned, as these usually contain too much salt for a baby. A food mill or baby-food grinder can be handy for vegetables that are hard or stringy. Offer only one new food at a time, waiting a few days before introducing another. In this way, should a certain food upset the baby, you will have a good idea which one it is.

A meal pattern that works well during this transition time is cereal and fruit in the morning and cereal and vegetables in the evening. Use a fresh or frozen vegetable from your own dinner before it is salted or seasoned.

Although one to two tablespoons of fruit is adequate, babies usually like the taste so much they are eager for more. Limit the baby to one-quarter or one-third cup per serving; too much fruit can cause intestinal upsets and diarrhea.

You can offer fruit juice instead, but limit the amount to three ounces a day. "Juice abuse" is a common mistake in infant feeding. Not only do babies not need more than three ounces, but juice often lessens their appetite for milk and solid foods. Overdependence on juice can lead to diarrhea and, especially when given in a bottle, to tooth decay. Avoid "fruit drinks," which contain mostly water, some juice, and sugar. Be careful with citrus, tomato, and pineapple juices—they can cause allergic reactions in some babies. Rashes, wheezing, nasal stuffiness, and diarrhea may be allergy symptoms. Juices bottled for infants are expensive and unnecessary. Once opened, fruit juices should not be stored in metal cans.

Juices are probably best offered from a cup. Most babies are ready to begin learning how to drink from a cup by the time they are seven or eight months old. At first you will need to hold the cup for the baby. Once she begins holding her own cup, be prepared for her turning the cup over to see what happens—all a part of the learning process. You can try a training cup, which comes with a tight-fitting lid and a spout and therefore won't spill; however, some babies suck from these, so the lesson goes unlearned.

One or two tablespoons of vegetable is sufficient for the baby. Vegetables high in nitrates, such as beets, carrots, and spinach, should be limited to this amount. When young infants are given excessive amounts of these vegetables, the nitrate can convert to nitrite in their bodies. This can cause the displacement of oxygen in the blood, leading to fast breathing and lethargy. *Methemoglobinemia*, as this condition is called, becomes less of a possibility after the baby is six months old and has more acid in her stomach.

Dark green and orange vegetables, such as broccoli, carrots, sweet potatoes, and squash, should be given no more than three or four times a week. Given too often, they can cause the baby's skin to turn yellow. This is completely harmless, however.

During this time you can also offer the baby breads and dry cereals. These offer B vitamins and iron. Although the baby may not actually eat much at first, she will be developing her chewing and self-feeding skills. Rice cakes and dry Rice Chex or Corn Chex are good first choices before trying wheat-based breads and cereals. The chance of an allergic reaction to wheat lessens once the baby is seven or eight months old, but you may want to put off offering wheat even longer if anyone in the family is allergic to it.

Try not to worry should your baby eat very little before she is eight months old. She will have her own food preferences, and she may refuse a certain food one week and happily eat it the next. She may refuse all foods for a while if she is not feeling well. And, as she becomes interested in feeding herself, she may also turn her head away from any food offered from a spoon. Although she'll be messy, you should let her feed herself. Give her another spoon, or allow her to use her fingers. Let her examine her food before deciding whether or not to eat it. By feeding herself, your baby will develop her grasping skills and hand-eye coordination. Be patient if she plays with her food instead of eating it; keep in mind that your breast milk is still the most important part of her diet.

From eight to ten months. Probably at some time between eight and ten months of age, your baby will become interested in what the rest of the family is eating. Again, I take my recommendations from Ellyn Satter and her wonderful guide to infant and toddler feeding, *Child of Mine: Feeding with Love and Good Sense* (1991).

Once table foods are offered, three major transitions follow. The first is adding another meal or two so the baby is eating three or four times a day. The second is adding high-protein foods—such as meat, poultry, fish, shell beans and lentils, eggs, cheese, tofu, and peanut butter—as the baby's intake of breast milk drops. The last transition is postponing breastfeeding until after the meal; this encourages the baby to take more solids.

This new meal pattern basically requires the addition of a midday meal and, perhaps, a small snack. Continuing to give a half cup of fortified infant cereal over one or two meals (or a meal and snack) is still important. Two servings of bread, at one-quarter slice a serving, complete the baby's requirement for grains. At least four daily servings of fruits and vegetables, at one or two tablespoons a serving, are recommended. Juice may substitute for one serving but should still be limited to three ounces a day.

The baby also needs at least two servings of high-protein foods every day. A serving of meat, poultry, fish, or eggs is about one tablespoon, or one-half ounce. Although chicken and fish (carefully boned) are fairly easy for the baby to manage, red meats may need to be shredded, ground, or minced. Avoid lunch meats and hot dogs, which are high in salt and nitrates and are not the best sources of protein. The baby can have an egg three or four times a week. Should allergies be a concern, cook the egg until solid and offer only the yolk. Other high-protein foods for a baby of this age include: one ounce of hard cheese, one-quarter cup of cottage cheese, one-half cup of shell beans or lentils, and two tablespoons of peanut butter. Commercially prepared "infant dinners" are a poor source of protein, being mostly vegetables and water with only a small amount of meat.

Should you prefer that your child have a vegetarian diet, this is easy so long as cheese and eggs are included. Do take the time to learn all you can about vegetarianism and the nutritional needs of infants and toddlers; *Child of Mine* and *The New Laurel's Kitchen* (see "Suggested Supplemental Reading") will get you started. You might also want to consult with a nutritionist, especially if you are considering a "vegan" (vegetable-only) diet. Young children on such diets are at substantial risk for B-vitamin deficiencies and, because of a lack of protein, general growth deficiencies. The federal Women, Infants, and Children (WIC) nutrition program or your local public health department can probably refer you to a nutritionist who can offer further guidance.

While your baby may not always get precisely the suggested amounts of grains, fruits, vegetables, and high-protein food every day, averaging close to these amounts over a week will ensure he is well nourished. But if by eight to ten months your baby will still take solids only sporadically at best, it may be time to give him a little extra encouragement. If his growth curve falls off, and, perhaps, he seems to be sick a lot, he may be becoming too emotionally dependent on the breast, and substituting nursing for eating a variety of nutritious foods. In this case, make sure you are nursing after meals, not before. If he is desperate for the breast, try to keep the nursing short, then encourage him to return his attention to other foods. Always include him in family meals, but offer food at other times of the day if he refuses it at mealtimes. If he resents your pushing solids, have someone else feed him or let him feed himself. Never assume that because he spits something out in disgust one day he won't take it a week later.

From ten to twelve months. After the baby is established on table foods, the final transition is adding milk along with the meal. Ideally this should be accomplished when the baby is between nine and twelve months of age. Whole milk is more digestible now that the baby is eating table foods. Low-fat milk is not a good choice because it does not provide the fat that the older baby or toddler needs. Evaporated milk, diluted one to one with water, can be used, however; this may be more convenient if the rest of your family drinks low-fat milk. Because evaporated milk is treated with high heat, it is more digestible than whole milk. And it is no more expensive. You can use soy formula or another hypoallergenic formula if your baby is allergic to milk. If your baby does not like milk of any sort, offer plenty of cheese and yogurt, and try tofu—it is also very high in calcium.

You may be wondering right now if we have just weaned your baby. In a sense, yes. Weaning is the *process* of expanding your baby's diet to include other foods. For many of you, nursing will continue to be important and convenient for early morning feedings, snacks, naps, bedtime, and general soothing and comforting.

The baby's fluoride supplements should be stopped now if your water is fluoridated to 0.3 parts per million.

Nursing Your Toddler

The toddler is trying to accomplish the major task of establishing himself as an individual. Although he is no longer a baby, he is still very dependent. One minute he is exploring and getting into everything, and the next he is turning to his mother for comfort and reassurance.

Many toddlers tend to nurse briefly. Some nurse just a few times a day, but many want the breast often. A toddler may nurse a few times one day, moreover, and many times the next. Even if he nurses infrequently, the antibodies in breast milk are still present and protective. The breast is important to the toddler not only for a quick snack and help in falling off to sleep, but for intermittent comfort and emotional refueling. Sometimes nursing is one of the toddler's few connections to a busy mother.

You may discover that nursing into toddlerhood is not only a convenient way of mothering, but that it is one of the few times during the day that your child holds still long enough for cuddling and affection.

Some nursing toddlers still wake at night for feedings. See "Survival Guide for the Later Months" for suggestions and coping strategies.

The young toddler may be quite insistent when he wants to nurse, regardless of the time or place. As he gets a bit older he will become more willing to wait a little while.

Children in many parts of the world are breastfed until they are two, three, or four years of age, yet nursing a walking, talking toddler is considered somewhat deviant in parts of Western society. Many toddlers are dependent on a bottle, pacifier, thumb, or blanket, and this is quite accepted, but a mother who is nursing a toddler may have to deal with veiled or point-blank suggestions that her child is too old for it. The concerns about nursing beyond infancy often reflect the fear that a child will become spoiled or overdependent. In fact, when a toddler's need for security is met, he becomes more self-assured and independent.

Mothers who are nursing toddlers usually enjoy socializing with others who are doing the same. La Leche League is not only supportive of women who breastfeed beyond the first year, but also offers meetings for those who are nursing young children. Norma Jane Bumgarner's book *Mothering Your Nursing Toddler* (1982) is an excellent resource for those nursing beyond infancy.

The Toddler's Diet

Toddlers are notorious as sporadic eaters. Their appetite decreases during this time—first because their growth slows down tremendously from that of the first year, and second because they are often too busy to eat. The toddler grows more in length than in weight. Weight gain typically slows to a pound or less every two months.

The toddler's feeding skills vary considerably. Sometimes she may feed herself, and other times she wants to be fed. Parents who worry about how little their child eats may be tempted to persuade, trick, or even force her to eat more. This turns meals into battles and may be the start of long-term feeding problems. As Ellyn Satter says, "You are responsible for *what* your child is offered to eat, *where* and *when* it is presented. She is responsible for *how much* of it she eats."

The suggested minimum servings of foods for the toddler are

similar to those for the older baby. A handy rule of thumb is this: give one tablespoon per year of age or one-quarter of the adult serving, whichever is easiest to figure for the particular food. You would therefore offer your toddler two tablespoons of peas or one-quarter of an apple. The suggested daily minimum servings for each food group are as follows:

- Fruits and vegetables: 4 servings
- Grains (bread, cereal, noodles, rice): 4 servings
- High-protein foods: 2 servings
- Milk: 2 to 3 cups

Offering a meal or nutritious snack every three to four hours is a good approach with a toddler. Don't always offer milk just because she likes it; if she drinks more than three cups a day it may replace other nutritious foods in her diet. Expect that your toddler may enjoy a certain food one day and refuse it the next. Make sure she comes to the table for meals and is offered whatever foods the family is eating. Do not play into her food whims by running out to the kitchen to fix something else for her when she refuses to eat.

Nursing during Pregnancy

Although many people frown on breastfeeding during pregnancy, there is no reason you cannot continue nursing your child when you find out another is on the way. Fears that nursing will lead to miscarriage or a malnourished newborn have no basis, even for mothers who are too queasy to eat much. Whether to wean is best left up to you—but if your child is less than a year old, it may be best to delay weaning at least until he is regularly eating solid foods and drinking from a cup.

Pregnancy often causes a decrease in milk supply. If your baby is much less than a year old and you notice your milk supply declining, you may need to supplement your milk with formula. Some nursing babies and toddlers wean themselves during their mothers' pregnancies. Others do not seem to mind the changes in the milk and show no signs of wanting to give up nursing.

Many women who nurse while pregnant experience tender breasts and sore nipples. These are due to the hormonal changes of pregnancy. Although this soreness usually goes away as the pregnancy progresses, there is no known cure for this problem except for weaning. Many women also feel especially tired at first—this again is a normal response to pregnancy. Plenty of rest helps combat fatigue, especially in the first trimester.

Some pregnant mothers may notice uterine contractions while nursing. No studies have shown that such contractions lead to premature labor, but if you have had a previous premature labor you should discuss this possibility with your doctor.

In the second and third trimesters, an excellent diet is essential for the nursing mother.

Tandem Nursing

Mothers who have nursed throughout all or most of their pregnancies may find themselves nursing an older baby or toddler along with the new baby. This may be overwhelming for some, particularly if the older child is nursing frequently. But many have found it to be a generally positive experience.

Because the breasts are receiving more stimulation than if the mother were nursing only one, the milk is usually plentiful. As a rule, the younger baby should be nursed first. Bumgarner's *Mothering Your Nursing Toddler* (1982) includes a detailed section on tandem nursing.

Weaning

Ideally, complete weaning occurs when both the baby and the mother are ready for it. Many times, though, a mother begins to think about weaning while her baby or toddler is still happily nursing. She may feel that weaning will make things easier—that it will put an end to night waking, make the baby more independent, or improve her own energy level. Some mothers have a self-imposed deadline for weaning and begin to feel pressured once it draws near. Others simply become fearful that their children will nurse forever if allowed. Most often, a mother considers weaning when other people suggest that the baby should no longer need to nurse. Criticism from friends, family, or health-care workers may be straightforward or subtle, but it often motivates a mother to end the nursing relationship.

All mothers have mixed feelings about nursing at times. Keep in mind that weaning will not help your child sleep through the night, improve your relationship with your partner, make you less tired

Putting two older nurslings to breast at once may mean getting them to sleep at once—and getting a much-needed break for yourself.

or less bored, or make the baby less dependent on you. Toddlers, especially, often demand to nurse more when their mothers become busier and when they receive little mothering except at the breast. At times that young children need more attention, ironically, mothers often feel most like they need some kind of a break. Weaning during these times can be terribly upsetting for a child, and for the rest of the family as well. Should the arbitrary date you had in mind for weaning arrive, there is no need to follow through if you and the baby are still enjoying nursing.

Everyone has her own opinion on how long a baby should nurse. Often this reflects her view of when a baby is no longer a baby. Many say children should be weaned at nine to twelve months, but year-old babies are just reaching 60 percent of adult capability for fighting infection, so breast milk still has immunological value for them. And no one can say when your baby or toddler will stop needing the breast for comfort. Your child has his own timetable for achieving independence, and weaning will not speed the process.

Knowing all this, you may still have trouble dealing with the disapproval of friends and family members. Families in particular can wield tremendous influence over a nursing relationship. You may be able to deal with criticism from others by either ignoring it or confronting it. Or you may choose to withdraw from those who are critical and find new friends who believe in nursing older babies; a mother-to-mother support group, such as La Leche League or the Nursing Mothers Counsel, is one place to do this. Finally, you might simply keep your nursing secret from those who don't approve.

Some babies stop nursing voluntarily at about nine to twelve months of age, especially first-born children. This may be because first-time mothers, fascinated by each developmental milestone, tend to encourage "grown-up" behavior by offering the breast less often. According to T. Berry Brazelton (1983) many infants at seven months and nine to twelve months show less interest in breastfeeding as a result of developmental events (such as crawling, standing, and walking). Perhaps some mothers interpret this temporary lack of interest as the baby's desire to wean.

When a baby is still nursing often and enthusiastically at the end of his first year, he will probably want to continue nursing throughout the second year and beyond. Some experts say a child rarely initiates weaning before the age of four. For this reason friends may tell you to wean by your baby's first birthday if you have definite feelings against nursing a three-year-old. You may fear that, if you wait, you will have a major struggle convincing your child to stop nursing in the months to follow. That toddlers seldom initiate weaning, however, doesn't mean they always fight it. Should you find yourself still happily nursing at your baby's first birthday, be assured that there will probably be several opportune times to wean and numerous techniques to accomplish weaning after a year of age and before the age of four.

You might rightly initiate weaning if you have definite feelings against nursing a toddler or nursing while pregnant. Weaning—or simply limiting the number of daily feedings—may also be best if you are starting to resent nursing. The decision to wean should be made carefully, not in reaction to a bad day or a temporary problem.

Timing is important once you've decided to wean. Keep in mind that weaning is a process rather than an event. Weaning initiated by the mother should ideally occur gradually and empathetically over several weeks, at least. And there are better times than others to initiate the process. If the child is particularly clingy and needy, if he has recently had a stressful experience such as moving or starting child care, or if you are actively trying to get him to sleep through the night, now is not the time to wean.

Some specific suggestions for weaning can be found in "Survival Guide for the Later Months." (For further advice, read *The Nursing Mother's Guide to Weaning* [see "Suggested Supplemental Reading"].) In general, mother-led weaning involves substituting for nursing something that the child enjoys as much. In this way weaning does not become a series of deprivations or rejections. If the pace of weaning is too rapid, most children will react with obvious unhappiness or increased dependency on a pacifier, a thumb, or a bottle. Occasionally weaning must be postponed for a few weeks because the child is simply unable to cope without nursing. Whether weaning is initiated by the mother or is a mutual undertaking, feelings of sadness are bound to arise as the final days arrive, marking the end of the precious months spent together nursing.

Once the nursings become infrequent, the breasts may look smaller and feel less firm. Still, most women can express milk for several months after nursing has stopped. The breasts typically regain their former size and shape within six months of weaning.

SURVIVAL GUIDE
for the Later Months

Biting
Night Waking
Nursing Strike
Weaning the Older Baby (Eight to Twelve Months)
Weaning the Toddler

Biting

Being bitten by a baby while nursing is a common yet unforgettable experience. Naturally, you let out a holler, take the baby from the breast, and tell her "No!" Just the right thing to do.

A baby most commonly bites before her teeth come in, often just before the top two teeth break through. Perhaps this is because her gums are sore. She is most likely to bite at the end of a feeding or when she is just snacking; she may have a playful look on her face as she goes about it. This behavior may continue for several days, but it usually ends as suddenly as it began.

Some mothers fear their babies will start biting once the first teeth have come in. This occasionally happens, but it is usually because other areas of the gums are sore, and not because the baby wants to try out her new incisors. While the baby is sucking, the tongue protects you by covering the lower teeth. In other words, so long as a baby is swallowing milk, she cannot bite.

Coping Measures for Biting

1. Keep your finger ready to end the feeding. Watch for a change in your baby's nursing pattern; as soon as she stops taking long even sucks and begins short choppy ones, end the feeding. If you notice a playful look on her face, end the feeding.

2. Should you miss the cues and get bitten, say "No!" loudly and sharply, and end the feeding. Do not nurse the baby again for at least half an hour.

3. Avoid letting the baby snack at the breast during this period of biting.

4. Offer the baby a cold damp washcloth or a chilled water-filled teething ring to chew on just before feedings.

Night Waking

Although some older babies and toddlers sleep well at night, many wake frequently, night after night. Your baby may in fact be waking more at night and napping less during the day than she did in the first few months. You may have thought that when your baby reached six months or older and started taking solid food that his nighttime wakings would diminish. You probably even know someone whose baby "sleeps through the night." But such a baby is atypical. When health professionals talk about sleeping through the night, they are referring to a six-hour stretch. Although some babies sleep a six-hour stretch, most breastfed babies wake two or more times a night. Many babies who slept long stretches in the early months wake more frequently later.

You may think something is wrong if your baby doesn't sleep through the night. You may wonder if she wakes because of teething, illness, hunger, thirst, digestive problems, wet diapers, chilling or overheating, superior intelligence, upcoming developmental milestones, or separation anxiety. Although any of these might perhaps contribute to night waking, the basic cause may simply be your baby's need for a snack and a cuddle.

As you may suspect, breastfed babies are less likely to sleep through the night. Chances are your friend's sleeping baby is already weaned or was never nursed at all. One study found that whereas weaned babies slept a median of nine to ten hours at a stretch at every age after four months, nursing babies slept in bouts of four to seven hours to the end of the second year (Elias et al., 1986).

Not only do breastfed babies sleep in shorter bouts than do bottle-fed babies, but nursing babies also sleep less overall. In the Elias study, weaned babies slept a median of thirteen to fourteen hours throughout the first two years, but nursing babies gradually lessened their total hours of sleep from a median of fourteen to a median of eleven hours.

Why do bottle-fed babies sleep in longer stretches than breastfed babies? Marsha Walker (1993), a lactation consultant, points out that babies formula-fed from birth have poor "vagal nerve tone"; that is, their autonomic nervous systems are measurably disordered. This makes them sleepier and less alert than breastfed newborns. Poor vagal tone in a newborn, by the way, is related to inferior motor and mental development for at least two years after birth.

Babies who are weaned after several months of breastfeeding may start sleeping through the night for other reasons. They certainly have waking episodes, as everyone does, but these babies fall back into deep sleep without any intervention from parents. Most have probably learned to go back to sleep alone—through the use of a thumb, pacifier, or bottle, through their parents' ignoring them, or perhaps with a sophisticated method such as scheduled awakenings, whereby a parent arouses a child in time to prevent spontaneous awakenings, until both spontaneous and scheduled awakenings are gradually eliminated. In most of these cases, the parents' desire for separation has overcome the baby's natural urge to be close to other human beings.

No one knows for sure why weaned children sleep more overall than those who are still nursing. It seems babies often nurse during light sleep; they release the nipple when they fall into deep sleep. This may be why a child who was obviously tired will, instead of falling asleep after a long nursing, wake up seeming completely refreshed. If nursing in a light-sleep state were counted as sleep, the average total hours of sleep might not vary at all between nursing and weaned children.

Whether or not you've identified a reason for night waking, you may be spending a considerable amount of energy trying to end it. Manipulating daytime naps, feeding solids late in the evening, giving pain relievers or cold remedies when the baby isn't sick or in pain, trying to keep the baby from falling asleep at the breast, consulting health-care providers, and trying different tactics in the middle of the night rarely work.

This is not to say that you shouldn't have your baby examined if you suspect a physical discomfort. She could be hurting from an ear infection (especially if she has had a runny nose in the past couple of weeks), or by teeth working their way in. Some babies who are distracted during many of their daytime nursings may wake often at night out of hunger.

Substituting pacifiers, bottles, or other comfort objects in the night is not likely to get you a full night's sleep, either. Most parents who try these things must get up at night to find them when their babies wake up crying. Besides, unless a bottle is filled with water, a baby risks developing tooth decay when she falls asleep at night drinking from one.

The only way you're likely to succeed at making your baby sleep through the night is to let her cry it out for a few nights or more. Several books tout this technique, perhaps the best known among them being Richard Ferber's *Solve Your Child's Sleep Problems: The Complete Practical Guide for Parents* (1985). The idea is to refuse to pick up your baby when she wakes during the night, but to let her cry herself back to sleep, until she learns that her crying is fruitless. Although this may seem drastic, many parents report that it has worked for them.

If you decide to try this strategy, choose a three- to four-day period in advance. When your baby wakes crying, go to her every five minutes. Lay her down; say, "It's night-night time"; and leave. Most babies cry up to an hour or so the first night, and for a shorter time the next two or three nights. If this technique solves your night-waking problem, you can still continue nursing during the day.

If this method seems too extreme or fails to work for you, you might consider the way nursing mothers all over the world have made night waking less disruptive: Sleep with your baby. Despite what people say, your baby won't be smothered by the covers or by your or your mate's shifting body. The baby won't keep you awake; babies with easy access to the breast rarely cry at night. After a few nights you'll adjust to the new sleeping companion, and her presence will not disrupt your sleep as much as would waking to her cries, getting out of bed, tending to her, and coming back to bed again. Neither you nor your baby will need to waken completely to nurse, and Dad won't need to waken at all.

If taking a baby into the parents' bed puts a damper on sexual activity, couples who have adopted this approach seldom complain about a lack of sex. Parents do mention how much they enjoy watching their baby sleep, cuddling her warm little body, and waking up with her in the morning.

Families have come up with many inventive ways to make the "family bed" more comfortable, safe, and convenient. You might buy a larger mattress, build a platform for mattresses placed side by side, or simply put your mattress on the floor. So your mattress stays dry, get a waterproof mattress pad; so *you* stay dry, double-diaper the baby or consider using disposables at bedtime. This will eliminate most nighttime diaper changes; when you or your mate must get up, a low-wattage nightlight will make things easier.

If you have doubts about sleeping with your baby, you might still try it for a couple of weeks before dismissing the idea. You can find more detailed advice on bed sharing in Tine Thevenin's *The Family Bed: An Age Old Concept in Child Rearing* (see "Suggested Supplemental Reading").

If you're still feeling worn out after you've found some way to get more sleep at night, you might examine your diet. Some lactating women may be vulnerable to fatigue because of vitamin B deficiencies. Although in such a case the baby will generally grow well and get the nutrients she needs from her mother's milk, her mother may suffer from low energy levels. Be sure you are eating plenty of whole grains, which are rich in B vitamins.

You might also consider supplementing your diet with brewer's yeast, a potent source of B vitamins that is considered more effective and faster-acting than B-complex supplements. Available in health-food stores, brewer's yeast can be taken as a tablet or as a powder to be mixed with juice or milk. Starting with the daily dose recommended on the label, you can slowly increase the amount to two to four times the daily recommendation (increasing the amount too quickly could cause diarrhea in you and your baby).

Nursing Strike

Although nursing strikes can occur at any time, they usually happen in the second half of the baby's first year. A nursing strike is distinguished from weaning by its suddenness. Some babies wean themselves between eight and twelve months, but they usually do so gradually.

Reasons for nursing strikes vary greatly. They may include teething, a cold, an ear infection, a painful herpes sore in the mouth, or a change in the taste of the milk. They sometimes happen after a prolonged separation between a baby and his mother, or after a baby has bitten his mother and been frightened by her response. Sometimes, when a baby has become used to a bottle and its rapid flow of milk, his refusal to nurse is a response to his mother's dwindling milk supply. Some authorities believe a nursing strike may precede mastery of a major motor skill, such as crawling, standing, or walking.

Although some mothers decide to turn a nursing strike into final weaning, in most cases the baby can be coaxed to resume nursing. Strikes typically last a few days, but they may go on for as long as two weeks.

Treatment Measures for Nursing Strikes

1. Try a change in position, or nurse in a quiet, darkened room.
2. So long as the baby refuses to nurse, pump or manually express your milk frequently throughout the day. Offer the milk in a cup rather than a bottle.
3. Try to determine the cause for the nursing strike. Consider having the baby examined to rule out an ear infection or other physical problem. Check your milk supply, especially if the baby has been nursing infrequently or has become increasingly dependent on a bot-

tle: Do your breasts feel empty most of the time? Is the milk slow to let down? Is the baby swallowing less?

4. Maintain frequent and close skin-to-skin contact with the baby without nursing. Offer the breast whenever the baby is sleepy.

Weaning the Older Baby (Eight to Twelve Months)

Weaning the older baby need not be hard, especially if she is crawling and busily exploring or has lost interest in some of her nursings. Ideally, weaning at any age should occur gradually, over several weeks at least. A good place to begin is with the nursing that the baby seems least interested in, most likely one during the day. Key to your success is providing an appealing substitute for the breast. This means offering not only something else to eat or drink, but also yourself. Nursing provides a mother's love and attention as well as food. You'll need to do a lot of cuddling and rocking, and activities like reading a book or playing on the floor together.

You must choose whether to wean to a cup or a bottle. Although the older baby is developmentally ready for a cup, if she has trouble swallowing from one, the bottle may be best. However, giving the baby a bottle can lead to other difficulties. If she is not carefully monitored, she can become overdependent on the bottle, lose interest in solid foods, and end up with serious tooth decay. If you wean the baby to a bottle, of course, you will probably need to wean her *from* it later on.

Unless the baby is well established on table foods and eating three meals a day, give formula before offering solid foods.

Although weaning may progress quickly for some babies, concluding in a month or two, other babies take longer, especially those who are especially fond of nursing or are reluctant to give up certain feedings. The first nursing in the morning and those before nap time and bedtime are often most loved by the older baby. It may take longer to eliminate these completely. For helpful advice, read *The Nursing Mother's Guide to Weaning* (see "Suggested Supplemental Reading").

Weaning the Toddler

Although the weaning process is similar at all ages, the toddler is often especially attached to the breast and deserves extra consideration. Weaning a toddler involves a good deal of time and attention.

Unfortunately, no one technique works for every mother and toddler. The best recommendations involve finding substitutions and distractions that may satisfy the child, while at the same time ensuring that his needs for food, love, and attention are met. No plan is likely to succeed, however, unless a mother is sure of her own desire to wean. Her attitude is most important to her success.

Before you begin, pay close attention to the child's nursing routine, and yours. Keeping a record for a few days, like the one below, may give you some valuable insights for developing an effective plan.

Time	Place	Interest level	Reason for nursing

Take note of when and where you nurse, the child's level of interest in nursing, and what you think prompted his demand for the breast. From the toddler's point of view, nursing may be just the thing whenever he is bored, frustrated, or tired, or he wants your attention or comfort—as well as when he is hungry.

From your observations, you should be able to identify which nursings are least crucial to your toddler and get some clues as to what type of substitutions will most likely satisfy him. Some nursings may be easily replaced with a nutritious snack or something to drink. Substitutions for toddlers may include any number of activities—playing with a special toy, reading a book, taking a walk, or visiting with another toddler. Warm-weather months may be an easier time to encourage weaning, as most toddlers enjoy exploring out of doors.

Although you may be able to substitute certain predictable daily nursings with other activities, if your toddler nurses sporadically all day you may sometimes need to coax him to postpone nursings. Delaying daytime nursings works well for some toddlers as long as some distraction is provided. This can be an effective way to further weaning.

Some of your nursings are probably associated with routines the two of you have established, and with recurrent situations in which your toddler wants to nurse to get your attention. Identify these instances so you can change the pattern. If you nurse in bed early in the morning, get up instead—get dressed and offer your child breakfast. If you have a favorite place to relax and nurse, stay away from it. If your toddler demands to nurse every time you talk on the phone, keep conversations short. If you sit in front of the television and nurse, do something else or he will want to continue with the usual pattern. Think creatively of ways your child can learn new routines.

You can also take advantage of your child's ability to understand language. Talk to him about nursing—especially if you are trying to postpone feedings. He may accept your wish to "save up the milk till nap time and night-night." Older toddlers may be able to agree to future weaning upon an upcoming birthday or other milestone, such as the start of preschool.

The bedtime nursing may continue as the child's favorite. Some mothers find this is a special time for themselves as well, and continue with it for weeks or months after other feedings have been abandoned. If you want to wean your toddler completely, your partner or another family member may be able to help the child establish a non-nursing bedtime routine.

For more advice on weaning your toddler, consult *The Nursing Mother's Guide to Weaning* (see "Suggested Supplemental Reading").

Resources for Nursing Mothers

Breastfeeding Support and Education

Nursing Mothers Counsel, Inc.
P.O. Box 50063
Palo Alto, California 94303
650-599-3669
www.nursingmothers.org
Nursing Mothers Counsel has chapters in various cities in California; in Denver, Colorado; and in Ft. Wayne, Indiana. Call for a local number.

Boston Association for Childbirth
    Education (BACE)
Nursing Mothers' Council
P.O. Box 600029
Newtonville, Massachusetts 02460
617-244-5102

La Leche League International
1400 North Meacham Road
Schaumburg, Illinois 60173
800-LA LECHE
847-519-7730
www.lalecheleague.org
Call between 9:00 A.M. and 3:00 P.M. CST for breastfeeding help or a referral to a local La Leche League group. Most white pages list a local La Leche leader's phone number under "La Leche League."

Lactation Professional Referral Services

International Lactation Consultant
    Association
4101 Lake Boone Trail, Suite 201
Raleigh, North Carolina 27607
919-787-5181
www.ilca.org
Call weekdays between 9:00 A.M. and 5:00 P.M. EST.

Breastfeeding National Network
    (Medela, Inc.)
800-TELL-YOU
www.medela.com
Call at any hour if you have Touch Tone dialing; if not, call weekdays between 7:30 A.M. and 6:00 P.M. CST.

Special Supplemental Nutrition Program for Women, Infants, and Children (WIC)

WIC is a federally subsidized program that provides nutritional information, counseling, and food to low- and moderate-income pregnant and nursing mothers and their young children. Some WIC programs also offer breast pumps to nursing mothers. Eligibility for WIC is determined by family income, as shown in the chart. The income figures are adjusted yearly, so current figures may be higher if you are reading this after June 30, 1999. A pregnant woman may be counted as two in figuring eligibility.

WIC Income Requirements, May 2, 1998 to June 30, 1999

Number of persons in family	annual	Maximum Gross Income monthly	weekly	hourly
1	$14,893	$1,242	$287	$ 7.17
2	20,073	1,673	387	9.67
3	25,253	2,105	486	12.17
4	30,433	2,537	586	14.67
5	35,613	2,968	685	17.17
6	40,793	3,400	785	19.67
7	45,973	3,832	885	22.17
8	51,153	4,263	984	24.67
over 8*	Add: 5,180	432	100	2.50

For each additional family member, add the amount shown to the maximum gross income for a family of eight.

To locate a WIC office near your home, look for a listing in the phone book or contact your county or community health department.

Nursing Bras

Although nursing bras are available at maternity shops and department stores, the selection of styles and sizes may be too limited for you. The companies listed here sell nursing bras by mail- and phone-order. Call or write for their catalogs.

Motherwear
320 Riverside Drive
Northampton, Massachusetts
   01062
800-950-2500
www.motherwear.com
Motherwear offers a wide variety of bra styles in sizes 32A to 48J.

Bosom Buddies, Inc.
1554 Emerson
Denver, Colorado 80218
303-860-0041
888-860-0041
www.bosombuddies.com
Bosom Buddies carries most brands of nursing bras, and special-orders from manufacturers as needed. The company provides fitting help by phone but is also willing to send bras in different sizes for you to try on; you can return those that don't fit.

Fancee Free Manufacturing
 Company
6609 Olive Boulevard
St. Louis, Missouri 63130
800-325-5088
Fancee Free carries many styles of nursing bras, in sizes 34C to 48J. Some styles have foam inserts for extra support and lift. Fancee Free bras are available in some maternity shops as well as by mail-order.

Medela
P.O. Box 660
McHenry, Illinois 60051
800-435-8316
www.medela.com
This leading breast-pump maker also carries soft-cup and underwire bras in sizes 32B to 46H, soft shoulder pads for use with any bra, and, for mothers who regularly pump their milk, a hands-free attachment kit for use with Medela bras. For referral to a local retailer, call 1-800-TELL-YOU.

Bravado
1159 Dundas Street East
Suite 140
Toronto, Ontario M4M3N9
Canada
800-590-7802
www.bravado.org
Bravado makes a comfortable, popular pull-on nursing bra of cotton and spandex, in five colors and in sizes from 32B to 46G and will custom-make larger sizes.

Colesce Coutures
P.O. Box 569390
Dallas, Texas 75356
800-487-4697
www.colesce.com
Colesce Coutures offers several styles of wire-free supportive bras, in over 200 sizes. Although the bras are not specifically designed for nursing mothers, the front flaps lower for breast access. A representative will come to your home and measure you for an exact fit. Call or write for a fitting or catalog.

Electric Breast Pump Rental

Medela, Inc.
P.O. Box 660
McHenry, Illinois 60051
800-TELL-YOU
www.medela.com
Call at any hour if you have Touch Tone dialing; if not, call weekdays between 7:30 A.M. and 6:00 P.M. CST. Medela will refer you to a local rental station where you can rent either a full-sized electric pump or the more portable Lactina Plus, a lightweight, fully automatic pump with an optional battery pack and an adapter for a car's cigarette lighter.

Hollister, Inc.
2000 Hollister Drive
Libertyville, Illinois 60048
800-323-4060
www.hollister.com
Call at any time to locate a pump rental station. Hollister will refer you to a local rental station where you can rent either a full-sized pump or the more portable Lact-Elite, a lightweight, fully automatic pump.

Breast Shells

Breast shells are used to correct inverted nipples during pregnancy and, sometimes, to protect injured nipples from friction against clothing. Many women find the flexible Soft Shells most effective and comfortable in treating inverted nipples.

Nurse-Dri Shields
Nurse-Dri Breast Shield Co.
P.O. Box 541
Corte Madera, California 94976
415-388-4818
$12.95 per pair, shipping included.

Medela Soft Shells
Medela, Inc.
(See address and phone number at left)
$14.00 per pair, plus $4.00 shipping.

Medela Hobbit Breast Shells
Medela, Inc.
P.O. Box 660
McHenry, Illinois 60051
800-435-8316
$12.00 plus $4.00 shipping.

Breast Milk Coolers

These insulated coolers are used to store and transport breast milk.

Medela Cooler Carrier
Medela, Inc.
P.O. Box 660
McHenry, Illinois 60051
800-435-8316
$22.00 plus $4.00 shipping. This cooler has room for a small manual or battery-operated pump as well as an insulated area for milk.

Medela Lactina Cooler Carrier
(See address and phone number above)
$33.00 plus $4.00 shipping. This cooler has room for the Lactina pump as well as an insulated area for milk.

Nursing Supplementation Devices

A nursing supplementation device provides supplementary milk or formula while a baby is breastfeeding. Such a device is most commonly used when a baby is adopted or a mother wishes to relactate after a period of not nursing. It may also help when a mother wishes to both build up and supplement a low milk supply, or when a baby has a weak or ineffective suck.

A supplementer usually consists of a plastic pouch to hold breast milk or formula and a thin, flexible tube that is placed on the breast, ending at the nipple. The baby must latch on to the nipple and the soft tube. As the baby nurses, he receives the supplement along with whatever milk his mother is producing. These devices should be used with the guidance of a lactation professional experienced with them. Currently they can be ordered from—

Supplemental Nutrition System
Medela, Inc.
P.O. Box 660
McHenry, Illinois 60051
800-435-8316
$43.00 plus $4.00 shipping.

Lact-Aid International
P.O. Box 1066
Athens, Tennessee 37371
423-744-9090
www.lact-aid.com
$38.50 plus shipping.

These devices may also be available in your area through a local lactation professional. Medela and Lact-Aid will be happy to refer you to any local source.

Nursing Pillows

My Best Friend Nursing Pillow
35 Leveroni Court
Novato, California 94949
800-555-5522
$39.95 regular, $45.00 extra large, plus $7.00 shipping.
This wearable pillow with a cushioned back support makes positioning the baby easier and sitting to nurse more comfortable.

Nurse EZ Twin
Basic Comfort, Inc.
445 Lincoln St.
Denver, Colorado 80203
800-456-8687
$42.95 plus $5.00 shipping.
The Nurse EZ Twin pillow circles a mother's waist to help her nurse more comfortably. The pillow is ideal for nursing twins simultaneously.

Nursing Stool

Medela Nursing Stool
Medela, Inc.
P.O. Box 660
McHenry, Illinois 60051
800-435-8316
$36.00 plus $4.00 shipping.

Modified Lanolin

Lansinoh
Lansinoh Laboratories
599-B Oak Ridge Turnpike
Oak Ridge, Tennessee 37830
800-292-4794
A 2-ounce tube of Lansinoh costs $9.95 plus shipping and handling. Call to order a tube or locate a local source. Lansinoh is carried at many drugstores and discount stores.

Pur-Lan 100
Medela, Inc.
P.O. Box 660
McHenry, Illinois 60051
800-435-8316
$2.50 for ¼ ounce; $6.00 for 1.3 ounces. Include $4.00 for shipping.

Electronic Baby Scale

Medela, Inc.
P.O. Box 660
McHenry, Illinois 60051
800-435-8316
Ask for the name of a nearby rental station or order directly from the company. Renting a scale costs approximately $28.00 per week.

Haberman Feeder

This feeder is designed for babies with cleft palates or other problems that make feeding difficult. Minimal effort is required for the baby to obtain milk.

Medela, Inc.
P.O. Box 660
McHenry, Illinois 60051
800-435-8316
$21.00 plus $4.00 shipping.

Breast Milk Storage Bags

These bags are constructed for leak-free milk storage. They are sturdier than bottle liners, which are often used for milk storage. To save time, milk bags can be used in place of bottles while pumping.

Mother's Milk Storage Bags
Breastfeeding Support Network
2028 West Ninth Avenue
Oshkosh, Wisconsin 54904
888-666-7224
For 25 bags, $7.20 plus $1.25 shipping.

Mother's Milk Freezer Bags
Hollister, Inc.
2000 Hollister Drive
Libertyville, Illinois 60048
800-323-4060
For 20 bags, $9.65 plus $3.00 shipping.

Determining Babies' Milk Needs during the First Six Weeks

Ten Percent Weight Loss

A newborn should lose less than 10 percent of her birth weight before she begins to gain weight. Find your baby's birth weight in the left column of the table. Look at the figure across from your baby's birth weight in the right column. If your baby weighs this amount or less, you'll want to compare her milk needs (see the following sections of this appendix) with your milk production, and take steps to increase her milk intake.

Birth Weight (in pounds-ounces)	10% Less	Birth Weight (in pounds-ounces)	10% Less	Birth Weight (in pounds-ounces)	10% Less
4-8	4-2	6-6	5-12	8-4	7-7
4-9	4-2.5	6-7	5-13	8-5	7-8
4-10	4-3	6-8	5-14	8-6	7-9
4-11	4-3.5	6-9	5-14.5	8-7	7-9.5
4-12	4-4	6-10	5-15	8-8	7-10
4-13	4-5	6-11	6-0	8-9	7-11
4-14	4-6	6-12	6-1	8-10	7-12
4-15	4-7	6-13	6-2	8-11	7-13
5-0	4-8	6-14	6-3	8-12	7-14
5-1	4-9	6-15	6-4	8-13	7-15
5-2	4-10	7-0	6-5	8-14	8-0
5-3	4-11	7-1	6-6	8-15	8-1
5-4	4-12	7-2	6-7	9-0	8-2
5-5	4-12.5	7-3	6-7.5	9-1	8-2.5
5-6	4-13	7-4	6-8	9-2	8-3
5-7	4-14	7-5	6-9	9-3	8-4
5-8	4-15	7-6	6-10	9-4	8-5
5-9	5-0	7-7	6-11	9-5	8-6
5-10	5-1	7-8	6-12	9-6	8-7
5-11	5-2	7-9	6-13	9-7	8-8
5-12	5-3	7-10	6-14	9-8	8-9
5-13	5-4	7-11	6-15	9-9	8-10
5-14	5-5	7-12	7-0	9-10	8-10.5
5-15	5-5.5	7-13	7-0.5	9-11	8-11.5
6-0	5-6	7-14	7-1	9-12	8-12
6-1	5-7	7-15	7-2	9-13	8-13
6-2	5-8	8-0	7-3	9-14	8-14
6-3	5-9	8-1	7-4	9-15	8-15
6-4	5-10	8-2	7-5	10-0	9-0
6-5	5-11	8-3	7-6	10-1	9-1

(continued)

Birth Weight (in pounds-ounces)	10% Less	Birth Weight (in pounds-ounces)	10% Less	Birth Weight (in pounds-ounces)	10% Less
10-2	9-2	10-12	9-11	11-6	10-4
10-3	9-3	10-13	9-12	11-7	10-5
10-4	9-4	10-14	9-13	11-8	10-5.5
10-5	9-4.5	10-15	9-13.5	11-9	10-6.5
10-6	9-5	11-0	9-14.5	11-10	10-7.5
10-7	9-6	11-1	9-15	11-11	10-8
10-8	9-7	11-2	10-0	11-12	10-9
10-9	9-8	11-3	10-1	11-13	10-10
10-10	9-9	11-4	10-2	11-14	10-11
10-11	9-10	11-5	10-3	11-15	10-12

Babies' Milk Needs During the First Five Days

Find your baby's age in the left column. At right is the amount of milk he needs at each of eight daily feedings.

Baby's Age, in Hours	Milk Needed per Feeding in Milliliters	in Ounces
24–48	15	½
48–72	20	⅔
72–96	30	1
96–120	45	1½

Babies' Milk Needs from Five Days to Six Weeks of Age

Follow these steps to determine how much milk your baby needs.

Step one. Weigh the baby naked, on an accurate scale, at least one hour after a feeding. Find the baby's weight in kilograms in the chart on the next page. If the baby weighs 7 pounds, 5 ounces, for example, look down the column headed "7" and across the row headed "5." The baby's weight in kilograms is 3.317.

Step two. To determine the approximate amount of milk a baby needs in a 24-hour period, multiply the baby's weight in kilograms by 6, and round the result to the nearest whole number.

Example: 3.317 kilograms × 6 = 19.902 ounces

If the baby weighs 3.317 kilograms, she needs approximately 20 ounces of milk per day.

Step three. Calculate how much milk the baby needs at each feeding. Divide the amount of milk the baby needs daily by the number of times she nurses in each 24-hour period.

Example: 20 ounces ÷ 8 = 2½ ounces

If the baby needs 20 ounces of milk per day and nurses eight times per day, she needs 2½ ounces of milk at each feeding.

| | | | | | Pounds | | | | | | |
Ounces	4	5	6	7	8	9	10	11	12	13	14
0	1.814	2.268	2.722	3.175	3.629	4.082	4.536	4.990	5.443	5.897	6.350
1	1.843	2.296	2.750	3.203	3.657	4.111	4.564	5.018	5.471	5.925	6.379
2	1.871	2.325	2.778	3.232	3.685	4.139	4.593	5.046	5.500	5.953	6.407
3	1.899	2.353	2.807	3.260	3.714	4.167	4.621	5.075	5.528	5.982	6.435
4	1.928	2.381	2.835	3.289	3.742	4.196	4.649	5.103	5.557	6.010	6.464
5	1.956	2.410	2.863	3.317	3.770	4.224	4.678	5.131	5.585	6.038	6.492
6	1.984	2.438	2.892	3.345	3.799	4.252	4.706	5.160	5.613	6.067	6.520
7	2.013	2.466	2.920	3.374	3.827	4.281	4.734	5.188	5.642	6.095	6.549
8	2.041	2.495	2.948	3.402	3.856	4.309	4.763	5.216	5.670	6.123	6.577
9	2.070	2.523	2.977	3.430	3.884	4.337	4.791	5.245	5.698	6.152	6.605
10	2.098	2.551	3.005	3.459	3.912	4.366	4.819	5.273	5.727	6.180	6.634
11	2.126	2.580	3.033	3.487	3.941	4.394	4.848	5.301	5.755	6.209	6.662
12	2.155	2.608	3.062	3.515	3.969	4.423	4.876	5.330	5.783	6.237	6.690
13	2.183	2.637	3.090	3.544	3.997	4.451	4.904	5.358	5.812	6.265	6.719
14	2.211	2.665	3.118	3.572	4.026	4.479	4.933	5.386	5.840	6.294	6.747
15	2.240	2.693	3.147	3.600	4.054	4.508	4.961	5.415	5.868	6.322	6.776

If the baby is taking eight feedings per day, however, you can skip step two, and instead multiply the baby's current weight in kilograms by 22.5. The result will be the amount of milk the baby needs at each feeding in milliliters.

Example: 3.317 kilograms × 22.5 = 74.6325 milliliters

A baby weighing 3.317 kilograms needs approximately 75 milliliters of milk per feeding. To find this amount in ounces, divide by 30.

Example: 75 milliliters ÷ 30 = 2½ ounces

The baby in our example needs 2½ ounces of milk at each of eight daily feedings.

If the baby is taking nine feedings every 24 hours, you can find how much milk she needs at each feeding by multiplying her weight in kilograms by 20.

Example: 3.317 kilograms × 20 = 66.34 milliliters

The baby weighing 3.317 kilograms and nursing nine times per day needs about 66 milliliters of milk at each feeding.

Example: 66 milliliters ÷ 30 = 2⅕ ounces

Since 30 milliliters equals 1 ounce, the baby needs 2⅕ ounces of milk nine times per day.

The Safety of Drugs during Breastfeeding
By Philip O. Anderson, Pharm.D., F.A.S.H.P., F.C.S.H.P.

If you are considering taking a drug while nursing, you are likely wondering what effects it may have on your baby and on milk production. Clear guidelines are sometimes hard to come by in this situation. This appendix will explain what you should consider before taking a particular drug, and how, if you take it, you can minimize its effects on your child.

The Excretion of Drugs into Milk

Almost any drug you take will reach your milk in some quantity. Although you would never want to expose your baby to a foreign chemical unnecessarily, the amount of a drug that appears in milk is usually not great enough to harm a nursing child. One group of researchers found that 87 percent of drugs taken by nursing mothers are transmitted to their babies in amounts of 10 percent or less of the mother's dose. Only about 5 percent of drugs reach the infant in amounts close to the mother's dose.

Several considerations are important when deciding whether to take a particular drug:

Your baby's age and maturity. Just as your baby becomes better able to move about as he grows older, his ability to metabolize and detoxify foreign chemicals and drugs improves with time. Premature infants have little ability to metabolize drugs; when a premie needs treatment for a medical condition, drugs are given in much smaller doses than they would be for a full-term newborn or an older infant. The amount of medication in a mother's milk that is safe for a one-month-old might be dangerous for a premature infant. Likewise, a baby who is several months old has a much greater capability of handling drugs in breast milk than does a one-month-old. And when an infant begins to eat solid food, he consumes less breast milk and, therefore, less of any drug it may contain.

Your needs. Maybe you have a serious medical condition that threatens your health and your ability to care for your child, and you must take medication for it. Or maybe you're suffering from only a minor discomfort, and can get by without drugs. Whatever your condition, you must evaluate its seriousness and the consequences of not taking a particular drug. Then weigh these consequences against the benefits of breastfeeding, as you see them. You may decide to pump your milk and discard it while you're taking the medication or, if necessary, give up nursing altogether rather than expose your baby to a potentially hazardous drug.

Only infrequently does a mother's medication make it necessary for her to completely stop nursing. Researchers in Canada found that many mothers who were prescribed an antibiotic for an infection failed to take the medication for fear of harming their nursing infants, even after being told that the drug was safe to use while nursing. Such action could easily cause a resurgence of the infection and the need for more potent antibiotics.

The duration of treatment. If you have a chronic health problem, such as high blood pressure, you may be taking a drug over a long period. But perhaps you need medication for only a few days, as is usual with many antibiotics, or even just once, as with an anesthetic for a dental procedure or a diagnostic agent for an X-ray. If only brief drug therapy is needed, you can usually avoid exposing your infant to harmful amounts of the drug with minimal disruption to your normal pattern of breastfeeding.

The history of the drug. If a drug has been used for many years—especially if it has been given frequently to infants or to nursing mothers—the risks it poses to the breastfed baby are quite predictable. This is not so, however, for drugs that are new on the market, for most herbal remedies, and for drugs that have never been used in children or infants. With no safety record to go on, health-care providers may vary in their assessments of the risks your baby faces from small amounts of the drug in your milk. You may get different advice from different physicians—your obstetrician and the baby's pediatrician, for example.

Unnecessary alarm and confusion is often caused by statements concerning nursing made by a drug's manufacturer in the *Physician's Desk Reference (PDR)* or in the package insert. These statements generally aren't written to help the nursing mother; instead, they usually reflect the manufacturer's desire for protection from legal liability in the absense of absolute knowledge about a drug's safety for breastfed babies. Unfortunately, many health-care providers use the *PDR* as their primary source of information on the use of drugs during lactation.

The persistence of the drug in the body. Some drugs are eliminated from the body after only a few hours, whereas others remain a long time and accumulate. Accumulation potential is measured by the "half-life" of the drug; it takes four to five half-lives for a drug to be eliminated from the body. Drugs with long half-lives are more likely to persist in milk than are "short-acting" drugs, those with short half-lives. Long-acting drugs are also more likely to accumulate in the baby and affect her health.

Coordinating feedings and dosage. If a drug is short-acting, or quickly eliminated, you may be able to time the doses in a way that will minimize the amount of drug in your milk at feedings. You might take a dose just after nursing, so the amount of drug in the milk peaks between feedings. If you are on a once-a-day medication, you might take it after the last feeding of the evening, and substitute milk expressed during the day or formula for the nighttime feedings; by morning the amount of drug in your milk may be down to an acceptably low level. These strategies work best with older infants who are nursing at infrequent intervals.

Part of the reason you can limit your baby's drug exposure this way is that drugs pass in both directions between your bloodstream and breast milk. As the drug levels in your bloodstream decrease, the drug in your milk will pass back into your bloodstream. When breastfeeding must be withheld because of drug therapy that may harm an infant, expressing milk is sometimes advocated in the mistaken belief that the drug will thereby be eliminated from the milk sooner. Because of the reverse passage of drugs from milk to the bloodstream and because only a very small fraction of the drug in your body is in your milk, pumping your breasts and discarding the milk ("pumping and dumping") has very little effect on the eventual amount of drug your baby gets from your milk. Pumping the breasts may be useful, though, in maintaining your milk supply and decreasing any pain from engorgement when you've temporarily stopped breastfeeding.

Route of administration. The way that you take a medication partially determines how much of the drug will get into your bloodstream and to your baby. Drugs you're given by injection go directly into your bloodstream and can reach the milk, but some injected drugs cannot be absorbed into the infant's bloodstream from her gastrointestinal tract. Medications you take by mouth usually appear in your bloodstream, except for some that are meant to work locally in the stomach or intestines. Significant amounts of drugs can be absorbed from drops and ointments placed in the eye. Vaginal and rectal products can also be absorbed into the bloodstream. Drugs taken through an inhaler generally reach the bloodstream in smaller amounts than the same drugs taken orally.

Since creams and ointments applied to the skin usually do not allow very much drug into the bloodstream, they are generally safe to use while nursing. Be careful, though, not to get a medicated ointment or cream on your baby's skin or allow him to get any into his mouth. If you are applying medication to your nipples, wipe them before nursing, and reapply the medication afterward.

The Effects of Drugs on Lactation

Not only may the drugs you take affect your baby directly, but some may influence your milk production. This can happen in a number of ways, since several hormones work together to control lactation. Some drugs are used deliberately to stimulate or stop milk flow; however, a few medications intended for another purpose have been shown to affect lactation. Those that have are identified in this appendix.

Side Effects in the Baby

Only infrequently must nursing be discontinued completely because of potential drug toxicity. Concern usually arises when the baby is a newborn or when the mother must take one of the most toxic drugs. But even drugs that are usually safe for nursing babies can occasionally cause mild but unpredictable allergic reactions, such as skin rashes, and sometimes more serious reactions. Minor side effects such as fussiness, drowsiness, and diarrhea also occur sometimes, but usually do not require medical attention. More serious side effects are rare.

If side effects or possible allergies become a problem for your baby while you're taking a drug, do not hesitate to seek help.

Common Drugs and Their Safety

In the following list, common drugs are grouped into categories and subcategories according to their uses. Noted are their potential effects on the breastfeeding infant and, where applicable, on lactation itself. Drug names that begin with a lowercase letter are generic; those that begin with a capital letter are brand names. A more complete listing of brand names is in the "Index to Common Drugs" at the end of this appendix.

If you can't find the drug you're looking for here, you might call the University of California, San Diego, Drug Information Service at 900-288-8273. Calls cost $3.00 for the first minute and $2.00 for each additional minute; most questions are answered in one to three minutes. Hours for this service are Monday through Friday, 9:00 A.M. to 5:00 P.M. Pacific time.

Acne products. Even though the manufacturer warns against it, *tretinoin* is safe to use during nursing if it is applied only to the face. Avoid touching your infant's skin with treated areas of your own skin, when you're nursing and when you're not. Other topical products, such as *benzoyl peroxide, clindamycin,* and *erythromycin* are also safe. *Isotretinoin,* which is taken by mouth, should not be used while nursing. Daily long-term use of *tetracycline* for acne is not desirable while nursing.

Anesthetics.

General anesthetics. Nitrous oxide is sometimes used for dental procedures and short outpatient procedures; it is rapidly eliminated from the milk. Injectable anesthetics such as *midazolam, propofol,* and *thiopental,* which are used for many short outpatient surgical procedures, have little or no effect on breastfed infants. Gaseous general anesthetics such as *desflurane, enflurane, halothane, isoflurane,* and *sevoflurane,* which are used in hospitals for major operations, have not been studied in nursing mothers and their babies. These drugs persist in the body longer than nitrous oxide, but appear unlikely to affect breastfed infants. Generally, by the time a mother feels sufficiently recovered from anesthesia to breastfeed, it is safe to resume nursing.

Local anesthetics. These drugs are given by injection for dental or other short procedures. Although many people refer to all of these drugs as "Novocaine" (the trade name for *procaine*), this old drug is rarely used now. Information on the effects of local anesthetics during nursing is available for only two drugs, *lidocaine* and *bupivacaine,* both of which are safe to use while nursing. Ask your physician or dentist if one of these can be used. Although other local anesthetics are unlikely to affect a breastfed baby, breastfeeding should be withheld as a precaution for about four hours after one of these other drugs is administered.

Antibacterials. Most drugs that are taken for infections reach the milk in only small quantities—quantities that would be too small to treat the same infections in your infant. Occasionally, though, these small drug amounts can disrupt the normal balance of microorganisms in a baby's mouth and intestines. This may result in diarrhea or diaper rash, caused by an overgrowth of yeast or other organisms in the bowel or, less often, thrush, an overgrowth of yeast in the mouth (see "Thrush Nipples," in "Survival Guide for the First Week," and "Fussiness and Colic," in "Survival Guide for the First Two Months"). Although these conditions generally are not serious and can be readily treated, it is important to watch for their signs while you are taking an antibacterial drug.

The likelihood of diarrhea or thrush occurring depends on the particular drug you are taking. Some antibacterials may cause other problems. In the unlikely event that blood appears in your infant's stool, stop breastfeeding, and call your physician immediately.

Aminoglycosides. These drugs (*gentamicin, tobramycin, amikacin*) are given primarily in the hospital, by injection. Amounts that appear in milk are very small and pose no danger to the breastfed infant.

Cephalosporins. These are similar to penicillins, and the same precautions apply. Occasionally allergies develop, so watch for signs of rash.

Cephalosporins, especially the more potent ones given by injection, may cause diarrhea and thrush.

Chloramphenicol. Some mothers who have used chloramphenicol report that their babies have been fussy during feedings or have refused the breast. Additionally, there is a small possibility that this drug may cause serious blood disorders in the infant. If the drug is essential, breastfeeding should be stopped, at least temporarily.

Clindamycin. Clindamycin is best avoided if possible, but a few days of therapy is probably safe, as long as the baby is closely monitored for diarrhea and bloody stools. Clindamycin presents less risk to the infant if it is given vaginally rather than orally or intravenously.

Erythromycin. This is a very safe drug that is often given directly to infants. It poses no unusual problems when taken by a nursing mother. See also "Acne Products." The closely related drugs *azithromycin* and *clarithromycin* appear to be equally safe.

Furazolidone. This drug is known to be poorly absorbed into the bloodstream after oral use. It is a safe alternative to metronidazole for *Giardia* infections if your infant is over one month old.

Isoniazid. This drug, used to treat tuberculosis, enters the milk in very small amounts. It poses a slight risk of damage to the baby's liver. Treating the mother with the drug, however, is safer than exposing the infant to tuberculosis. Watch the infant for signs of jaundice (yellowing of the skin and eyes).

Metronidazole. Breastfeeding should be stopped temporarily during use of this medication, but can be resumed 24 hours after the last dose. In the treatment of *Trichomonas* infections, metronidazole can be given as a single dose. For *Giardia* infections, a safer alternative is furazolidone if the infant is over one month old. For postoperative (including C-section) infections, consider clindamycin as a alternative.

Nitrofurantoin. This drug appears in small amounts in breast milk; these amounts are generally not harmful to infants over one month of age, but the drug should be avoided with younger babies.

Penicillins. These are very safe drugs that are often given directly to infants as treatment for infections. Occasionally allergies develop to penicillins, so the baby should be watched for rashes. If you see signs of rash, diarrhea, or thrush, call your health-care provider.

Quinolones. Ciprofloxacin, ofloxacin, trovafloxacin (and several others) have not been well studied in nursing infants and are not given directly to infants or children because of their possible harm to the developing joints. It is best to avoid these drugs, if possible, or to withhold breastfeeding while they are used. *Norfloxacin* is a quinolone that is excreted into milk in lesser amounts and is poorly absorbed by infants. Norfloxacin is sometimes an acceptable and safe alternative for urinary tract infections during nursing.

Sulfonamides (sulfas). Septra and *Bactrim* are common drugs that contain *trimethorprim* and the sulfonamide *sulfamethoxazole. Sulfisoxazole* is another common sulfa. Large doses of sulfas given directly to newborn infants can increase the risk of jaundice (yellowing of the skin and eyes). Other medications are usually preferred if the baby is premature or under two months of age. Combination tablets containing the red dye *phenazopyridine,* such as *Azo-Gantrisin* or *Azo-Gantanol,* should be avoided, particularly with newborns. Phenazopyridine is also the ingredient in *Pyridium.* This drug decreases pain on urination, but is not necessary to treat a bladder infection.

Tetracyclines. These are generally not given to children because they can cause permanent staining of the teeth. The amounts that appear in milk, however, are very small and are somewhat inactivated by the calcium in milk. In fact, no report has ever been made of tooth staining caused by a tetracycline in breast milk. Tetracyclines are therefore safe for a nursing mother to take for short periods, but should be used only if no other drug will work. One tetracycline, *minocycline,* can cause the milk to turn black. See also "Acne products."

Vancomycin. This drug is excreted into milk in only small amounts and is not absorbed into the baby's bloodstream. Vancomycin drug is safe to use during nursing.

Antifungals. Since *Amphotericin B* and *nystatin* aren't absorbed into the baby's bloodstream, you can safely use them in your infant's mouth or on your nipples to treat thrush (*Candida* infections), or take them by mouth yourself.

Clotrimazole (dissolved from a troche) and *miconazole* have been safely used in the mouths of infants with thrush, often successfully after nystatin has failed, and these antifungals are also safe to use for vaginal infections. Numerous related drugs, such as *butoconazole, oxiconazole,* and *terconazole,* are also available for vaginal use. Since little is known about their absorption into the bloodstream of a nursing infant, however, it is preferable to use clotrimazole or miconazole when a vaginal antifungal is needed.

You should not take *ketoconazole* orally or apply it to your nipples when you're breastfeeding, because this drug can be absorbed into the baby's bloodstream and poses some risk of liver damage.

Fluconazole is a potent, low-risk antifungal that is taken orally; a single dose for a vaginal infection is safe during nursing when other drugs have failed. At least two weeks of therapy is required in this situation.

Antiparasitics. Insecticides are used to treat scabies, a skin condition caused by mites, and pediculosis, or infestation with lice. An old medication that should no longer be used, *lindane,* is a very fat-soluble insecticide that can persist in milk and in the baby's body a long time. Although no harm due to lindane has been reported in breastfed infants, this drug is best avoided. If you do use lindane for scabies, you should forego breastfeeding for 48 hours after you wash off the drug (it is normally left on for 8 to 12 hours). Safer alternatives include *pyrethrins (Rid and A-200,* for example) or *permethrin (Nix)* for lice, and *permethrin (Elimite)* for scabies.

Mebendazole. Mebendazole is used for various worm (parasite) infestations. Since it is poorly absorbed from the intestinal tract, it is unlikely to cause adverse effects in breastfed infants. Contrary to an early report, it does not inhibit lactation.

Antivirals.

Acyclovir. Recent studies indicate that this antiviral drug is well tolerated by nursing infants.

Amantadine. This antiviral agent for influenza may decrease lactation and should therefore be avoided while nursing.

Antinauseants.

Most drugs used for nausea and vomiting are phenothiazine derivatives (see "Psychotherapeutic Agents"), such as *prochlorperazine, promethazine,* and *thiethylperazine,* taken in low doses. Another commonly used drug is *trimethobenzamide.* These drugs may cause transient drowsiness or, rarely, abnormal movements in infants, but are safe to use for a short time. Newer antinauseants such as *dolasetron, ondansetron,* and *granisetron* are used for more severe nausea, due to cancer chemotherapy or general anesthesia. Although these drugs have not been studied in breastfeeding women, they are not absorbed well into the infant's bloodstream if they do get into the mother's milk, so the risk they pose to the baby seems minimal.

Pain, arthritis, and migraine medications.

Acetaminophen. This drug is safe to use during lactation.

Aspirin. When large doses are taken daily, as for arthritis, problems can sometimes occur. Generally, it is best to avoid aspirin; ibuprofen is a better choice. If you take an occasional aspirin, do not breastfeed for at least one hour.

Nonsteroidal anti-inflammatory agents. Ibuprofen, diclofenac, and *flurbiprofen* appear in only minute amounts in milk; they seem safe to use while nursing an infant of any age. If your baby is over one month old, you can also safely use *fenoprofen, ketoprofen, naproxen, tolmetin,* and long-acting drugs such as *diflunisal, piroxicam,* and *sulindac.* The more toxic drugs *ketorolac, mefenamic acid,* and *indomethacin* should not be used during breastfeeding.

Narcotics. Drowsiness due to narcotics in milk occurs more commonly in infants than formerly thought—about 20 percent of breastfed babies whose mothers have taken narcotics are affected. The degree of drowsiness varies with the dosage, and babies under one month old are particularly susceptible. Limiting the dosage to one tablet (such as 30 milligrams of *codeine,* 5 milligrams of *hydrocodone* or *oxycodone,* or 65 milligrams of *propoxyphene*) every four hours is advisable; if needed, acetaminophen or ibuprofen can be taken in addition. Single injections of narcotics during nursing usually cause no problems, but intravenous narcotics given during labor can sometimes interfere with the establishment of lactation. *Meperidine* is the worst in this regard, *morphine* causes fewer problems, and *fentanyl* the least. Epidural administration causes fewer nursing problems. *Tramadol* has not been well studied, but it appears that only small amounts appear in milk. Tramadol is probably safe to use while nursing an older infant.

Ergotamine. This is a component of several products, such as *Cafergot,* used in the treatment of migraine headaches. Some ergot alkaloids cause vomiting in breastfed infants whose mothers have taken the drugs. Although ergotamine itself has not been studied, avoiding it while breastfeeding seems prudent.

Sumatriptan. Very little of this drug appears in milk, even when sumatriptan is given by injection, and the small amount that reaches the milk is poorly absorbed by the infant. Similarly, new drugs for migraine (*naratriptan, rizatriptan, zolmitriptan*) have not been studied during breastfeeding, so sumatriptan is preferable.

Dichloralphenazone. This component of *Midrin* releases chloral hydrate in the mother's body and can cause drowsiness in the breastfed infant.

Cancer chemotherapy. This group includes the drugs used to treat cancer, severe arthritis, and certain skin diseases. Because these agents are among the most toxic used in medicine, very few women have breastfed while taking them. Little is known about the passage of these drugs into milk, but even small amounts, should they reach the baby, could cause harm.

Because these drugs are used for only very severe conditions, it is usually more important for the mother to take the drug than it is for her to nurse her baby. Generally, therefore, breastfeeding should not be undertaken. Occasionally, some short-acting chemotherapy drugs are given in intermittent regimens that may allow a woman to resume nursing after stopping temporarily.

Immunosuppressive agents. These drugs are administered after an organ is transplanted to prevent its rejection. A few mothers have safely breast-fed their infants while taking *azathioprine* following kidney transplantation. *Cyclosporine* and *tacrolimus* are also used as immunosuppressants following organ transplantation. Limited experience indicates that it may be safe to nurse while using cyclosporine, but the infant should be carefully monitored. There has been less experience with tacrolimus, so nursing is inadvisable while taking this drug.

Anticoagulants. Some anticoagulants (such as *heparin, enoxaparin,* and *dalteparin*) are injected; others (such as *warfarin*) are taken orally. Injected anticoagulants can be safely used during lactation because they do not pass well into milk nor are they absorbed orally by the infant. Although warfarin was thought for many years to endanger the breastfeeding infant, newer evidence indicates that this drug is probably safe to use as well.

Ticlopidine and *clopidogrel* act in a different way to decrease blood platelet function. Neither has been studied during nursing, and so they both should be avoided.

Anticonvulsants. Anticonvulsants are used to treat epilepsy and other seizure disorders. Because these medications are used continuously and are often long-acting, they should be taken with caution during breastfeeding. Your baby may show no effects other than subtle behavioral changes, so be vigilant. Infants of mothers taking anticonvulsants tend to have more difficulty nursing and tend to wean earlier than other babies. You may need to have your infant's blood drawn to determine if the drug is affecting her.

Carbamazepine. This drug is known to pass into milk in significant amounts. Although most breastfed infants of women taking the drug show no effects from it, two such infants have had liver problems. Watch for jaundice (yellowing of the skin and eyes) while using carbamazepine.

Clonazepam. There is not much information on this benzodiazepine drug during breastfeeding, but it may make the baby drowsy.

Lamotrigine. There is little information on the use of this new drug while nursing, but two infants have been breastfed without harm while their mothers took it.

Phenobarbital. This drug has been given directly to infants for many years, usually with no severe adverse effects. You can probably use it safely during breastfeeding, although it may make the baby drowsy and less interested in nursing. The baby's behavior, weight gain, and blood levels should be monitored if there is concern. Women taking phenobarbital sometimes have to stop nursing.

Phenytoin. This drug has been used for many years by breastfeeding women. It is usually safe.

Primidone. This is similar to phenobarbital; the same precautions apply.

Valproic acid. Only very small amounts of this drug enter milk; rarely, however, the drug may cause liver damage or interference with blood platelets. Infants should be watched for unusual bruising or signs of jaundice (yellowing of the skin and eyes).

Cough, cold, allergy, and asthma medications. The various drugs used for these respiratory conditions are often taken together in combination products. These combination products are best avoided during breastfeeding. Usually only one or two symptoms are really troublesome, and a single-ingredient product can treat them effectively. For example, hay fever and other allergies can be treated with an antihistamine alone, and a cough can be treated with a cough syrup that has only one or two active ingredients. Drugs taken as nasal sprays or by inhaler generally reach the milk in lesser quantities than those taken orally. Sustained-release products should be avoided. Common sore throat lozenges (such as *Sucrets, Chloraseptic,* and *Hall's*) are safe to use.

Antihistamines. Antihistamines are used in many products for allergy, colds, coughs, and inducing sleep, although their use for colds is not justified. They can reach the infant through breast milk in amounts large enough to cause drowsiness or fussiness. High doses of antihistamines, particularly when in combination with a decongestant, may perhaps decrease milk flow. Use no more than necessary to control symptoms; often a single dose at bedtime is sufficient. If you are planning to use an oral product, choose one with 2 milligrams or less of *chlorpheniramine* or *brompheniramine* per dose, or 25 milligrams or less of *diphenhydramine* per dose, and avoid sustained-release products. *Loratadine* and *fexofenadine* are well tolerated by infants and are preferred over the older sedating antihistamines. *Cetirizine* is a newer antihistamine that can cause drowsiness and may possibly affect lactation. It is not a good choice while nursing.

Most nonprescription medications for motion sickness, such as *dimenhydrinate* and *meclizine*, are also antihistamines. One or two doses of these medications should have no effect on your infant other than temporary drowsiness.

Asthma inhalers and nasal inhalers. These may contain a bronchodilator (such as *albuterol, salmeterol* or *ipratropium*) or a corticosteroid (such as *beclomethasone, fluticasone, flunisolide,* or *triamcinolone).* All of these reach the mother's bloodstream in very low levels, so levels in breast milk are also low. Try to avoid swallowing excess medication after using an inhaler, because swallowed medication can enter the blood from the intestinal tract and reach the milk. Rinse your mouth and throat, and spit out the excess medication.

Decongestants. Nasal sprays *(Afrin, Nostrilla)* are preferable to oral drugs, especially if your baby is a newborn. A saltwater spray (such as *Ocean*) or rinse is quite safe to use during nursing. Oral decongestants can cause agitation or fussiness in your infant, and, most important, they may decrease your milk supply. If you are planning to use an oral product, choose one with 30 milligrams or less of *pseudoephedrine* or *phenylpropanolamine* per dose; avoid sustained-release products.

Theophylline. *Aminophylline* and other theophylline products have been well studied in breast milk. Occasionally they can cause jitteriness and agitation in infants, usually newborns. In general, they are safe.

Cough medicines. The two most common of these drugs are *guaiafenesin* and *dextromethorphan,* both of which are safe to use during breastfeeding.

Heart and blood pressure drugs. These drugs are rarely used in women of breastfeeding age, and information about them is therefore limited. Very little is known, in particular, about newer agents in the group.

ACE inhibitors. *Benazepril, captopril,* and *enalapril* are safe to use while nursing. No other drugs in this class have been studied during breastfeeding.

Angiotensin-2 blockers. None of these drugs have been studied in nursing women or in infants. It is best to avoid these medications until more is known.

Beta blockers. The oldest drug in the group, *propranolol,* is also the best studied and safest. *Metoprolol* and *labetalol* appear safe to use, too. These drugs reach the milk in insignificant amounts.

Some of the newer, long-acting drugs, such as *acebutolol, atenolol, nadolol, sotalol,* and *timolol,* reach the milk in higher quantities, and are also more likely to accumulate in the infant's bloodstream. These should be avoided while breastfeeding a newborn.

Calcium channel blockers. Information on *diltiazem, nifedipine, nitrendipine,* and *verapamil* is limited, but amounts in milk do not appear to be large enough to affect the nursing infant.

Clonidine. Clonidine and the related drug *guanfacine* may decrease prolactin secretion, and thereby reduce the milk supply. Clonidine reaches the milk in high levels, and breastfed infants have blood concentrations of the drug approaching those of their mothers. Other blood pressure drugs are preferred, but if these drugs can't be avoided, they should be used with caution during breastfeeding.

Digoxin. This drug is excreted into milk in only small amounts. It can be used safely during lactation.

Hydralazine. Amounts of this drug excreted into milk are small. Hydralazine can be used safely during lactation.

Methyldopa. Amounts of this drug excreted into milk are small. Methyldopa has been used safely during nursing for many years.

Procainamide. Amounts that reach the milk are small. This drug appears safe to use while nursing.

Reserpine. Because this drug can cause nasal stuffiness in infants, it should be avoided during lactation.

Diuretics. Large doses of diuretics, especially the most potent ones and those that are long-acting, can decrease milk production; in fact, diuretics have been used for this purpose. Their passage into milk has not been well studied, but small amounts might in rare instances cause rashes or other allergic reactions in infants.

Furosemide. This potent drug has been used to suppress lactation. It should be used cautiously, in small doses.

Hydrochlorothiazide. Given once daily in usual doses, this drug appears safe. Larger doses given several times daily could suppress lactation.

Other thiazides. Long-acting thiazides should be avoided during breastfeeding.

Chlorthalidone. This very long-acting diuretic should not be used during breastfeeding because it suppresses lactation. It may also accumulate in the infant's body.

Spironolactone. This drug appears in insignificant amounts in milk.

Ergot alkaloids. *Ergonovine* and *methylergonovine* are often given to mothers right after delivery to diminish uterine bleeding. Methylergonovine is preferred because ergonovine can suppress lactation. With the usual doses and the normal length of treatment, these drugs cause no problems in breastfed newborns. Large amounts, however, can cause nausea, vomiting, and diarrhea in the baby. These effects may also occasionally occur when the drugs are used beyond the immediate postpartum period. *Bromocriptine* has been used after birth to suppress lactation, but is no longer approved for this use because it can be severely toxic to the mother.

Gastrointestinal drugs. Many of the drugs in this class act in the stomach and intestine and are not absorbed into the bloodstream; they cannot, therefore, appear in milk. Other gastrointestinal drugs are absorbed, and can affect your infant through your breast milk. If a choice exists, choose a drug that is not absorbed.

Antacids. These are poorly absorbed and are therefore safe to use during breastfeeding.

Absorbable laxatives. Many of the more potent laxatives are absorbed into the bloodstream and have caused increased frequency of stools in breastfed infants. *Aloe, cascara,* and *senna* can affect the breastfed infant if taken in high doses, but are safe to use occasionally in small amounts.

Nonabsorbable laxatives. Bulk-forming laxatives such as bran and other fibers *(Metamucil, Fibercon)* are not absorbed into the bloodstream and are therefore safe to use. Likewise, stool softening agents such as *docusate* are not absorbable. *Bisacodyl* is a stronger laxative that is also not absorbed into your bloodstream. Saline cathartics such as *Phospho-Soda* and *milk of magnesia* are poorly absorbed and do not affect the composition of milk. *Glycerin* suppositories are safe to use.

Antidiarrheals. Attapulgite is not absorbed and can be used safely to firm loose or watery stools. *Loperamide* and *diphenoxylate* have not been well studied, but one or two small doses daily should pose little risk to nursing infants. *Bismuth subsalicylate (Pepto-Bismol)* is best avoided because of the large amount of absorbable salicylate it contains. Salicylate in large amounts can be toxic to the baby.

Cisapride. This intestinal stimulant, similar to metoclopramide, has unknown effects on the milk supply. Low concentrations of cisapride appear in breast milk, but the drug's effects on breastfed infants are also unknown. Use this drug with caution while nursing.

Histamine H-2 antagonists. During breastfeeding, *famotidine* and *nizatidine* are the preferred drugs in this class, especially if the baby is young, because they reach the mother's milk in the lowest amounts. *Ranitidine* is less desirable in this respect, but probably safe, and *cimetidine* is the least desirable of this group. If your baby is older and is no longer nursing at night, you can safely take a single daily dose of any of these drugs at bedtime just after the baby's last feeding of the day.

Mesalamine derivatives. Diarrhea and bloody stools have occurred on rare occasions in infants of mothers using one of the mesalamine derivatives, *mesalamine, olsalazine,* or *sulfasalazine.* These drugs may be used cautiously during nursing, but the baby must be closely observed.

Metoclopramide. This medication is used to stimulate normal intestinal movement. It has also been used to increase the milk supply in women who are producing insufficient quantities of milk, such as mothers of premature or sick infants, and in adoptive mothers. Metoclopramide does not appear to harm infants if it is used for two weeks or less. Because this drug may cause or worsen depression, however, it is best avoided in women with a history of depression, and it should not be used for long periods of time.

Proton pump inhibitors. Omeprazole is the only drug of this type that has been studied during nursing, and it has been studied in only one mother and her baby. Levels of omeprazole in the milk were very low, and the newborn infant was breastfed without harm. It may be best to avoid these drugs, however, until more is known.

Sucralfate. This locally acting drug is poorly absorbed into the bloodstream and therefore poses no risk to breastfed infants.

Herbals.

There is a mistaken tendency to think that because herbal medications are "natural," they never are toxic. This is not true. Each herbal product must be evaluated individually on its own merits and risks. Unfortunately, almost none of these products have been studied during lactation, and very few have been studied in infants. Because these products are poorly regulated in the United States, the quality and amounts of ingredients and even the ingredients themselves can vary widely from batch to batch and from one manufacturer to another. Additionally, because plant products may contain dozens of chemicals that can cause allergies, they may be more likely than other drugs to cause problems such as skin rashes in an infant or lead to plant allergies later in life. For all these reasons, it is somewhat of a gamble to use herbal medications during nursing. Information on some of the currently popular herbals follows.

Blessed thistle. This herb is being used to stimulate lactation, but there are no scientific studies that confirm its effectiveness. In fact, there have been no studies at all of the herb's effects during lactation. Blessed thistle appears to be fairly safe, but allergies have been reported.

Dong quai. There have been no studies of this herb during lactation. Dong quai contains two potentially toxic components: one is a known carcinogenic (cancer-causing) chemical, and the other can cause allergic skin reactions with light exposure. The risks of using this herb make it unacceptable during nursing.

Echinacea. There have been no studies of this herb during lactation or in infants. But echinacea appears to be fairly free from adverse effects.

Fenugreek. Most commonly used as a spice, fenugreek seeds are also used to stimulate lactation and increase milk supply. Although there have been no scientific studies on this use, fenugreek is a safe food substance that is used as the flavoring in artificial maple syrup.

Ginkgo biloba. There have been no studies on the use of ginkgo during lactation. Side effects are generally mild, but allergic skin reactions have occurred, and these could occur in your nursing infant.

Ginseng. Several different plants are referred to as ginseng. Although the most common forms (*Panax* species) appear to be fairly safe in adults, there is some evidence that they may have estrogen-like activity. Siberian ginseng (*Eleutherococcus* species) taken by one mother caused masculinization (pubic and forehead hair and swollen, red nipples) in her breastfed infant.

Kava kava. There have been no studies on the use of kava kava during lactation, but chronic use can cause dry, discolored, flaky skin and muscle weakness. Whether enough is transmitted through breast milk to cause these effects in a nursing infant is unknown.

Ma huang. This common herbal ingredient in diet products contains an amphetamine-like stimulant that can suppress lactation and may affect a nursing infant. These diet products, many of which contain other stimulants as well, should definitely be avoided during lactation. *See also* "Weight-loss Products."

Pycnogenol. There have been no studies of this product during lactation. The compounds in it appear to be without side effects.

St. John's wort. This herb appears to be effective in relieving mild depression. There have been no studies of St. John's wort during lactation, and it has not been studied in infants. With exposure to light, the herb may cause allergic skin reactions in fair-skinned persons. Also, the wisdom of self-medication for a serious condition such as depression is doubtful. St. John's wort should be avoided during lactation.

Hormones.

Several classes of drugs fall into the category of hormones, and each class must be considered separately. Because hormones are potent agents that might affect a baby's development, it is of paramount importance to consider both the dosage and the duration of therapy.

Antithyroid agents. Recent data indicate that, with due caution, breastfeeding during treatment with *propylthiouracil* is safe. The other antithyroid drug is *methimazole*. Although a moderate to large dose of methimazole can be dangerous to a breastfed infant, low doses appear to be safe. With any antithyroid drug, your doctor may recommend monitoring your infant's blood for adequate thyroid function.

Clomiphene. This synthetic hormone-like drug affects the activity of estrogen in the body and stimulates ovulation. There is no information on the drug's effects during nursing. Because clomiphene could have serious adverse consequences on the sexual maturation of your infant, and because it could remain in your body for weeks after you take it, you should discontinue nursing if you use this drug.

Estrogens. Estrogens have been used after birth to suppress lactation, but they are no longer used this way because they are sometimes toxic. Estrogen products such as *Premarin* and *Estrace* can probably interfere with nursing after oral or vaginal administration.

Contraceptives. Hormonal contraceptives can be divided into two categories: combination and progestin-only. The combination products contain estrogen; they decrease lactation, although long-term effects on infants' growth and development have not been found. The "morning-after" contraceptive is essentially a higher dose of a combination contraceptive taken twice in one day. This brief exposure should not adversely affect your infant and should have only a minimal and temporary effect on lactation. If you plan to use hormonal contraception, progestin-only oral products such as *norethindrone (Micronor, Nor-Q.D.)* or *norethynodrel (Ovrette)*, or progestins given by injection *(Depo-Provera)* or implantation *(Norplant)* are preferable. Because hormonal contraceptives can interfere with the establishment of lactation, you should wait at least six weeks after your baby's birth before taking any.

Corticosteroids. Drugs in this category include *cortisone, methylprednisolone, prednisone,* and *triamcinolone.* Low doses and short courses of therapy (up to two weeks) appear to pose no harm to breastfed infants. Of concern are long courses of treatment (several weeks to months) with moderate to large doses. Although only a small fraction of each dose appears in breast milk, no one knows what these amounts might do to the developing infant.

DHEA. This hormone-like drug is available without a prescription. There have been no studies of DHEA during lactation, but it is a chemical normally present in the body. Women of childbearing age, however, have near maximum amounts in their body. Because additional DHEA taken as a supplement may affect the infant or suppress lactation, you should avoid taking this drug during nursing.

Insulin. Insulin therapy for diabetes mellitus is like thyroid replacement in that it restores that which is missing. Diabetic mothers using insulin can nurse their infants, but may need to reduce each insulin dose to about 75 percent of its prepregnancy level. Since insulin is inactivated in the baby's stomach, none that enters the milk will be absorbed into the infant's bloodstream.

Progesterone. This natural hormone is sometimes given in suppositories for premenstrual syndrome. It is also found in one type of intrauterine contraceptive device, or IUD *(Progestasert).* Amounts of progesterone that appear in breast milk are small, and they are not absorbed by the infant.

Thyroid. Thyroid products have one major, valid use—to replace the thyroid hormone that is lacking in the bloodstream. When a woman takes proper doses, her thyroid levels become approximately normal. Thyroid replacement, therefore, poses no risks to the breastfed infant. However, large daily doses of thyroid hormone (more than about 100 micrograms of *levothyroxine*) may affect the infant.

Lipid-lowering drugs. None of the cholesterol-lowering drugs have been studied during nursing. Because cholesterol is essential for the proper development of the infant's brain and nervous system, cholesterol-lowering drugs that can enter the milk should not be taken during nursing. The most potent and commonly used among these drugs are called "statins"; they include *atorvastatin, cerivastatin, fluvastatin, lovastatin, pravastatin,* and *simvastatin.* Other drugs that can enter the milk are called "fibrates"; they include *clofibrate, fenofibrate,* and *gemfibrozil.* All of these drugs should be avoided during nursing. *Cholestyramine* and *colestipol* are resins that work only in the mother's intestinal tract and therefore can be used during nursing. It is not known whether high-dose *niacin* can affect the nursing infant.

Psychotherapeutic agents. For most of these agents, little is known about their excretion into milk or their effects on infants. Undertake nursing with caution if you are using one of these drugs.

Major tranquilizers. These drugs include the *phenothiazines,* such as *chlorpromazine, thioridazine, trifluoperazine, perphenazine,* and *fluznphenazine;* the closely related *thioxanthenes,* such as *thiothixene;* and the *butyrophenones,* such as *haloperidol.* Small amounts of these drugs appear in breast milk, and occasionally they cause drowsiness in breastfed infants. Long-term effects on breastfed infants are not well known; however, there is currently no evidence that the small amounts excreted into milk are harmful, and one study found no altered development in infants exposed to these drugs through breast milk. Nursing is not recommended during *clozapine* therapy because a serious side effect—a decrease in white blood cells—has occurred in breastfed infants.

Antidepressants. There is controversy about how the small amounts of tricyclic antidepressants, such as *amitriptyline, imipramine, doxepin, nortriptyline,* and *desipramine* may affect the growth and development of the breastfed infant, but no harmful long-term effects have ever been shown to occur. Drowsiness can result with some of the more sedating drugs, such as doxepin, which should be avoided. Nortriptyline appears to be the safest of all the antidepressants during breastfeeding. It appears in only small amounts in milk, and little or none reaches the infant's bloodstream. If possible, take tricyclic antidepressants only in the evening after the final nursing of the day.

Because *fluoxetine* is very long-acting, it should not be used when a nursing baby is less than one or two months old. Colic, fussiness, and decreased weight gain have occurred in young babies whose mothers were using fluoxetine. Infants over six months can probably tolerate the drug better. *Citalopram* should not be used by breastfeeding women, since it appears in fairly large amounts appear in milk and may cause drowsiness in an infant. The related drugs *fluvoxamine* and *paroxetine* have been studied less, but are shorter-acting than fluoxetine, and so should be better tolerated by a baby.

Sertraline has been well studied during lactation and does not seem to affect nursing infants. It is a good choice when an antidepressant is needed during nursing.

Other antidepressants, such as *amoxapine, bupropion, maprotiline, nefazodone* and *trazodone,* have been less well studied, so no judgment can be made on their safety. *Venlafaxine* appears in relatively high amounts in breast milk. Experience with it during breastfeeding is very limited, but no side effects have been seen in nursing babies. Still, it should be avoided during nursing, if possible.

The monoamine oxidase inhibitors *phenelzine* and *tranylcypromine* are very potent drugs and should not be used while breastfeeding.

Lithium. This drug reaches breast milk in significant levels and can accumulate in the bloodstream of the premature or newborn infant. A healthy infant may be breastfed during lithium therapy, but careful monitoring—including, perhaps, of his lithium blood level—is essential. Since an infant may show symptoms of lithium poisoning if he becomes dehydrated due to diarrhea or a viral illness, you should stop breastfeeding if your infant becomes ill for any reason.

Sedatives and sleep medications. Several types of drugs are included in this category. Although all of them can make your infant drowsy, some are more likely to do so than others. The drugs also differ in how long they persist in the body, which affects their tendency to accumulate in infants.

Barbiturates. Drugs in this class include *amobarbital, butalbital, pentobarbital, phenobarbital, secobarbital,* and others. All may occasionally cause drowsiness in a breastfed infant, but none are particularly hazardous to the baby otherwise, unless he becomes so drowsy that he nurses less.

Benzodiazepines. Of all sedative drugs, these are currently the most frequently used. They include *diazepam, chlordiazepoxide, flurazepam, triazolam,* and *alprazolam.* Although these drugs are safe in an adult, an infant does not readily metabolize them; they can accumulate in the infant's body. This may make a baby drowsy, and, in some cases, may interfere with the binding of bilirubin in the bloodstream. These problems are accentuated in premature and newborn babies. Preferable benzodiazepines, including *oxazepam* and *lorazepam,* are short-acting and reach breast milk in lesser amounts, and are therefore unlikely to cause drowsiness.

Buspirone. Since no information exists on the effects of this drug during lactation, buspirone is best avoided during nursing.

Chloral hydrate. Though old, this drug is still used sometimes. It has caused drowsiness in infants, but it is safe for occasional use.

Over-the-counter sleep medications. These usually contain *diphenhydramine;* the general precautions for the sedating antihistamines apply. (See "Cough, Cold, Allergy, and Asthma Medications.")

Iodine and iodide. Rarely, iodide drugs such as *potassium iodide (SSKI)* are prescribed as expectorants. Use of *povidone iodine,* even on the skin or as a douche, can also result in high iodine blood levels in the mother. Iodine becomes concentrated in milk and subsequently in your infant's thyroid gland, possibly causing abnormal thyroid function; iodide rashes have also occurred in breastfed infants. Iodides should not be used during lactation. See also "Radio-opaque Agents."

Interferons. Several interferon drugs are available. These drugs are large molecules that are unlikely to pass into milk, as was found in a study of a breastfeeding woman who was taking interferon alfa. Also, the drugs are active only when given by injection, so any interferon that were to reach the milk would have little effect on a nursing infant.

Muscle relaxants. Most of these drugs have not been studied during nursing. Muscle relaxants taken by mouth, such as *carisoprodol, chlorzoxazone, diazepam,* and *methocarbamol,* are sedatives, and can be expected to cause drowsiness in breastfed infants. *Cyclobenzaprine* causes less sedation and probably doesn't reach high levels in milk, but it has not been studied during nursing. In general, it is best to avoid these drugs while breastfeeding, if possible. Taking ibuprofen or acetaminophen along with mild to moderate exercise will usually ease muscle spasms and pain as well as muscle relaxants could.

Vaccines and skin tests. No vaccine or skin test (such as the one for tuberculosis [PPD]), when given to a mother, is known to pose a hazard to her breastfed infant. Killed vaccines, including *diphtheria-tetanus, hepatitis A* and *B, injectable polio,* and *influenza* vaccines, are inactive in breast milk. Although live vaccines are occasionally transmitted through breast milk, they do not endanger the baby. Live vaccines include *measles, mumps, rubella, oral typhoid, varicella,* and *oral polio.* The U.S. Centers for Disease Control (CDC) states that no vaccination of any type should be withheld from a woman or delayed because she is breastfeeding.

Weight-loss products. Excessive weight loss by any method during lactation should be avoided, because many fat-soluble environmental contaminants (such as some insecticides) are stored in body fat. When body fat is lost, contaminants are released into the bloodstream and appear in the fat of breast milk in larger than usual amounts. In addition, some weight loss agents can affect infants or the milk supply. *Chromium picolinate* is probably safe, however, in doses of 200 micrograms or less daily. Many weight-loss products contain vitamins that may also be in multivitamin products prescribed by your doctor. If you take the two products together, your vitamin intake may be excessive.

Radiologic diagnostic agents. A number of compounds are used in the X-ray diagnosis of various conditions. These compounds fall into three categories: MRI contrast agents, radio-opaque contrast agents, and radioactive agents. The radiologist administering the tests will probably have guidelines on breastfeeding with the specific agents. X-rays of your teeth or broken bones pose no hazard to your breastfed infant.

MRI contrast agents. These agents, *gadodiamide* and *gadopentetate,* contain *gadolinium* rather than iodine, and are relatively safe and rapidly eliminated. Wait six to twelve hours after taking one of these agents before resuming nursing.

Radio-opaque agents. These are generally compounds that contain iodine, but they vary in the amount of iodine that can pass into milk. Many have no free iodine and therefore pose little risk to the breastfed infant. Others require that the mother stop nursing for several hours after use.

Radioactive agents. Breastfeeding must be stopped for a time after these agents are administered. The period of time varies depending on the agent and the dose given; a few of these agents persist in breast milk for so long that the baby must be completely weaned. For nursing mothers with overactive thyroid glands, the most commonly prescribed of these agents are *iodine-123* (for diagnosis) and *iodine-131* (for treatment). Although iodine-123 is eliminated in two to three days, it leaves the long-lasting by-product *iodine-124.* Experts disagree about the safety of these drugs, but it seems prudent to stop nursing permanently after using them. *Technetium (pertechnetate)* is a suitable alternative for diagnostic use.

After exposure to some of these agents, your body could give off significant amounts of radiation, particularly at close range. This means that not only will you have to stop breastfeeding, but you may not be able to hold your baby for some time, since doing so would expose her to significant radiation.

Nonmedical drugs. Since drugs used for nontherapeutic purposes are not essential to the well-being of the mother, and since their effects on a breastfed infant are often unknown, their use is generally discouraged. Additionally, even small amounts could cause positive drug tests in your infant's urine, which with some drugs could lead to legal problems.

Alcohol. Alcohol readily passes into the milk. Large amounts of alcoholic beverages consumed over a short time can make a baby drunk and can inhibit the let-down reflex. Right after you drink an alcoholic beverage, your infant may suck more but consume up to 25 percent less milk. Heavy daily drinking can lead to hormonal imbalances in a breastfed infant, and even small to moderate amounts of alcohol taken daily or nearly every day while nursing appear to cause delayed muscular development and coordination in infants, although the severity of this problem depends on the amount of alcohol used. An occasional alcoholic beverage probably does not pose a serious danger to the infant, but it is prudent to wait at least two hours per drink before nursing, and to refrain from daily or near-daily alcohol use.

Amphetamines. Amphetamine and *methamphetamine* ("crystal," "crystal meth") have not been formally studied during nursing. However, they are potent stimulants. Breastfeeding mothers who take these drugs often have fussy infants who cry a lot, cannot be comforted easily, and do not sleep well. Amphetamines probably also inhibit the mother's milk production. These drugs should not be used during nursing; if they are, the mother should temporarily stop nursing for 24 to 48 hours after taking them.

Caffeine. Low to moderate intake of beverages containing caffeine is unlikely to cause problems in the infant, since the amount of caffeine that reaches the milk is usually small. But very high caffeine intake (more than ten cups of coffee per day, for example) can make the baby jittery and agitated.

Cocaine. Cocaine is extremely toxic to infants because they metabolize it slowly. Great agitation and continuous crying are often noted in breastfed infants of cocaine users; some of these babies have convulsions; and some have even died from cocaine poisoning. Cocaine must be avoided during nursing. A mother who does take cocaine should stop breastfeeding for at least 24 to 48 hours afterward.

Marijuana. There are few reports of the effects of marijuana in breastfed babies. After a single use, marijuana levels in milk are apparently low, but the active component of the drug is very fat-soluble and can build up in the body with daily or near-daily use. Because milk has a high fat content, marijuana levels are probably high in the milk of chronic users. Note, too, that an infant in the same room with a smoker will breathe in significant quantities of marijuana. Breastfed infants whose mothers use marijuana have shown delayed muscular development and coordination.

Phencyclidine (PCP). Large amounts of this drug have been measured in the breast milk of users. PCP must be entirely avoided during breastfeeding.

Narcotics. Large doses can cause narcotic effects and addiction in breastfed infants. Narcotic addicts should not breastfeed. The safety of *methadone* maintenance during breastfeeding depends on the methadone dose.

Hallucinogens. Information is lacking on the effects of these drugs during breastfeeding; however, levels in milk should be low by the time the mother has stopped feeling the effects of the drug.

Tobacco. Nicotine from smoking tobacco appears in breast milk. Other toxic substances in smoke probably reach the milk as well. Smoking interferes with lactation, causing smokers to stop nursing and start supplementing sooner than nonsmokers. If you smoke, your infant is more likely to have colic symptoms and more respiratory infections than if you did not smoke. Additionally, although breastfeeding reduces the risk of sudden infant death syndrome (SIDS), smoking negates this advantage. If you can't stop smoking while you are nursing, you should (1) decrease your smoking as much as possible, (2) avoid smoking just before nursing, and (3) avoid smoking in the same room with your baby. Using a *nicotine* patch or nicotine chewing gum during breastfeeding is probably safer than smoking, although studies have not been performed on nicotine patches or gum during lactation.

Index to Common Drugs

Each brand name is listed in capital letters; the corresponding generic name is given after it. All generic names that do not appear as headings in the text are followed here by cross-references to the relevant sections. The names of combination products are followed by lists of the ingredients they contain; see the separate entry for each ingredient. Not all brands are listed, so if you can't find the name of a particular product in this list, look under the generic name of its ingredient or ingredients.

Selected References

American Academy of Pediatrics. "Report on the Assessment of Scientific Evidence Relating to Infant-Feeding Practices and Infant Health." *Pediatrics* 74 (1984).

———. "Policy Statement: Breastfeeding and the Use of Human Milk." *Pediatrics* 100 (1997): 1035–39.

Auerbach, Kathleen G. "Employed Breastfeeding Mothers: Problems They Encounter." *Birth* 11 (1984): 17–20.

Auerbach, Kathleen G., and Laurence Gartner. "Breastfeeding and Human Milk: Their Association with Jaundice in the Neonate." *Clinics in Perinatology* 14 (1987): 89–107.

Auerbach, Kathleen G., and E. Guss. "Maternal Employment and Breastfeeding: A Study of 567 Women's Experiences." *American Journal of Disease in Childhood* 138 (1984): 958–60.

Bauer, G., et al. "Breastfeeding and Cognitive Development of Three Year Old Children." *Psychology Report* 68 (1991): 1218.

Bishop, N., M. McGraw, and N. Ward. "Aluminum in Infant Formulas." *Lancet* 1 (1989): 490.

Brazelton, T. Berry. *Infants and Mothers: Differences in Development.* Rev. ed. New York: Delta/Seymour Lawrence, 1983.

Brewster, Dorothy Patricia. *You Can Breastfeed Your Baby . . . Even in Special Situations.* Emmaus, Penn.: Rodale Press, 1979.

Brown, Marie Scott, and Joan T. Hurlock. "Preparation of the Breast for Breastfeeding." *Nursing Research* 24 (1975): 448–51.

Byers, T., et al. "Lactation and Breast Cancer: Evidence for a Negative Association in Pre-Menopausal Women." *American Journal of Epidemiology* 121 (1985): 664–74.

Davis, M. K., D. A. Savitz, and B. I. Graubard. "Infant Feeding and Childhood Cancer." *Lancet* 2 (1988): 365–68.

DeCarvalho, M., M. Hall, and D. Harvey. "Effects of Water Supplementation on Physiological Jaundice in Breast-fed Babies." *Archives of Disease in Childhood* 56 (1981): 568–69.

Ehrenkranz, R., and B. Ackerman. "Metoclopromide Effect on Faltering Milk Production by Mothers of Premature Infants." *Pediatrics* 78 (1986): 614–20.

Elias, Marjorie F., et al. "Sleep/Wake Patterns of Breastfed Infants in the First 2 Years of Life." *Pediatrics* 77 (1986): 322–29.

Ferber, Richard. *Solve Your Child's Sleep Problems: The Complete Practical Guide for Parents.* New York: Simon and Schuster, 1985.

Frantz, Kittie B., Paul M. Fleiss, and Ruth A. Lawrence. "Management of the Slow-Gaining Breastfed Baby." *Keeping Abreast Journal* 3 (1978): 287–308.

Friedland, G., and R. Klein. "Transmission of the Human Immunodeficiency Virus." *New England Journal of Medicine* 317 (1987): 1125–35.

Gwinn, M. L., et al. "Pregnancy, Breastfeeding, and Oral Contraceptives and the Risk of Epithelial Ovarian Cancer." *Journal of Clinical Epidemiology* 43 (1990): 559–68.

Hahn-Zoric, M., et al. "Antibody Responses to Parenteral and Oral Vaccines Are Impaired by Conventional and Low Protein Formulas as Compared to Breastfeeding." *Acta Paediatrica Scandanavica* 79 (1990): 1137–42.

Huggins, Kathleen, and Sharon Billon. "Twenty Cases of Persistent Sore Nipples: Collaboration Between Lactation Consultant and Dermatologist." *Journal of Human Lactation* 9 (1993): 155–60.

Jensen, Rima. "Fenugreek—Overlooked But Not Forgotten." *UCLA Lactation Alumni Association Newsletter* 1 (1992): 2–3.

Kavanaugh, Karen, et al. "Getting Enough: Mothers' Concerns about Breastfeeding a Preterm Infant after Discharge." *JOGNN* 24 (1995): 23–32.

Keating, J. P., G. J. Schears, and P. R. Dodge, "Oral Water Intoxication in Infants: An American Epidemic." *American Journal of Disease in Childhood* 145 (1991): 985–90.

Kennedy, Kathy, et al. "Consensus Statement on the Use of Breastfeeding as a Family Planning Method." *Contraception* 39 (1989): 477–96.

Koetting, C. A., and G. M. Wardlaw. "Wrist, Spine, and Hip Bone Density in Women with Variable Histories of Lactation." *American Journal of Clinical Nutrition* 48 (1988): 1479–81.

Kowalchik, Claire, and William H. Hylton, eds. *Rodale's Illustrated Encyclopedia of Herbs*. Emmaus, Penn.: Rodale Press, 1987.

Labbok, M. H., and G. E. Hendershot. "Does Breastfeeding Protect Against Malocclusion? Analysis of the 1981 Child Health Supplement to the National Health Interview Survey." *American Journal of Preventative Medicine* 3 (1987): 227–32.

La Leche League International. *The Womanly Art of Breastfeeding*. Franklin Park, Ill.: La Leche League International, 1997.

Lawrence, Ruth A. *Breastfeeding: A Guide for the Medical Profession*. St. Louis: C.V. Mosby, 1994.

———. *A Review of the Medical Benefits and Contraindications to Breastfeeding in the United States*. Arlington, Virginia: National Center for Education in Maternal and Child Health, 1997.

Layde, P. M., et al. "The Independent Associations of Parity, Age of First Full-Term Pregnancy, and Duration of Breastfeeding with the Risk of Breast Cancer." *Journal of Clinical Epidemiology* 42 (1989): 963–73.

Lucas, A., et al. "Breastmilk and Subsequent Intelligence Quotient in Children Born Preterm." *Lancet* 339 (1992): 261–64.

Mayer, E. J., et al. "Reduced Risk of IDDM among Breastfed Children." *Diabetes* 37 (1988): 1625–32.

McJunkin, J. E., W. G. Bithoney, and M. C. McCormick. "Errors in Formula Concentration in an Outpatient Population." *Journal of Pediatrics* 111 (1987): 848–50.

McTiernan, A., and D. B. Thomas. "Evidence for a Protective Effect of Lactation on Risk of Breast Cancer in Young Women." *American Journal of Epidemiology* 124 (1986): 353–58.

Meier, Paula. "A Program to Support Breastfeeding in the High-Risk Nursery." *Perinatology/Neonatology* 4 (1980): 43–48.

———. *Professional Guide to Breastfeeding Premature Infants.* Columbus, Ohio: Abbott Laboratories, 1997.

Meier, Paula, and G. Anderson. "Responses of Small Preterm Infants to Bottle- and Breast-feeding." *Maternal-Child Nursing* 12 (1987): 97–105.

Merrett, T. G., et al. "Infant Feeding and Allergy: Twelve Month Prospective Study of 500 Babies Born in Allergic Families." *Annals of Allergy* 61 (1988): 13–20.

Michigan Department of Public Health. *Minutes of the Panel on Recommendations Relating to PBB and Nursing Mothers,* 1976.

Mitchell, E. A., et al. "Cot Death Supplement: Results from the First Year of the New Zealand Cot Death Study." *New Zealand Medical Journal* 104 (1991): 71–76.

Morrow-Tlucak, M., R. H. Haude, and C. B. Ernhart. "Breastfeeding and Cognitive Development in the First Two Years of Life." *Social Science Medicine* 26 (1988): 635–39.

Morse, Janice M., and Margaret J. Harrison. "Social Coercion for Weaning." *Journal of Nurse Midwifery* 32 (1987): 205–10.

Moscone, S. R., and M. J. Moore. "Breastfeeding During Pregnancy." *Journal of Human Lactation* 9 (1993): 83–88.

Neifert, M. R., and J. M. Seacat. "Contemporary Breastfeeding Management Clinics." *Perinatology* 12 (1995): 319–42

Rickert, V. I., and C. Merle Johnson. "Reducing Nocturnal Awakening and Crying Episodes in Infants and Young Children: A Comparison Between Scheduled Awakenings and Systematic Ignoring." *Pediatrics* 81 (1988): 203–12.

Riordan, Jan[ice]. *A Practical Guide to Breastfeeding.* St. Louis: C.V. Mosby, 1983.

Riordan, Jan[ice], and Kathleen Auerbach. *Breastfeeding and Human Lactation.* Boston: Jones and Bartlett, 1998.

Riordan, Janice, and Francine Nichols. "A Descriptive Study of Lactation Mastitis in Long-term Breastfeeding Women." *Journal of Human Lactation* 6, no. 2: 53–58.

Satter, Ellyn. *Child of Mine: Feeding with Love and Good Sense.* Palo Alto, Calif.: Bull Publishing, 1991.

Walker, Marsha. "A Fresh Look at the Risks of Artificial Infant Feeding." *Journal of Human Lactation* 9 (1993): 97–107.

Weintraub, R., G. Hams, M. Meerkin, and A. Rosenberg. "High Aluminum Content of Infant Milk Formulas." *Archives of Disease in Childhood* 61 (1986): 914–16.

Wickizer, Thomas M., Lawrence B. Brilliant, Richard Copeland, and Robert Tilden. "Polychlorinated Biphenyl Contamination of Nursing Mothers' Milk in Michigan." *American Journal of Public Health* 71 (1981): 132–37.

Woolridge, M. W., and Chloe Fisher. "Colic, 'Overfeeding,' and Symptoms of Lactose Malabsorption in the Breast-fed Baby: A Possible Artifact of Feed Management?" *Lancet* 2 (1988): 382–84.

Victora, C. G., et al. "Use of Pacifiers and Breastfeeding Duration." *Lancet* 341 (1993): 404–6.

Suggested Supplemental Reading

Most of the books listed here are available in bookstores. If you can't find or order them locally, contact Cascade HealthCare Products or ICEA Bookcenter, both of which publish catalogs. Cascade and ICEA Bookcenter accept telephone orders.

Cascade HealthCare Products
  (Birth and Life Bookstore)
141 Commercial Street N.E.
Salem, Oregon 97301
503-371-4445
800-443-9942 (orders only)

ICEA Bookcenter
P.O. Box 20048
Minneapolis, Minnesota 55420
612-854-8660
800-624-4934 (orders only)

La Leche League pamphlets are available from—

La Leche League International
1400 North Meacham Road
Schaumburg, Illinois 60173
847-519-9585

Childbirth Graphics pamphlets are available from—

Childbirth Graphics
P.O. Box 21207
Waco, Texas 76702-1207
800-299-3366

Bumgarner, Norma Jane. *Mothering Your Nursing Toddler*. Schaumburg, Ill.: La Leche League International, 1982.

Danner, Sarah Coulter, and Edward R. Cerrutti. *Nursing Your Baby with a Cleft Palate or Cleft Lip*. Rochester, N.Y.: Childbirth Graphics, 1994.

This pamphlet can be ordered for $2.00 from Childbirth Graphics.

Fraiberg, Selma H. *The Magic Years*. New York: Charles Scribner's Sons, 1959.

A classic text on child development from infancy to six years.

Good, Judy. *The Diabetic Mother and Breastfeeding*. Schaumburg, Ill.: La Leche League International, 1987.

La Leche League publication 17, this pamphlet is available for $1.50.

Gotsch, Gwen. *Breastfeeding a Baby with Down Syndrome*. Schaumburg, Ill.: La Leche League International, 1998.

This pamphlet is available for $1.50 plus shipping from La Leche League. Ask for publication 23a.

Gromada, Karen. *Mothering Multiples*. Schaumburg, Ill.: La Leche League International, 1998.

Huggins, Kathleen, and Linda Ziedrich. *The Nursing Mother's Guide to Weaning*. Boston: Harvard Common Press, 1994.

Jones, Sandy. *Crying Baby, Sleepless Nights*. Boston: Harvard Common Press, 1992.

Kleiman, Karen R., and Valerie D. Raskin. *This Isn't What I Expected: Overcoming Postpartum Depression*. New York: Bantam Books, 1994.

Pryor, Gale. *Nursing Mother, Working Mother*. Boston: Harvard Common Press, 1997.

Robertson, Laurel, Carol Flinders, and Brian Ruppenthal. *The New Laurel's Kitchen*. Berkeley: Ten Speed Press, 1986.

Satter, Ellyn. *Child of Mine: Feeding with Love and Good Sense*. Expanded ed. Palo Alto, Calif.: Bull Publishing, 1991.

Thevenin, Tine. *The Family Bed: An Age Old Concept in Child Rearing*. Minneapolis: Tine Thevenin, 1976.

Available from Birth and Life Bookstore, ICEA Bookcenter, and La Leche League.

Index

About the Author

A registered nurse who was awarded a Master of Science degree by the University of California, San Francisco, and certified as a lactation consultant by the University of California, Los Angeles, Kathleen Huggins directs a breastfeeding clinic and telephone counseling service at a county hospital in California. She lectures on breastfeeding across the United States for organizations that include the International Lactation Consultant Association and Nursing Mothers Counsel, and she is well known for her experimental research on such subjects as persistent sore nipples, the potential for milk production in women with hypoplastic breasts, and the use of fenugreek to boost milk production. Since the publication of its first edition in 1986, *The Nursing Mother's Companion* has won a top rating from the *Journal of Human Lactation*. The book is listed among the Top Ten Recommended Books for Pregnant Women and Their Families by Lamaze International, and it serves as a textbook for the Nursing Mothers Counsel. With Linda Ziedrich, Kathleen Huggins has also written *The Nursing Mother's Guide to Weaning*. Huggins lives in California with her husband and two children.

Other childcare and parenting books
from The Harvard Common Press

Harvard Common Press books are available at bookstores nationwide. You may also order directly from the Publisher by calling 617-423-5803 or 888-657-3755. Our complete catalog is available in print and at our website, www.harvardcommonpress.com.

THE NURSING MOTHER'S GUIDE TO WEANING
by Kathleen Huggins, R.N., M.S., and Linda Ziedrich
$10.95 paper, ISBN 1-55832-065-2

Kathleen Huggins, author of the bestselling *The Nursing Mother's Companion,* and Linda Ziedrich provide invaluable advice on a subject that has caused distress for countless mothers—when and how to wean. They describe the safest, least stressful ways to wean at every age, from early infancy through toddlerhood and beyond.

"Always considerate of the needs of babies and mothers, *The Nursing Mother's Guide to Weaning* offers practical and truly helpful advice on this significant life transition."—Penny Simkin, P.T.

NURSING MOTHER, WORKING MOTHER:
THE ESSENTIAL GUIDE FOR BREASTFEEDING
AND STAYING CLOSE TO YOUR BABY AFTER YOU RETURN TO WORK
by Gale Pryor
$19.95 cloth, ISBN 1-55832-116-0
$10.95 paper, ISBN 1-55832-117-9

With straightforward information and an encouraging tone, Pryor advises on everything from how to switch gears after the work day ends to maintaining one's milk supply, where to pump at work, and how to store and transport milk safely and conveniently.

"Written as only one who has done it could write it, this book nurtures the new mother and teaches her how to manage what many, perhaps even her doctor, say can't be done. Gale Pryor is like the experienced older sister who wants the best for this new mother and her baby, and she says, 'Yes, you can. Here's how.'"
—William Sears, M.D., and Martha Sears, R.N.

25 THINGS EVERY NEW MOTHER SHOULD KNOW
by Martha Sears, R.N., with William Sears, M.D.
$14.95 cloth, ISBN 1-55832-068-7
$8.95 paper, ISBN 1-55832-069-5

Authors of numerous popular books on baby care, the Searses have distilled the wisdom they've gleaned over the years into a small, clear-headed volume of advice. This guide, covering such matters as feeding methods, sleeping arrangements, crying (the baby's and the mother's), the father's role, and family support, shows mothers that, although baby care takes time and devotion, it needn't be lonely or totally exhausting.

"This thoughtful, insightful book grasps the essential ingredients of the role and joys of being a mother."—Marshall H. Klaus, M.D., and Phyllis H. Klaus, M. ED., C.S.W.

YOU AND YOUR NEWBORN BABY: A GUIDE TO THE FIRST MONTHS AFTER BIRTH
by Linda Todd, M.P.H.
$11.95 cloth, ISBN 1-55832-055-5
$6.95 paper, ISBN 1-55832-054-7

A practical and sensitive guide to a mother's physical and emotional recovery after birth, to infant care, and to the baby's early development. Linda Todd offers advice on breastfeeding vs. bottlefeeding, postpartum depression, the special needs and roles of fathers, siblings, grandparents, and other loved ones, and many other topics, all in a warm and encouraging style.

"A gentle, helpful book that will enable parents to respond to their new baby's needs."—Sheila Kitzinger

THE PREEMIE PARENTS' COMPANION:
THE ESSENTIAL GUIDE TO CARING FOR YOUR PREMATURE BABY
IN THE HOSPITAL, AT HOME, AND THROUGH THE FIRST YEARS
by Susan L. Madden, M.S.
Foreword by William Sears, M.D.
Introduction by Jane E. Stewart, M.D.
$27.95 cloth, ISBN 1-55832-134-9
$14.95 paper, ISBN 1-55832-135-7

In a warm and supportive manner, Madden moves parents beyond their uncertainty to actively participate in their preemie's care. She teaches parents what they need to know, helping them to confidently care for their child both in the hospital and at home, through the first developmentally crucial years.

"Susan Madden offers practical suggestions and critical strategies to any parent struggling with the daily challenges of raising, comforting, and connecting with a fragile and sensitive premature baby. The up-to-date medical, clinical, and developmental information combined with the practical suggestions for parents makes this book an extremely valuable resource."
—Margaret S. Mahoney, L.C.S.W.

NINE MONTHS AND A DAY:
A PREGNANCY, LABOR, AND DELIVERY COMPANION
by Adrienne B. Lieberman and Linda Hughey Holt, M.D., F.A.C.O.G.
$7.95 paper, ISBN 1-55832-150-0

This easy-reference book helps expectant mothers to take an informed role in their prenatal care and delivery. The authors cover a wide range of topics, while helping a woman to anticipate and cope with each of the changes her body will undergo and providing supportive counsel on the more complex decisions she may have to make during pregnancy.

"*Nine Months and a Day* gives extremely important information for both a woman and her partner. It is written in an organized and easy-to-read manner and is truly an essential 'companion' for a woman before, during, and after her pregnancy."—Julie Tupler, R.N.

A GOOD BIRTH, A SAFE BIRTH:
CHOOSING AND HAVING THE CHILDBIRTH EXPERIENCE YOU WANT
THIRD REVISED EDITION
by Diana Korte and Roberta Scaer
$21.95 cloth, ISBN 1-55832-042-3
$15.95 paper, ISBN 1-55832-041-5

A Good Birth, A Safe Birth provides detailed information about childbirth options, with advice on finding an appropriate doctor and hospital, questions an expectant mother may ask to make sure she gets the kind of childbirth she wants, the benefits and drawbacks of medications, and much more.

"A most important book. One of the few books every woman should read during her pregnancy."—Marshall H. Klaus, M.D.

THE VBAC COMPANION:
THE EXPECTANT MOTHER'S GUIDE TO VAGINAL BIRTH AFTER CESAREAN
by Diana Korte
$21.95 cloth, ISBN 1-55832-128-4
$12.95 paper, ISBN 1-55832-129-2

Diana Korte helps women who have delivered by cesarean to make an informed decision about whether or not to have a VBAC the next time around. Korte addresses concerns, such as rupture of uterine scars or difficult labor, and helps negotiate the maze of doctors, hospitals, and insurers.

"*The VBAC Companion* is yet another masterpiece on birthing from Diana Korte. I recommend it with great enthusiasm to every woman who has had a cesarean and to anyone who wants to be well prepared and well informed about childbirth."—John Kennell, M.D.

CRYING BABY, SLEEPLESS NIGHTS:
WHY YOUR BABY IS CRYING AND WHAT YOU CAN DO ABOUT IT
REVISED EDITION
by Sandy Jones
$17.95 cloth, ISBN 1-55832-046-6
$12.95 paper, ISBN 1-55832-045-8

A reassuring, comprehensive guide to the many causes of infant crying. Jones helps parents determine what their baby's cries mean, and offers them practical suggestions for making their babies happier and for coping with their own emotions.

"If 'sleeping like a baby' sounds like an ironic jest, you need this book. Mixing equal parts of sympathy for the crying baby and the hapless parents, Jones has made an excellent book even better."—Adrienne B. Lieberman

GETTING TO DRY:
HOW TO HELP YOUR CHILD OVERCOME BEDWETTING
by Max Maizels, M.D., Diane Rosenbaum, PH.D., and Barbara Keating, R.N., M.S.
$27.95 cloth, ISBN 1-55832-130-6
$14.95 paper, ISBN 1-55832-131-4

The experts at the country's leading center for treating childhood enuresis offer proven techniques to bring bedwetting to a happy end. The authors cover the pros and cons of various anti-wetting strategies, while offering friendly advice about how to replace punishment and shame with rewards and praise.

"A wonderful, straightforward, and enlightened book for parents and health-care providers alike, by authors with extensive experience. This book will really help thousands of families."—Mark Stein, PH.D.

HELPING CHILDREN COPE WITH SEPARATION AND LOSS
REVISED EDITION
by Claudia Jewett Jarratt
$12.95 paper, ISBN 1-55832-051-2

A compassionate, practical book for any adult who wants to help a child recover from the stages of denial and mourning that follow the loss of a loved one, whether from a death, divorce, move, hospitalization, or simply the politics of friendship.

"This is a book of warmth and wisdom, a resource for all caregivers to children in time of need."—*Publishers Weekly*

SMART LOVE:
THE COMPASSIONATE ALTERNATIVE TO DISCIPLINE
THAT WILL MAKE YOU A BETTER PARENT
AND YOUR CHILD A BETTER PERSON
by Martha Heineman Pieper, PH.D., and William J. Pieper, M.D.
$22.95 cloth, ISBN 1-55832-142-X

This husband-and-wife team of experienced professionals—and parents of five—show that putting children's inner happiness, rather than their outward behavior, first will make them better behaved, and more responsible, confident, happy, and successful. With real-life examples, they help parents find the medium between "anything goes" and too-tough discipline.

"Excellent suggestions on how to be nurturing and compassionate, so that you can help your child become well-adjusted and happy."—Ann Landers